D1001133

Is a Little Pollution Good for You?

**ENVIRONMENTAL ETHICS AND SCIENCE POLICY SERIES**
General Editor: Kristin Shrader-Frechette

**Democracy, Risk, and Community**
Technological Hazards and the Evolution of Liberalism
*Richard P. Hiskes*

**Environmental Justice**
Creating Equality, Reclaiming Democracy
*Kristin Shrader-Frechette*

**Taking Action, Saving Lives**
Our Duties to Protect Environmental and Public Health
*Kristin Shrader-Frechette*

**Across the Boundaries**
Extrapolation in Biology and Social Science
*Daniel P. Steel*

**Is a Little Pollution Good for You?**
Incorporating Societal Values in Environmental Research
*Kevin C. Elliott*

# Is a Little Pollution Good for You?

## Incorporating Societal Values in Environmental Research

KEVIN C. ELLIOTT

2011

OXFORD
UNIVERSITY PRESS

Oxford University Press, Inc., publishes works that further
Oxford University's objective of excellence
in research, scholarship, and education.

Oxford New York
Auckland Cape Town Dar es Salaam Hong Kong Karachi
Kuala Lumpur Madrid Melbourne Mexico City Nairobi
New Delhi Shanghai Taipei Toronto

With offices in
Argentina Austria Brazil Chile Czech Republic France Greece
Guatemala Hungary Italy Japan Poland Portugal Singapore
South Korea Switzerland Thailand Turkey Ukraine Vietnam



Published by Oxford University Press, Inc.
198 Madison Avenue, New York, New York 10016

www.oup.com





Library of Congress Cataloging-in-Publication Data
Elliott, Kevin Christopher
Is a little pollution good for you? : incorporating societal values in environmental
research / by Kevin C. Elliott.
p. cm.—(Environmental ethics and science policy series)

ISBN 978-0-19-975562-2
1. Environmental responsibility. 2. Environmental ethics.
3. Pollution—Case studies. 4. Social values—Case studies. I. Title.
GE195.7.E48 2010
179'.1—dc22 2010007927

9 8 7 6 5 4 3 2

Printed in the United States of America
on acid-free paper

For Cris and Janelle, who did so much to prepare me for this project,
and for Janet, who gave me the support to complete it

# Preface

Compared to many philosophy books, this volume is directed at a rather diverse range of audiences. I came to this research as a philosopher of science hoping to achieve two major goals: (1) to examine the range of methodological and interpretive judgments that permeate policy-relevant scientific research and (2) to explore ways of making these judgments more responsive to a range of public values—not just to the "deep pockets" that have abundant resources available to spend on research. In brief, I was interested in how science and democracy relate to one another. This is a project that intersects with many different scholarly disciplines, research projects, and practical concerns.

*Nearly everyone with an interest in the environment*—concerned citizens, environmentalists, scientists, industry groups, and policy makers—should find the book's major case study, hormesis, of interest. Hormesis involves seemingly beneficial effects produced by low doses of substances that are normally toxic. Some scientists argue that this phenomenon could have important policy implications, such as weakening government regulations of toxic substances. Large sums of money are at stake in debates about government regulatory policy, and many interest groups are intensely concerned about these issues. Therefore, the book's careful analysis of the methodological and interpretive judgments associated with hormesis research (especially in chapter 2) should be helpful to a variety of groups who want to understand the scientific issues at stake more clearly. Chapter 7 examines similar judgments associated with two other phenomena, endocrine disruption and multiple chemical sensitivity (MCS), which are also relevant to environmental policy.

*Research ethicists* will also hopefully find much of interest in the book's analysis of the hormesis, endocrine disruption, and MCS cases. Chapter 4 reviews a variety of questionable research practices that have been perpetrated by vested interest groups with a stake in the outcome of scientific research. The chapter argues that university conflict-of-interest policies are not sufficient to prevent worrisome effects of vested interests on academic research, and it suggests several alternative strategies. Chapter 6 examines the responsibilities of scientific experts when they communicate controversial or inconclusive scientific findings to policy makers and the public. Recently, heavily politicized debates about topics like climate change have highlighted the importance of these ethical issues.

*Policy makers and researchers* may appreciate the fact that the book also intersects with recent work on science and technology policy. In particular, chapter 5 examines current efforts to incorporate various forms of public participation or broadly based deliberation in science policy making. The chapter points out that even though public participation and deliberation have become increasingly important in the spheres of policy making and technology development, they have not been implemented as widely in the context of scientific research. Chapter 5 argues that, given the range of value judgments involved in scientific practice, it is worth putting greater effort into determining when policy-relevant areas of science would benefit from various formal mechanisms for deliberation.

*Philosophers, historians, and sociologists of science and technology* will see that the book builds on a significant body of previous work in these disciplines. The hormesis case constitutes a new and detailed case study of the ways that value judgments permeate policy-relevant science. The book especially emphasizes that linguistic decisions about how to categorize and label phenomena permeate the hormesis, MCS, and endocrine disruption cases. It is striking to see the societal significance of these decisions in a field like toxicology, where one might expect wording to be of little importance. Chapter 3 synthesizes a good deal of previous philosophical scholarship on the role that nonepistemic values ought to play in scientific research. It argues that, in policy-relevant research, these values should not be systematically excluded from any of the categories of value judgments considered in the book: (1) the choice of research projects and the design of studies; (2) the development of scientific categories and choice of terminology; (3) the interpretation and evaluation of studies; and (4) the application of research to the formulation of public policy.

There are pros and cons involved in writing a book that intersects with so many subjects. On one hand, it may not do justice to any of them. On the other hand, we may learn a great deal by drawing connections between related fields. I hope that my many different audiences will find that the blend of research projects and disciplinary perspectives yields some promising lines of inquiry.

Kevin C. Elliott
Columbia, SC
January 2010

# Acknowledgments

Portions of chapters 4, 5, and 6 are adapted from three of my articles: "Scientific Judgment and the Limits of Conflict-of-Interest Policies," *Accountability in Research: Policies and Quality Assurance* 15 (2008): 1–29 (© Taylor and Francis Group, LLC); "A Case for Deliberation in Response to Hormesis Research," *Human and Experimental Toxicology* 27 (2008): 529–38 (© 2008 Sage Publications); and "An Ethics of Expertise Based on Informed Consent," *Science and Engineering Ethics* 12 (2006): 637–61 (© 2006 Opragen Publications, with kind permission of Springer Science and Business Media). Smaller portions of chapters 2 and 7 draw from two other articles: "The Ethical Significance of Language in the Environmental Sciences: Case Studies from Pollution Research," *Ethics, Place, and Environment* 12 (2009): 157–73 (© 2009 Taylor and Francis), and (with Daniel McKaughan) "How Values in Scientific Discovery and Pursuit Alter Theory Appraisal," *Philosophy of Science* 76 (2009): 598–611 (© 2010 by the Philosophy of Science Association).

It is humbling to consider how many people have assisted me in the creation of this book. My research on hormesis, which ultimately gave rise to this volume, began while I was a graduate student in the Program in History and Philosophy of Science (HPS) at the University of Notre Dame. I was assisted by two fellowships during my time there: a Notre Dame Presidential Fellowship and a Pew Younger Scholars Fellowship from the Pew Charitable Trusts. My work took a significant step forward when I attended a conference on hormesis in January 2000, thanks to support from Don Howard, the director of the HPS program, and Kristin Shrader-Frechette, the O'Neill Family Chair in Philosophy. I continued to work on the book while serving as a faculty member with a joint appointment in the Department of Philosophy at Louisiana State University and at the Pennington Biomedical Research Center (PBRC) of the LSU System. My thanks go to John Whittaker, the philosophy chair who created the unique position that I held, and to Claude Bouchard, the executive director of PBRC, who provided me with ample time and support to work on the project. I completed the project at the University of South Carolina, where I have received invaluable guidance from my colleagues.

Numerous scholars provided valuable feedback as I worked through the ideas in the manuscript. Although I cannot thank them all personally, I am grateful for numerous questions at conference presentations and university talks that clarified and challenged my thinking. Janelle Elliott, Matt Kisner, Travis Rieder, and Kristin Shrader-Frechette deserve special thanks for reading the entire manuscript at various stages of its development. Kristin's scholarship and advice pervade this book. I am also grateful to the members of the Philosophy of Science, Technology, Engineering, and Medicine (PSTEM) and Ethics reading groups at the University of South Carolina, who read and discussed portions of the manuscript with me. Informal discussions with a variety of others, including Michael Dickson, Heather Douglas, Dan McKaughan, and Justin Weinberg, also sharpened portions of the manuscript. I am especially thankful to Justin for suggesting the book's cover photograph. The editors and reviewers at Oxford University Press, including Tamzen Benfield, Peter Ohlin, and Lucy Randall, were extremely helpful as well.

I am also thankful for numerous scientists who were willing to humor a philosopher in need of advice. Anne McNabb and Louis Guillette provided helpful information about low-dose chemical effects, especially endocrine disruption. George Hoffmann and Paul Mushak also read portions of the manuscript and provided very helpful comments. I especially want to thank Ed Calabrese. Although this volume does not always endorse his claims regarding the hormesis phenomenon, I have found him to be a very gracious source of ideas and advice. Over the course of in-person conversations, email exchanges, and phone calls, I have learned a great deal from him.

More personally, I owe a significant debt of gratitude to my parents, Cris and Janelle. It is largely because of their encouragement and the effort that they channeled into my education that I have had the opportunity to write this book. My sister, Juliann, helped me to produce aesthetically satisfactory figures and assisted me in developing the book's cover. My son, Jayden, and my daughter, Leah, kept me sane by making sure that I had plenty of other entertainment and activities. Jayden perceptively asked me recently, "Daddy, why do you spend more than 50 percent of your life typing?" Most of all, I express my thanks to my wife, Janet. During the past ten years, she has continually made concessions so that I could study or think or write. She was also the one who lifted my spirits when I was discouraged and gave me wise advice when I needed it. Thus, it is both fitting and a pleasure to dedicate this book to my wife and best friend, Janet, along with my parents, Cris and Janelle. They prepared me for this project and gave me the support to complete it.

# Contents

# Is a Little Pollution Good for You?

# 1

# Introduction

## Societal Values and Environmental Research

During recent decades, the world has witnessed intense citizen action in response to a wide range of environmental concerns. For example, consumers have largely quashed the introduction of genetically modified (GM) foods into the European market, in part because of worries about the potential risks to human health, as well as the environmental and social effects of these products. Similarly, countless citizen groups throughout the United States have mobilized in an effort to block plans for new chemical plants, waste dumps, incinerators, and even the national repository for high-level nuclear waste at Yucca Mountain, Nevada.[1] Activists have highlighted their concerns about the environmental and human rights consequences of globalization by engaging in well-publicized protests, including the classic 1999 "battle of Seattle" against the World Trade Organization (WTO). The manufacturer of the growth regulator Alar was forced to stop marketing the product in the United States because of the public uproar in the spring of 1989 over the possibility that residues of the chemical on apples might prove carcinogenic, especially to children.[2] Citizen actions like these have been motivated in part by the perception that expert scientists and policy makers have either misjudged the seriousness of environmental risks or have become beholden to interest groups that want to downplay the significance of the problems.[3]

However, these citizen actions raise both theoretical and practical questions about how to handle cases in which members of the public disagree with experts or at least want more of a say in how society investigates and responds to environmental problems. As political scientist and science-policy expert David Guston puts it, "The delegation of significant authority from political to scientific actors is arguably the central problem in science policy, both analytically and practically."[4] From a theoretical perspective, we

1. Shrader-Frechette, *Environmental Justice*.
2. See Jasanoff, *Fifth Branch*.
3. Irwin, *Citizen Science*; Shrader-Frechette, *Taking Action, Saving Lives*.
4. Guston, "Institutional Design for Socially Robust Knowledge," 63.

must determine how to reconcile the prominent place of scientific expertise in policy making with a democratic commitment to equal accountability of government to all citizens. As long as expert knowledge can be regarded as a neutral body of information on which all citizens can agree, it does not raise problems for this democratic ideal. However, when experts' pronouncements come under fire, it is unclear how to address those disagreements in a manner that does not violate the liberal democratic principle of neutrality between competing worldviews or sectarian positions.[5]

Policy makers also face a variety of practical challenges as they attempt to balance the role of technical experts and citizens in decision making. For example, the influential Harvard University law professor Cass Sunstein insists that "Democratic governments should respond to people's values, not to their blunders."[6] In other words, he argues that policy makers should find ways to respond to societal values regarding public health and environmental welfare while insulating the scientific elements of government decision making from public influences. Others argue that Sunstein's attempts to maintain a barrier between scientific analyses and public values result in a problematic form of technocracy.[7] Finding the best ways to integrate scientific expertise with citizens' values is not a simple task.

Analysts who represent a range of disciplines have addressed this complex interface between scientific knowledge and democratic politics. For example, many sociologists have attempted to create opportunities for greater public involvement in science by altering its "rarefied" image as a source of universal, objective, privileged knowledge. These thinkers highlight the negotiated character of scientific knowledge, the "boundary work" that scientists must perform in an effort to distinguish science from other sources of knowledge, and the "local knowledge" of ordinary citizens, which can rival scientific expertise.[8] Science-policy analysts have proposed a range of methods for "democratizing" science: engaging citizens more fully in the review of federal grant applications, increasing support for community-based research and "participatory technology assessment," creating government offices for technology assessment, and making the expert deliberations of advisory committees more transparent and accountable to the public.[9] Philosophers of science have contributed to these discussions by framing the relationship between science and democracy in terms of questions about

5. Turner, "What Is the Problem with Experts?" 123–24.

6. Sunstein, *Laws of Fear*, 126.

7. Kahan et al., "Fear of Democracy"; Shrader-Frechette, "Review of *Risk and Reason* by Cass Sunstein."

8. See, for example, Irwin, *Citizen Science*; Gieryn, *Cultural Boundaries of Science*; Jasanoff, *Fifth Branch*; Wynne, "Sheep Farming after Chernobyl."

9. See, for example, Guston, "Forget Politicizing Science."

the role of value judgments in scientific research.[10] They have emphasized that researchers must make difficult decisions regarding what questions to pursue, what methodologies and statistical analyses to use, what background assumptions to accept, how to interpret ambiguous data, and how to apply laboratory findings to complex, real-life scenarios.[11] Many philosophers have argued that a variety of ethical and societal values have a legitimate role to play in making these judgments, especially when the research has ramifications for public policy.[12] Thus, despite differences among the disciplinary perspectives considered here, they converge around the goal of more successfully integrating scientific knowledge with the concerns of citizens.

## OVERVIEW OF THE BOOK

While drawing from scholarship associated with a number of disciplines, the present book is oriented within a philosophy-of-science framework. It examines how societal values can be more effectively incorporated into a number of judgments associated with policy-relevant environmental research. It defines societal values as qualities or states of affairs that societies or social groups regard as good or desirable. Typical examples include fairness, justice, diversity, efficiency, health, liberty, stability, privacy, and community. Although these values are widely held in contemporary societies, they sometimes come into conflict with each other, and as a result different communities may have differing aims or priorities. Some philosophers have responded to these disagreements by offering sophisticated accounts of what an "ideal" or "well-ordered" scientific portfolio (i.e., one that reflects an adequate range of societal values) would look like.[13] Nevertheless, many of the most serious barriers to incorporating societal values in scientific practice involve *not* a lack of vision about what democratically informed science would be like but *rather* practical problems that make it difficult to attain that goal. In particular, contemporary research tends to be dominated by the values of just a few

10. As chapters 2 and 3 emphasize, this book does not use the term "values" solely to refer to ethical and political considerations but instead uses it in the way that most philosophers of science do to refer to any quality that scientists regard as desirable in a theory or hypothesis. Thus, "value judgments" refer here to any scientific decisions that require weighing the multiple strengths and weaknesses of debated scientific claims or methodologies.

11. Brown, *Perception, Theory, and Commitment*; Kuhn, "Objectivity, Value Judgment, and Theory Choice"; Longino, *Science as Social Knowledge*; McMullin, "Values in Science," in Newton-Smith; McMullin, "Values in Science," in Asquith and Nickles.

12. Cranor, *Regulating Toxic Substances*; Douglas, "Inductive Risk and Values in Science"; Kitcher, *Science, Truth, and Democracy*; Longino, *Science as Social Knowledge*.

13. See, for example, Kitcher, *Science, Truth, and Democracy*.

groups (especially industry and the military) that happen to have "deep pockets."[14] Although market forces often cause the interests of big business and those of the public to coincide, there are also many circumstances in which this is not the case, as we will see in chapter 4.[15]

The influence of powerful interest groups on science can be felt in a number of ways. On one hand, members of the public often receive inadequate scientific information about problems that merit public input, partly because of industry strategies that include direct suppression of scientific data, control of the media, "capture" of federal regulatory agencies, revolving doors between high-level industry and government positions, massive public-relations expenditures, think tanks, campaign contributions, lobbying, and front groups.[16] On the other hand, much of contemporary research on environmental issues has become "special-interest science," influenced by the values of specific interest groups rather than a wider range of societal perspectives.[17] Kristin Shrader-Frechette analyzes a variety of strategies that the purveyors of private-interest science employ in order to obtain results that support their values: (1) using problematic tests, models, or data; (2) employing small samples and short-term studies that decrease the likelihood of uncovering hazards; (3) depending on theoretical estimates rather than empirical measures of harm; (4) failing to do uncertainty analysis; and (5) developing diversionary arguments, such as insisting on human experiments (which are typically unethical) before regarding pollutants as harmful.

14. Consider, for example, that an estimated 65 percent of the money spent on research and development in the United States in 2006 came from industry, whereas 28 percent came from the federal government; see Koizumi, "Federal R&D in the FY 2009 Budget," accessed on 11/24/08. Moreover, in the same year, defense spending accounted for more than 55 percent of the federal R&D budget; see Intersociety Working Group, *Congressional Action on Research and Development*, accessed on 11/24/08. Thus, nondefense federal R&D spending is dwarfed by industrial research funding. In support of the contention that the power of vested interest groups to direct scientific research is a particularly fundamental barrier to "democratizing" science, see Longino, "Science and the Common Good." Kitcher also places much more emphasis on the problematic effects of capitalist influences on scientific research in his more recent article, "Scientific Research—Who Should Govern?"

15. See Krimsky, *Science in the Private Interest*. Corporate and public interests are especially likely to diverge in situations in which a product could be regulated because of concerns about its side effects on environmental or human health. In those cases, there are difficult trade-offs between "consumer" risks and "producer" risks. See, for example, Shrader-Frechette, *Ethics of Scientific Research*; Wilholt, "Design Rules."

16. See, for example, Beder, *Global Spin*; Fagin, Lavelle, and the Center for Public Integrity, *Toxic Deception*; Markowitz and Rosner, *Deceit and Denial*; McGarity and Wagner, *Bending Science*; Rampton and Stauber, *Trust Us, We're Experts!*; Shrader-Frechette, *Taking Action, Saving Lives*. See especially the second chapter of Shrader-Frechette's book for an excellent summary of these strategies.

17. Krimsky, *Science in the Private Interest*; McGarity and Wagner, *Bending Science*; Shrader-Frechette, *Taking Action, Saving Lives*.

In response to these problems, this book aims to develop and promote more effective avenues for incorporating a representative array of societal concerns in policy-relevant science. This project is grounded in the conviction that it is less important at present to decide exactly what the "ideal" scientific portfolio would look like than to develop some practical methods for nudging science closer to that ideal.

With this goal in mind, I pursue two preliminary projects that in turn set the stage for three major lessons for integrating societal values in policy-relevant research. First, I analyze how policy-relevant science incorporates four major types of judgments: choosing research projects and study designs; creating categories and terminology; evaluating and interpreting evidence; and applying research results to public policy. Whereas discussions about "democratizing" science sometimes focus on a narrow set of decisions associated with choosing research projects for funding, we will see that science is "shot through" with a much wider range of important judgments. My second preliminary project is to argue that, under at least some circumstances, societal values have a legitimate role to play in all four categories of judgments. This is not to say that societal influences on science can never be criticized or regarded as illegitimate. The point is that sometimes a range of different methodological or interpretive judgments are all compatible with standards for good scientific practice. I argue that societal values can have a role to play in making these decisions. Building on these two preliminary projects, I propose three lessons to help scientists, policy makers, citizens, and ethicists integrate a representative range of societal values into these judgments.

The lessons provided in this work are significant insofar as they address all three of the major "bodies" identified by Sheila Jasanoff as crucial for obtaining trustworthy scientific information that addresses societal problems. These include the "bodies of knowledge" that scientists produce, the "advisory bodies" or committees through which experts provide advice for policy makers, and the "bodies of the experts" themselves (i.e., the bodies of those who disseminate information and offer judgment in policy domains).[18] The first lesson of the book, that university conflict-of-interest policies are significantly limited in their ability to prevent interest groups from "hijacking" academic research, gives rise to some alternative suggestions for safeguarding our *bodies of knowledge*. The second lesson is that we need to more carefully diagnose forms of broadly based deliberation that are appropriate

18. Jasanoff, "Judgment under Siege," 211. Although Jasanoff develops her "three-body problem" in response to the specific difficulty of maintaining accountable and trustworthy expert advice, this book shows that the three bodies that she identifies are central to establishing effective relationships between science and democratic decision making in general.

in response to particular areas of policy-relevant research. This lesson is designed to improve the *bodies* (i.e., committees and other deliberative forums) *through which we develop advice* for policy makers. The third lesson, that the principle of informed consent can serve as a basis for a promising ethics of expertise, provides guidance for *experts themselves*.

Scientific research projects related to chemical pollution serve as the book's primary case studies. Industry currently produces six trillion pounds of more than seventy-five thousand different synthetic chemicals each year, generating annual sales of roughly $1.5 trillion.[19] In 2008, the most recent year for which information is available, very conservative estimates indicate that industry in the United States released (through disposal or other methods) about 3.9 billion pounds of toxic chemicals into the environment.[20] There is widespread agreement that exposing organisms to this pollution at high dose levels constitutes a significant threat to environmental and public health. For example, industrial and agricultural toxicants appear to be responsible for at least sixty thousand avoidable cancer deaths annually, and expenditures for occupational diseases and injuries (many of which are caused by toxic substances) total $240 billion.[21] Nevertheless, the low-dose effects of chemical pollution continue to be a matter of intense disagreement among scientists, policymakers, and activist groups.[22] These scientific disputes are aggravated by the significant amounts of money at stake both in governmental regulation of toxicants and in legal liability for harms they allegedly cause. For instance, according to estimates from the Census Bureau, industry spends more than $25 billion in the United States each year on operating costs and capital expenditures for pollution abatement.[23]

19. Fagin, Lavelle, and the Center for Public Integrity, *Toxic Deception*; McGinn, "Reducing Our Toxic Burden," 77.

20. The figure of 3.9 billion pounds comes from the EPA's toxics release inventory (http://www.epa.gov/TRI/tridata/tri08/national_analysis/index.htm, accessed on 12/21/09). This figure dramatically underestimates actual releases because (1) it includes data on only about 650 particularly toxic chemicals (out of the roughly eighty thousand chemicals in use), (2) it does not include small businesses, and (3) it does not include data that industry illegally withholds. For example, the U.S. General Accounting Office (GAO, now known as the Government Accountability Office) and other watchdog groups have raised a number of concerns about the reliability of air pollution reports from industry; see U.S. GAO, *Air Pollution*; Shrader-Frechette, *Taking Action, Saving Lives*, 32.

21. Shrader-Frechette, *Taking Action, Saving Lives*.

22. For arguments that low-dose chemical pollution is not harmful, see, for example, Ames, Magaw, and Gold, "Ranking Possible Carcinogenic Hazards"; Efron, *Apocalyptics*; Fumento, *Science under Siege*; Milloy, *Junk Science Judo*; Whelan, *Toxic Terror*. For arguments that low-dose chemical pollution is harmful, see, for example, Ashford and Miller, *Chemical Exposures*; Colborn, Dumanoski, and Myers, *Our Stolen Future*; Krimsky, *Hormonal Chaos*; Wargo, *Our Children's Toxic Legacy*.

23. U.S. Census Bureau, *Pollution Abatement Costs and Expenditures*, accessed on 10/22/08.

These expenses are generally more than offset for the population as a whole once savings in health care and other sectors are taken into account, but the costs remain particularly salient to regulated industries.[24]

Much conflict stems from the fact that researchers are forced to make numerous controversial judgments in the course of studying chemical pollution and providing advice to regulators.[25] For example, some scientists claim that up to 5 percent of the U.S. population may suffer from extreme sensitivity to toxic chemicals. This phenomenon, which is frequently called "multiple chemical sensitivity" (MCS), may be linked to a number of other mysterious medical problems, including "Gulf War syndrome," "sick-building syndrome," and even chronic fatigue syndrome and fibromyalgia.[26] Other scientists insist, however, that the phenomenon is psychologically induced and that toxic chemicals do not directly cause any of the physiological problems associated with MCS.[27] Scientists are forced to weigh the strengths and weaknesses of opposing scientific studies when advising policy makers and the general public about this illness.

In another debated area of research, some scientists claim that many chemicals may mimic hormones such as estrogen, thereby causing (at surprisingly low doses) a wide variety of disorders: disrupted animal behavior, declining species populations, and human health problems ranging from declining male sperm counts to increasing rates of reproductive cancers, immune disorders, and behavioral problems.[28] As in the MCS case, experts must make controversial judgments when estimating the extent to which these endocrine-disrupting chemicals are causing specific harmful effects not only for wildlife but also for humans.

Toxicologists are also exploring the apparently contradictory hypothesis that some normally toxic chemicals exhibit hormesis, which consists of seemingly beneficial low-dose effects.[29] In chapter 2 I argue that it is extremely difficult to develop a satisfactory definition for this phenomenon. Unless otherwise specified, it is characterized throughout the book as a biphasic dose-response relationship that is caused by "compensatory biological processes following an initial disruption in homeostasis" (see figures 1.1 and

24. The U.S. Office of Management and Budget claims that, between 1992 and 2002, the societal benefits of the EPA's regulations were three to five times greater than their costs. See the OMB website, http://www.whitehouse.gov/omb/inforeg/2003_cost-ben_final_rpt.pdf, accessed on 11/3/05.

25. See, for example, Cranor, *Regulating Toxic Substances*; Mayo and Hollander, *Acceptable Evidence*.

26. Ashford and Miller, *Chemical Exposures*.

27. See chapter 7 for a more complete discussion of these disagreements.

28. Colborn, Dumanoski, and Myers, *Stolen Future*; Krimsky, *Hormonal Chaos*.

29. For a comparison of endocrine disruption and hormesis, see Weltje, vom Saal, and Oehlmann, "Reproductive Stimulation by Low Doses of Xenoestrogens."

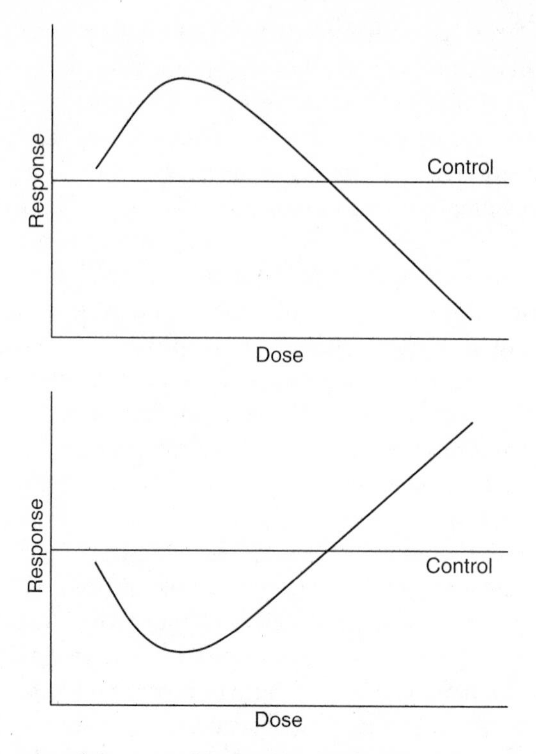


**Figure 1.1.** Examples of the general form of hormetic dose-response relationships. The top curve could represent a hormetic relationship between the dose of a growth inhibitor and plant growth, whereas the bottom curve could represent the relationship between alcohol intake and human mortality.

1.2).[30] In other words, it consists of cases in which the direction of some biological response (e.g., growth, fecundity, or enzyme activity) changes with decreasing dose as a result of biological feedback mechanisms. These feedback processes allow organisms to respond to low doses of stressors by temporarily overshooting the return to homeostasis after they have been disrupted. For example, the growth of peppermint plants is initially inhibited at all dose levels by treatment with the growth retardant phosphon, but after two to five weeks of treatment, the plants exposed to low doses of phosphon appear to overcompensate for this stress. This results in a hormetic dose-response curve in which the plants treated with low doses grow faster than the controls, whereas those treated with high doses grow slower than the controls.[31]

30. Calabrese and Baldwin, "Defining Hormesis," 91. Calabrese and Baldwin choose to count biphasic relationships produced not only by compensatory biological processes but also by what they call "direct stimulation" as instances of hormesis.

31. Calabrese and Baldwin, "General Classification of U-shaped Dose-response Relationships."

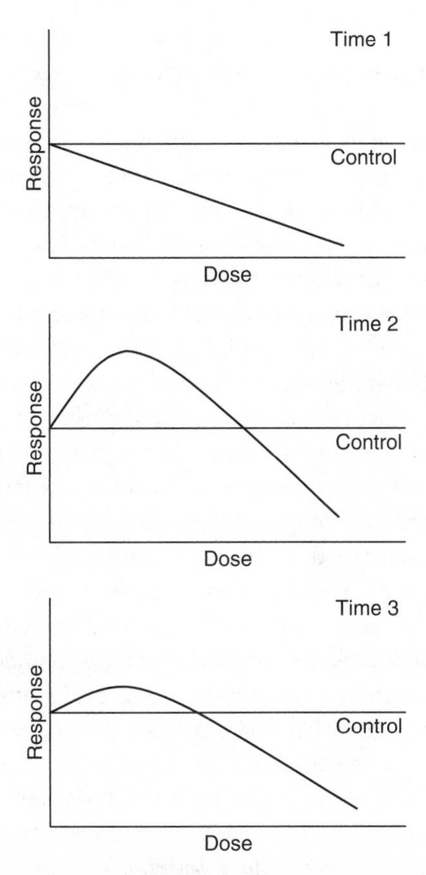


**Figure 1.2.** An illustration of the ways that dose-response relationships produced by compensatory biological processes change over time. The top curve illustrates an initial disruption in homeostasis, with the response (e.g., growth) inhibited at all dose levels. The middle curve shows how compensatory processes can stimulate the response to levels higher than that of controls. The bottom curve shows how the low-dose stimulation above control levels gradually decreases over time.

Building on previous work by Kristin Shrader-Frechette, one can identify at least four distinct claims made by proponents of hormesis.[32] First, claim H is that, in some biological models, some low-dose toxicants and carcinogens exhibit hormesis on some biological endpoints. Second, claim HG is that hormesis is widely generalizable across biological models, chemical classes, and endpoints.[33] Third, claim HP is that hormesis is the predominant dose-response model, meaning that it accurately represents the low-dose effects of toxicants more frequently than do alternatives, such as

32. Claims H, HG, and HD were previously identified in Shrader-Frechette, "Ideological Toxicology."

33. Calabrese and Baldwin, *Chemical Hormesis*; Calabrese, Baldwin, and Holland, "Hormesis."

the threshold model.[34] Fourth, claim HD is that "a strong case can be made for the use of hormesis as a default assumption in the risk-assessment process."[35] Although most researchers would agree with claim H, the other three claims (regarding its generalizability, predominance, and applicability for public policy) are disputed by many scientists in the regulatory and medical communities.[36] This book focuses especially on these debates over hormesis and uses examples associated with endocrine disruption and multiple chemical sensitivity to strengthen its conclusions.

Some commentators might argue that hormesis constitutes a problematic case study, based on the charge that it has insufficient scientific legitimacy to merit a book-length investigation and that much of the recent attention given to the phenomenon originates in special-interest groups.[37] In response to this charge, it is true that much of the support for the phenomenon has come from researchers with connections of some sort to polluting groups like industry or the military, but there are exceptions to this generalization.[38] Moreover, the fact that polluters are interested in hormesis arguably increases rather than decreases its relevance. Because various interest groups have supported research on the phenomenon, many of the avenues through which value judgments can affect policy-relevant research have come under scrutiny in this case. Furthermore, hormesis has received a good deal of attention in the scientific and popular press; thus, it is very important to unravel and highlight these value judgments so that the public can be informed about them. The hormesis phenomenon has been discussed in dominant toxicology textbooks, cited in more than a thousand articles from the Web of Science database, and reviewed in publications such as *Science, Nature, Scientific American, Fortune, U.S. News and World Report*, and the *Wall Street Journal*.[39] Nevertheless, analysts in the

34. Calabrese and Baldwin, "Toxicology Rethinks Its Central Belief"; Calabrese and Baldwin, "Hormetic Dose-response Model Is More Common"; Calabrese et al., "Hormesis Outperforms Threshold Model." The differences between the hormetic and threshold dose-response models are discussed further in chapter 2.

35. Calabrese and Baldwin, "Hormesis: U-shaped Dose Responses."

36. For criticisms of claims HG, HP, and HD, see Axelrod et al., "'Hormesis'—An Inappropriate Extrapolation"; Thayer et al., "Fundamental Flaws"; Mushak, "Hormesis and Its Place."

37. I received a dismissive response of this sort from an individual who reviewed one of my recent journal articles.

38. For the claim that most of the motivation for hormesis research is coming from industry, see vom Saal, "Hormesis Controversy." For work on hormesis that does not appear to be directly connected to the concerns of polluters, see the research of Mark Mattson, who is chief of the Laboratory of Neurosciences at the U.S. National Institute of Aging; for example, Mattson, "Hormesis Defined."

39. For discussions of hormesis in the popular press, see Begley, "Scientists Revisit Idea"; Boyce, "Is There a Tonic in the Toxin?"; Raloff, "Counterintuitive Toxicology"; Renner, "Hormesis"; Stipp, "A Little Poison Can Be Good for You." For an example of a very prominent toxicology textbook that discusses hormesis, see Klaassen, *Casarett and Doull's Toxicology*. A search in the Web of Science electronic database on Dec. 12, 2009, with "hormesis" as the topic yielded 1,089 articles.

humanities and social sciences have subjected it to relatively little critical examination, even though proponents of claims HG, HP, and HD have argued that it could have a wide variety of scientific and societal ramifications.[40]

Based on claims H, HG, and HP, for example, Edward Calabrese has suggested that hormesis could affect disciplines as diverse as toxicology, pharmacology, medicine, ecology, psychology, and agriculture.[41] Moreover, appealing to claim HD, he insists that hormesis "is counter to the cancer risk assessment practices by U.S. regulatory agencies . . . which assume that cancer risk is linear in the low-dose area."[42] Lester Lave also suggests that hormesis could provide the basis for a new phase in U.S. regulatory policy (presumably based on his acceptance of claim HD).[43] Nevertheless, these assertions should be closely scrutinized, in part because they come from individuals with ties to powerful groups that stand to benefit from looser pollution regulations—although one should keep in mind that neither Calabrese nor Lave has been afraid to challenge polluters when they think the evidence warrants it.[44] Other university and government scientists argue that Calabrese's and Lave's claims depend on a variety of questionable assumptions: that hormesis is generalizable, that it is beneficial from the perspective of the entire organism, that beneficial effects last for an extended period of time, that humans are not already receiving toxic doses higher than hormetic levels, and that it would be possible to regulate toxic substances precisely enough to maintain levels in the hormetic zone.[45]

40. One of the few publications with analysis of hormesis from a humanities standpoint is *Human and Experimental Toxicology* 27(9) (September 2008), which focuses on "Hormesis and Ethics"; the articles are also available in the *BELLE Newsletter* 14(3) (January 2008), http://www.belleonline.com/newsletters.htm, accessed on 11/25/08. For discussion of the ramifications of hormesis, see Calabrese and Baldwin, "Toxicology Rethinks Its Central Belief," and Calabrese, "Hormesis: Why It Is Important."

41. See Calabrese and Baldwin, "Applications of Hormesis"; Calabrese and Baldwin, "Hormesis: The Dose-response Revolution"; Calabrese, "Hormesis: From Marginalization to Mainstream."

42. Calabrese and Baldwin, *Chemical Hormesis*, VIII-1.

43. Lave, "Hormesis: Policy Implications"; Lave, "Hormesis: Implications for Public Policy." For further discussion of the regulatory implications of hormesis, see Barnes, "Reference Dose (RfD)"; see also Calabrese, Baldwin, and Holland, "Hormesis"; Calabrese and Baldwin, "Toxicology Rethinks Its Central Belief"; Connolly and Lutz, "Nonmonotonic Dose-response Relationships."

44. Calabrese's ties are discussed in chapter 4. Lave codirects the Carnegie Mellon Electricity Industry Center, which receives a major portion of its funding from the Electric Power Research Institute; see http://wpweb2.tepper.cmu.edu/ceic/index.htm and http://www.corrosionimpact.net/information/authors/lave.htm, both accessed on 10/17/08. For examples of their work that clashes with the interests of "deep pockets," see Lave and Seskin, "Air Pollution and Human Health"; Calabrese and Blain, "Single Exposure Carcinogen Database." Also, in the 1990s, Calabrese called for more stringent environmental pollution standards than those accepted by the Shell Oil Company and the U.S. Army in a proposed cleanup of the Rocky Mountain Arsenal outside of Denver; see http://www.cdphe.state.co.us/regulations/wqccregs/100241wqccbasicstandardsforgroundwater.pdf, accessed on 12/17/09.

45. See Foran, "Regulatory Implications of Hormesis"; Kitchin and Drane, "Critique of the Use of Hormesis"; Axelrod et al., " 'Hormesis'—An Inappropriate Extrapolation"; Thayer et al., "Fundamental Flaws"; Mushak, "Hormesis and Its Place."

It is worth noting that these conflicts over pollution research, which feature heavily in the present book, also serve to illustrate and highlight the dynamics of other debates associated with policy-relevant science.[46] For example, Gary Meffe and C. Ronald Carroll argue that one of the most important insights to bear in mind when applying environmental science to policy making is to recognize and address the pervasive uncertainty surrounding the science.[47] One has only to look at contemporary debates over climate change to see the importance of uncertainty, the difficult judgments that accompany it, and the efforts of powerful interest groups to influence those judgments.[48] Although the vast majority of scientists now agree that human actions are contributing to climate change, they find it more difficult to estimate the amount of warming that will occur and the precise effects that will follow from those temperature changes. For example, it is difficult to determine the likelihood that major ice sheets in Greenland or West Antarctica will melt or the probability that the Gulf Stream will be significantly altered. Furthermore, as evidenced by conflicts over the Stern Review on the Economics of Climate Change, economists face controversial judgments of their own when predicting the costs and benefits of policies that respond to global warming.[49] Some political actors (again, frequently those associated with powerful interest groups that have a large financial stake in policy decisions) appeal to this uncertainty to criticize aggressive action against climate change, while others insist on the importance of taking precautionary, preventive actions.[50] Therefore, the analysis of the hormesis case and other pollution controversies in the following chapters should shed light on other disputes associated with policy-relevant science.

## CHAPTER SUMMARIES

Chapter 2 addresses the book's first major project (i.e., analyzing the roles that value judgments play in science) by examining research on hormesis in

46. Cranor, *Toxic Substances*; Krimsky, *Hormonal Chaos*; Shrader-Frechette, *Risk and Rationality*.

47. Meffe, Carroll, and contributors, *Principles of Conservation Biology*; see also Norton, *Searching for Sustainability*.

48. See, for example, Beder, *Global Spin*; Rampton and Stauber, *Trust Us, We're Experts!*; Shrader-Frechette, *Taking Action, Saving Lives*.

49. The Stern Review concluded that it would be much cheaper to take actions now to *prevent* harm from climate change than to wait and respond to the *effects* of climate change. Other economists challenged both the science on which the report was based and its approach to discounting future costs. The Stern Review is available at http://www.hm-treasury.gov.uk/independent_reviews/stern_review_economics_climate_change/sternreview_index.cfm, accessed on 6/29/07. For an overview of debates about the report, see Leonhardt, "Battle over the Costs of Global Warming."

50. Gardiner, "Ethics and Global Climate Change."

detail. The chapter considers how judgments enter into four elements of scientific practice: (1) the choice of research projects and the design of studies; (2) the development of scientific categories and the choice of terminology; (3) the interpretation and evaluation of studies; and (4) the application of research to the formulation of public policy. Whereas chapter 2 provides a descriptive account of the manner in which values *do* play a role in hormesis research, chapter 3 addresses the normative question of what sorts of values *ought* to influence these four elements of science. One might assert, for example, that societal values have a legitimate role to play in choosing the areas of research that receive the most government funding, but one might insist that the interpretation of study results should remain insulated from nonscientific influences. Chapter 3 argues instead that, in cases of policy-relevant research on topics like hormesis, societal values should not be completely excluded from any of the four aspects of scientific practice analyzed here. This is partly because scientists have ethical responsibilities to consider the effects of their work on the public and partly because they are forced to interpret their results under uncertainty.

This analysis of the hormesis case raises the question of how to incorporate societal values in a manner that is responsive to public concerns but that does not damage the objectivity of science. This is a very complex question, but the next three chapters propose lessons for incorporating societal values in each of the crucial bodies proposed by Jasanoff: the body of scientific knowledge, the expert bodies that provide advice to policy makers, and the bodies of the experts themselves.[51] The fourth chapter considers how to safeguard the *body of scientific knowledge* from being overwhelmed by the influences of vested interest groups. It argues that the current financial conflict-of-interest (COI) policies employed by most universities are insufficient to keep academic work responsive to a representative array of societal concerns. Although a majority of research currently takes place outside the academy, universities are of special importance because they have traditionally been a primary source of public-interest science, serving as relatively neutral providers of information about policy-relevant topics.[52] The chapter suggests several alternative strategies that may complement current COI policies. These include creating registries of scientific studies, developing adversarial proceedings or consensual deliberative forums to evaluate research, and encouraging more independently funded research projects.

Chapter 5 considers one of the strategies proposed in the preceding chapter, namely, the promotion of consensual deliberative forums and participatory approaches for responding to scientific research and technology

51. Jasanoff, "Judgment under Siege."

52. Krimsky, *Science in the Private Interest.*

policy. The chapter notes that there has been relatively little systematic effort to initiate participatory responses to controversial areas of policy-relevant science. Instead, community involvement in scientific research has generally arisen in an ad hoc fashion in response to local hazards, whereas large-scale efforts to promote broadly based deliberation have generally addressed new *technologies* or *risks* rather than scientific *research* itself. Chapter 5 suggests a model that could help citizens, policy makers, and academics to more systematically "diagnose" what sorts of participatory, deliberative mechanisms would be most appropriate in response to significant areas of scientific research. The chapter illustrates what this process of diagnosis might look like in the hormesis case. Ideally, the result of more careful diagnosis will be more socially responsive *bodies* (i.e., committees or advisory groups) *that provide advice* about what areas of research to pursue, how to engage in the most meaningful and reliable studies, and what policy lessons to draw from current research.

Chapter 6 examines how *experts themselves* can facilitate more informed democratic decision making in response to policy-relevant research. The chapter argues that, if experts are to respect a range of societal values, they should not provide information about controversial areas of research in a manner that unjustifiably favors their own value orientation. Rather, they should seek to provide information in a way that enables others to apply their own values to the issues under consideration. Scientific organizations are currently struggling to determine how they can fulfill these responsibilities. For example, scientists affiliated with the Society for Conservation Biology have often debated the extent to which they can advocate particular environmental policies without inappropriately imposing their own values on society or losing the trust of those who appeal to them for advice.[53] Chapter 6 suggests that an ethics of expertise based on the principle of promoting informed consent may provide a helpful framework and set of guidelines for experts to follow. It also shows how these guidelines could apply to the hormesis case.

One potential objection to the arguments in chapters 2 through 6 is that they focus on one particular case study (namely, hormesis). One might therefore ask to what extent the conclusions can be generalized to other cases. In order to address this concern, chapter 7 illustrates how two additional case studies related to pollution research (i.e., multiple chemical sensitivity and endocrine disruption) support the claims made in the preceding chapters. In particular, one can discern in these cases the same four categories of value judgments that one finds in hormesis research: (1) choosing research projects and designing studies; (2) developing categories and

53. Marris, "Should Conservation Biologists Push Policies?" See also the special section on "Conservation Biology, Values, and Advocacy," *Conservation Biology* 10 (1996): 904–20.

choosing terminology; (3) interpreting and evaluating studies; and (4) applying research to individual and social decision making. Moreover, the multiple-chemical-sensitivity and endocrine-disruption cases strikingly illustrate the importance of the three strategies proposed in chapters 4 through 6 (i.e., the need for new approaches to address financial COIs, the value of diagnosing the most appropriate deliberative mechanisms for responding to policy-relevant research, and the guidance provided by an ethics of expertise based on informed consent).

## CONCLUSION

Winston Churchill famously claimed, "Democracy is the worst form of government except for all those others that have been tried." The present book makes a similar point about the governance of policy-relevant research. Admittedly, a variety of difficulties are associated with integrating a broad range of societal values in scientific work—the possibility of increased costs, the challenge of adjudicating between various constituencies, and the difficulty of educating stakeholders about scientific issues. Nevertheless, the alternatives—especially the domination of policy-relevant research by a few interest groups with deep pockets—are much more disconcerting. It is therefore of great importance that we reflect on how scientific research and societal values currently relate to one another and how they can be brought together more effectively. Numerous studies have examined how values of various sorts permeate science, but the present volume contributes a new and detailed case study, together with several specific lessons for incorporating societal values in scientific judgments. Moreover, the hormesis case study deserves detailed scrutiny from as many quarters as possible because public-policy decisions to accept claims HG, HD, or HP could significantly affect the pollution risks faced by the public. The analysis provided in the following chapters should help to facilitate that needed reflection.

# 2

# The Hormesis Case

Prominent hormesis researcher Edward Calabrese claims that "Data over the past decade have indicated that the field of toxicology made a crucial error regarding its most fundamental and central feature—that is, the dose response."[1] Recall from the previous chapter that hormesis consists of instances in which the direction of some biological response (e.g., growth, disease incidence, enzyme activity) changes with decreasing dose as a result of biological feedback mechanisms. Calabrese argues that toxicologists have failed to recognize that hormetic dose-response relationships predominate over others.[2] Moreover, he insists that this error has both scientific importance and significant ramifications for public health and economic well-being. According to Calabrese, many pollutants that normally increase rates of cancer incidence or cause other harmful effects at high doses are likely to decrease the incidence of these harmful effects (below control levels) when present at low concentrations. Thus, he suggests that it may be feasible to weaken pollution regulations, thereby saving money and improving public health at the same time.[3]

The present chapter examines the hormesis case study and highlights the key methodological and interpretive questions that one needs to consider in order to evaluate Calabrese's claims about the hormesis phenomenon. As chapter 3 discusses, these methodological choices have frequently been labeled "value judgments" by philosophers of science. Because the concept of a value judgment requires a good deal of unpacking, however, the present chapter merely identifies these crucial choices and saves reflections about their nature and significance for subsequent chapters.

Analyzing the methodological and interpretive choices associated with hormesis research should be of interest to a wide variety of citizens and

1. Calabrese, "Hormesis: Why It Is Important."

2. Calabrese and Baldwin, "Toxicology Rethinks Its Central Belief"; Calabrese and Baldwin, "Hormetic Dose-response Model Is More Common"; Calabrese et al., "Hormesis Outperforms Threshold Model."

3. See, for example, Calabrese and Baldwin, "Toxicology Rethinks Its Central Belief"; Calabrese, "Hormesis: Once Marginalized."

scholars. Philosophers, historians, and sociologists of science have been especially interested in the ways that various sorts of judgment enter scientific practice, but the importance of this topic extends far beyond those particular academic fields. Anyone concerned about the relationship between science and democracy needs to consider how the scientific enterprise incorporates not only technical analysis but also significant interpretive decisions. Moreover, since the hormesis phenomenon may play an important role in future debates about environmental regulation, clarifying these sorts of judgments in the present case study should help a wide variety of policy makers, scientists, concerned citizens, and interest groups who want to respond to it.

The first section of this chapter orients the reader to the hormesis case study. It provides an overview of the key characters who are presently debating the hormesis hypothesis and the typical arguments that they present. The next section provides a brief history of hormesis research that explains how we arrived at the current debate. Each of the following four sections examines a particular way in which methodological or interpretive questions enter scientific work on hormesis. They are ordered very roughly according to the sequential process of conducting research; thus, the first section analyzes decisions about the choice of projects, the proposal of hypotheses, and the design of studies. The next section considers choices associated with the development of scientific terminology, including the creation and labeling of categories. The third section examines judgments associated with the evaluation and interpretation of studies, and the final section considers decisions about the application of research in individual and social decision making.[4]

These four categories are neither mutually exclusive nor exhaustive. The divisions proposed here are useful primarily for organizing one's reflections about scientific judgments; they do not reflect sharp distinctions in actual scientific practice. For example, through a host of feedback loops, decisions associated with one category (e.g., the interpretation of evidence) end up influencing other categories (such as the choice of research projects). Moreover, judgments influence science in a variety of ways that are not considered here; the present book focuses on this fourfold organizational structure because it covers many of the important choices that have been discussed in the science-studies literature and that are central to the hormesis case.

4. Others have made similar distinctions among different categories of value judgments; see, for example, Douglas, "Inductive Risk and Values in Science"; Longino, *Science as Social Knowledge*; Machamer and Wolters, "Introduction." The major difference between these previous works and the categorization in this chapter is that they do not include a separate category for the role of values in developing scientific categories and terminology.

Three different sorts of claims should be distinguished as one reads this chapter: (1) the descriptive claim that methodological or interpretive decisions play a role in particular aspects of scientific practice; (2) the normative claim that values of a particular sort (e.g., societal values) *should* or *should not* play a role in those decisions; and (3) the more restricted normative claim that *specific* values (e.g., concern for public health) as opposed to *other* values (e.g., promoting economic growth) should or should not influence those decisions. This chapter addresses the first type of claim; it describes four sorts of judgments that arise in the course of hormesis research. Chapter 3 takes up the second (i.e., normative) sort of claim and argues that societal values and concerns should not be completely excluded from any of the four categories of judgments considered here. Chapters 4, 5, and 6 tackle the third sort of claim by considering how to bring specific societal values to bear on policy-relevant research.

## SETTING THE STAGE

To date, Edward Calabrese has clearly been the most influential and persistent defender of the claims that hormesis is widely generalizable, that it predominates over other dose-response relationships, and that it should be the default model for assessing risks from toxic chemicals (i.e., claims HG, HP, and HD). He is a long-time professor in the School of Public Health and Health Sciences at the University of Massachusetts, Amherst, and the prolific author of more than ten books and hundreds of articles. He claims that his interest in hormesis originated when he discovered as a student that the plant-growth inhibitor phosphon seemed to stimulate growth in peppermint plants when administered at low doses.[5] When he heard about research in the 1980's on hormetic effects produced by ionizing radiation, he decided to investigate whether the phenomenon was produced by toxic chemicals as well.[6] He and his colleague Linda Baldwin searched through thousands of previous toxicology articles to find potential examples of hormesis. These studies are discussed further in the subsequent sections of this chapter.

Calabrese has been joined by several collaborators and by a range of other figures who have begun exploring the hormesis phenomenon in specific contexts. Perhaps his most notable recent collaborator is Mark Mattson, the equally prolific chief of the Laboratory of Neurosciences at the National Institute of Aging in Baltimore. Together, they edited the book *Hormesis:*

5. See, for example, Begley, "Scientists Revisit Idea"; Boyce, "Is There a Tonic in the Toxin?"

6. Personal communication from Edward Calabrese, Dec. 17, 2009.

*A Revolution in Biology, Toxicology, and Medicine.*[7] Mattson comes to hormesis research with an interest in neurodegenerative disorders and environmental influences on aging and health. For example, he has studied beneficial effects associated with fasting and with exposure to natural chemicals in the diet.[8] He challenges the common notion that the beneficial effects of eating fruits and vegetables stem from antioxidants that protect cells from oxidative damage. Instead, he suggests that "noxious" chemicals (e.g., natural pesticides) in the plants may activate adaptive stress response pathways in human cells, resulting in beneficial health effects due to hormetic mechanisms. Moreover, he argues that the beneficial effects associated with exercise and caloric restriction also stem from hormesis.[9]

The proponents of claims HG, HP, and HD employ a set of common arguments that we will encounter throughout this book.[10] First, they frequently appeal to Calabrese's literature searches of previous toxicology studies as evidence for the generalizability of hormesis. They point out that in hundreds of previous studies he found biphasic dose-response relationships involving many different biological endpoints (e.g., growth, enzyme activities, fecundity), as well as many types of organisms (e.g., bacteria, yeast, mammals). They note that, in one of Calabrese's literature searches, he found hormetic dose-response relationships in close to 40 percent of the studies that were appropriately designed to uncover evidence of hormesis.[11] They also argue that, insofar as living organisms have been exposed to harmful environmental factors throughout their evolutionary history, it makes sense that these life forms would have developed compensatory strategies for responding to those threats. For example, they appeal to specific cellular mechanisms that stimulate the expression of protective proteins (e.g., DNA repair or antioxidant enzymes) in response to toxic substances.[12] Based on these findings, some hormesis researchers claim that the models used by U.S. regulatory agencies for estimating the low-dose risks associated with toxic chemicals are far too protective and thus needlessly harmful to the economy.[13]

So far, regulatory agencies have not been convinced by these arguments, and they have been joined by a chorus of scientists who raise concerns about

7. Mattson and Calabrese, eds., *Hormesis.*

8. See, for example, Mattson, Son, and Camandola, "Viewpoint"; Mattson, "Hormesis Defined."

9. Mattson, "Hormesis Defined."

10. A good recent source for the claims described in this paragraph is Mattson and Calabrese, eds., *Hormesis.*

11. Calabrese and Baldwin, "Frequency of U-shaped Dose Responses."

12. See, for example, Mattson, "Hormesis Defined"; Mattson, "Fundamental Role of Hormesis in Evolution."

13. See, for example, Calabrese and Baldwin, "Toxicology Rethinks Its Central Belief"; Calabrese, "Hormesis: Once Marginalized."

claims HG, HP, or HD. Two of these critics are the independent researchers and consultants Kenny Crump and Paul Mushak. They have questioned the methodologies associated with Calabrese's literature studies, including various features of his statistical analyses and terminological choices.[14] Another prominent critic is Devra Davis, who has coauthored several articles that challenge Calabrese's claims about hormesis.[15] She is the director of the Center for Environmental Oncology at the University of Pittsburgh Cancer Institute. She has also authored two popular books, *When Smoke Ran like Water* and *The Secret History of the War on Cancer*, which highlight the connections between environmental exposures to toxic substances and a range of human health problems.[16] Frederick vom Saal, professor in the Division of Biological Sciences at the University of Missouri, Columbia, is also frequently cited by the media as a counterpoint to Ed Calabrese. As an expert on endocrine disruption, vom Saal agrees with Calabrese that the low-dose effects of many toxic chemicals are difficult to predict based on effects at higher doses, but he argues that low-dose effects are often *more harmful* than previously thought.[17]

Those who question the applicability of hormesis to regulatory policy typically make one or more of the following arguments, which I examine in more detail in the following sections. First, they often question whether Calabrese's literature studies have provided as much evidence for the generalizability of hormesis as the proponents of claim HG typically suggest.[18] Some critics question whether the conceptual category of "hormesis" is even needed, given that we already have the general notion of nonmonotonic (i.e., U-shaped or J-shaped) dose-response relationships.[19] Second, they argue that, no matter how frequently hormesis occurs, it probably does not have significant ramifications for government regulatory policy.[20] They claim that, when one considers chemicals not individually but as mixtures, sensitive individuals (such as children) are already exposed to levels above the beneficial hormetic range. Also, given the multiple biological effects produced by most chemicals, the critics question whether seemingly

14. Crump, "Evaluating the Evidence for Hormesis"; Crump, "Limitations in the National Cancer Institute Antitumor Drug Screening Database"; Mushak, "Hormesis and Its Place"; Mushak, "Ad-hoc and Fast Forward."

15. Axelrod et al., "'Hormesis'—An Inappropriate Extrapolation"; Thayer et al., "Fundamental Flaws."

16. Davis, *When Smoke Ran like Water*; Davis, *Secret History of the War on Cancer.*

17. See, for example, vom Saal, "Hormesis Controversy"; Weltje, vom Saal, and Oehlmann, "Reproductive Stimulation by Low Doses of Xenoestrogens."

18. See, for example, Mushak, "Ad-hoc and Fast Forward"; Axelrod et al., "'Hormesis'—An Inappropriate Extrapolation."

19. See, for example, Thayer et al., "Fundamental Flaws."

20. See, for example, Foran, "Regulatory Implications of Hormesis"; Thayer et al., "Fundamental Flaws."

beneficial hormetic effects on one endpoint (e.g., growth or expression of protective enzymes) generally translate into beneficial effects for an organism as a whole over the course of a lifetime.[21]

Finally, some critics worry that the hormesis phenomenon is likely to be used as an additional tool in the repertoire of those who are constantly trying to bring regulatory activities to a standstill.[22] Regulatory agencies currently use empirical evidence to identify "reference doses," at which substances do not increase health risks. To do this, agencies frequently take the level at which no adverse effects were observed in experimental studies and divide it by "uncertainty factors" of 10 or 100 or 1000 so as to minimize the chances of exposing sensitive individuals to unsafe levels of toxic substances. By appealing to hormesis, industry groups might be able to argue that regulators should avoid using safety factors and instead perform detailed (and time-consuming) research to determine the precise levels at which normally toxic chemicals begin to produce beneficial effects.[23] I examine these arguments made by hormesis researchers and their opponents in much more detail throughout the remainder of this chapter, but first it may be helpful to provide a historical overview of how we arrived at the current situation.

## BRIEF HISTORY OF HORMESIS RESEARCH

As early as the 1500s, Paracelsus famously claimed that "All things are poison and nothing is without poison, only the dose permits something not to be poisonous." He suggested that a variety of minerals could have medicinal properties if administered at the right dose levels. In subsequent centuries, homeopathic physicians argued that minute quantities of substances that normally produce harmful effects could be used to treat sick people who suffer from similar symptoms. Contemporary proponents of claim H (i.e., that hormesis occurs) frequently look back to the work of Hugo Schulz in the 1880s as the starting point for twentieth-century studies of hormesis.[24] Schulz

21. See, for example, Shrader-Frechette, "Ideological Toxicology."

22. For information about the efforts of industry groups to slow regulatory activities to a standstill, see Fagin, Lavelle, and the Center for Public Integrity, *Toxic Deception*.

23. I thank a referee at Oxford University Press for highlighting this point.

24. See, for example, Calabrese and Baldwin, "Chemical Hormesis: Its Historical Foundations"; Calabrese and Baldwin, "Marginalization of Hormesis"; Calabrese and Baldwin, "Tales of Two Similar Hypotheses." See also Calabrese, "Hormesis: Why It Is Important." Marc Lappé and A. R. D. Stebbing also cite Hugo Schulz as the important initiator of hormesis research, but D. Henschler argues that Rudolf Virchow actually identified hormetic effects more than thirty years before Schulz; see Lappé, *Chemical Deception*; Stebbing, "Theory for Growth Hormesis"; Henschler, "Origin of Hormesis."

observed that low doses of some poisonous substances increased yeast fermentation (relative to control levels), whereas higher doses decreased fermentation (again relative to control levels). He and the homeopathic physician Rudolph Arndt became well known for the claim that, at low doses, toxic substances generally stimulate biological endpoints such as growth or fertility. This stimulatory effect became known as the Arndt-Schulz law.[25]

In 1896, Ferdinand Hueppe (a distinguished bacteriologist and student of Nobel laureate Robert Koch) published an influential textbook in which he claimed to have observed, in bacteriological studies, the same phenomenon of poisons producing low-dose stimulation (relative to controls) of biological endpoints such as growth or longevity. Calabrese and Baldwin noted that, because of Hueppe's international influence, the concept of low-dose stimulation of specific biological endpoints (relative to controls, by poisons that inhibited those same endpoints at higher doses) came to be known more generally as Hueppe's rule rather than the Arndt-Schulz law.[26]

Between the late nineteenth century and the 1930s, other international research on plants, bacteria, fungi, and yeast also revealed apparent biphasic effects produced by poisons. The toxic substances, which included metal salts, organic compounds, and pesticides, stimulated endpoints such as growth, respiration, bacterial and fungal nitrogen fixation, fungal spore germination, and yeast fermentation. From 1924 to 1930, a German journal (translated as *Cell Stimulation Research*) published studies that illustrated these sorts of low-dose effects.[27] Southam and Ehrlich first proposed the term "hormesis" (from the Greek word *hormo*, meaning 'to excite') in 1943 to describe this phenomenon of biphasic effects produced by toxic substances.[28]

Following the initial burst of interest in biphasic effects in the early decades of the twentieth century, toxicologists appeared to lose much of their interest in the phenomenon. In a set of recent papers on the history of hormesis research, Calabrese and Baldwin suggest several explanations for what they regard as the demise of the hormesis hypothesis (presumably referring to claims H or HG, the hypotheses that hormesis occurs or is

25. Calabrese and Baldwin, "Chemical Hormesis: Its Historical Foundations."

26. Ibid.

27. Ibid.

28. Southam and Ehrlich, "Effects of Extracts." An important ambiguity in the use of Southam and Ehrlich's definition of hormesis is that they explicitly employed only the notion of low-dose *stimulation* in their definition, but later researchers such as Calabrese and Baldwin sometimes use the term "hormesis" to refer also to low-dose *inhibition* of endpoints such as tumor formation; see Calabrese and Baldwin, "Toxicology Rethinks Its Central Belief." Subsequent sections of this chapter address this ambiguity and clarify different concepts of hormesis.

highly generalizable) during the middle decades of the twentieth century.[29] They argue that the hypothesis was linked to so much scientific evidence and was associated (at least tangentially) with the work of such influential scientists (including Louis Pasteur, Robert Koch, Wilhelm Ostwald, and Charles Richet) that its demise is quite surprising.

In order to account for the failure of hormesis to receive more research interest, Calabrese and Baldwin rely on several sociological explanations. For example, they note that some hormesis researchers and many proponents of the medical practice of homeopathy attempted to use hormesis to explain the effects of homeopathic remedies, thus linking the phenomenon with a disreputable and severely criticized medical research program. Furthermore, Calabrese and Baldwin argue that the low-dose region of the dose-response curve did not, in the mid-twentieth century, appear to have many practical implications that could provide an incentive for further research.[30] Finally, they suggest that close educational connections between important critics of hormesis (such as A. J. Clark) and many of the biostatisticians who pioneered the development of dose-response models further minimized the potential for hormetic effects to be integrated into mainstream toxicological research.[31]

Paul Mushak argues that, whereas Calabrese and Baldwin lean toward the interpretation that hormesis was unfairly marginalized during the mid-twentieth century, the primary reasons for a lack of interest in the phenomenon may have been fairly pedestrian.[32] He points out that the low-dose properties of toxicants were not the primary focus for most researchers, so they would have tended to regard biphasic effects in that region as relatively unimportant anomalies. Moreover, he claims that it would have been difficult to interpret hormetic dose-response curves at that point in the history of toxicological research, partly because risk assessment models did not develop significantly until the 1980s. Finally, he notes that even when scientists became interested in hormesis in the 1990s, it took a decade to develop a definition—one that, as we will see later in this chapter, still faces problems. Mushak interprets this as further evidence that studies of the hormesis phenomenon have simply illustrated the typically slow workings of science and not any overt hostility to it. Later in this chapter we will encounter a number of other reasons that many scientists continue to be skeptical

29. Calabrese and Baldwin, "Chemical Hormesis: Its Historical Foundations"; Calabrese and Baldwin, "Marginalization of Hormesis"; Calabrese and Baldwin, "Tales of Two Similar Hypotheses."

30. Calabrese and Baldwin, "Marginalization of Hormesis."

31. Ibid.

32. Mushak, "Hormesis and Its Place."

of strong claims about hormesis, such as HG, HP, and HD (concerning the generalizability of hormesis, its predominance over other dose-response models, and its relevance for risk assessment).

Despite the relative lack of focus on hormesis for several decades, interest in the phenomenon never completely disappeared during the twentieth century. Marc Lappé suggests that during this time researchers associated it primarily with the endpoint of longevity.[33] He reports that, in the 1950s, scientists proposed a variety of potential explanations for the anti-aging effects of various stressors. In the 1960s, a major textbook on aging even included a chapter about hormetic effects.[34] By the 1970s, however, most scientists appeared to believe that hormesis had been clearly documented only for the antiaging effects of low caloric consumption and a low temperature environment (for cold-blooded organisms).[35] Thus, the growth of interest in the phenomenon in the 1980s and 1990s does appear to represent a shift in perspective for the biology and toxicology communities.

A number of factors may have played a role in its resurgence, but the most important consideration appears to be its potential significance for the regulation of toxic chemicals. For more than fifty years, toxicologists in the United States have been working to establish standards for safe human exposure to hazardous substances. Unfortunately, low-dose effects are usually small and therefore difficult to measure using statistical analyses. Scientists have proposed various models that are consistent with the observed (higher-dose) data from empirical studies, but these models have very different implications for the extrapolation of low-dose effects.[36] For most noncarcinogenic substances, scientists have assumed the existence of threshold doses. In other words, they claim that some dose level exists below which a substance ceases to be toxic. This assumption fits well with the notion that organisms have adaptive capabilities that enable them to respond effectively to low levels of environmental stressors. According to some models of carcinogenesis, however, even one molecule of a carcinogen can increase cancer risk. If such models are correct, it would mean that *no* threshold exists, at least for carcinogens. At present, federal agencies such as the Environmental Protection Agency (EPA), the Occupational Safety and Health Administration (OSHA), and the Food and Drug Administration (FDA) employ *threshold* models for estimating the low-dose effects of most toxicants, but they employ *linear, no-threshold* models for carcinogens.[37]

33. Lappé, *Chemical Deception*, 111.
34. Shock, *Biological Aspects of Aging*.
35. Lappé, *Chemical Deception*, 111.
36. Paustenbach, "Survey of Health Risk Assessment."
37. National Research Council (NRC), *Science and Judgment in Risk Assessment*, 31.

Acceptance of claim HD (i.e., that hormesis should be the default model for risk assessment) could dramatically reshape the policy landscape and result in less stringent regulations.[38] This potential significance of hormesis for regulatory decision making plausibly played an important role in the decisions of the EPA, the National Institute of Environmental Health Sciences (NIEHS), the Nuclear Regulatory Commission, the Texas Institute for the Advancement of Chemical Technology, and the U.S. Air Force to provide research grants for Calabrese to initiate new studies of hormesis. This funding added to the money already provided to his closely associated Biological Effects of Low Level Exposures (BELLE) organization by various industry groups (e.g., Canadian Electric Utilities, Dow-Corning, the Electric Power Research Institute, ExxonMobil, the GE Foundation, Gillette, Ontario Hydro, and RJReynolds).[39]

Based in part on this funding, a growing number of papers on hormesis were published by various scientists in the 1980s and 1990s. For instance, A. R. D. Stebbing published a seminal paper in 1982, in which he suggested that low-dose stimulation of growth or body weight by toxic substances might be the result of biological overcompensation responses to disruptions in an organism's homeostasis.[40] At the same time, T. D. Luckey suggested that low doses of ionizing radiation appeared to be advantageous, and a conference inspired by his book on that topic was held in 1985.[41] In 1987, the journal *Health Physics* published an issue with a number of articles on radiation hormesis. In that issue, Edward Calabrese and his coworkers provided an overview of the evidence for chemical hormesis as well.[42]

Soon after Calabrese's article in *Health Physics* appeared, a team headed by P. J. Neafsey published evidence that low doses of many carcinogens may extend the life span of animals.[43] Other researchers drew attention to the occurrence of U-shaped dose-response curves (reflecting opposite effects at low versus at high doses, as in figure 1.1 in chapter 1), although they expressed skepticism about the extent to which those U-shaped curves were the result of any one particular mechanism.[44] Following this initial revival of

38. Calabrese and Baldwin, "Toxicology Rethinks Its Central Belief."

39. This information about Calabrese's funding comes from his curriculum vitae from 2002; see http://people.umass.edu/nrephc/EJCCVApril02.pdf, accessed November 2003. See also Kaiser, "Sipping from a Poisoned Chalice." Frederick vom Saal argues that the chemical industry was motivated to study hormesis partly because it wanted to counteract growing evidence (especially from research on endocrine disruptors) that very low doses of toxic substances could be more harmful than previously thought; see vom Saal, "Hormesis Controversy."

40. Stebbing, "Hormesis."

41. Calabrese, "Hormesis: From Marginalization to Mainstream."

42. Calabrese, McCarthy, and Kenyon, "Occurrence of Chemically Induced Hormesis."

43. Neafsey et al., "Gompertz Age-specific Mortality Rate Model."

44. Davis and Svendsgaard, "U-shaped Dose-response Curves"; Davis and Svendsgaard, "Nonmonotonic Dose-response Relationships."

interest in the phenomenon, Calabrese and his coworker Linda Baldwin performed several extensive literature studies designed to provide support for claims H, HG, HP, and HD (namely, the existence, wide generalizability, predominance, and regulatory default status of hormesis).[45] Since then, numerous researchers have begun examining hormetic dose-response relationships in a wide variety of contexts. The following sections of this chapter focus on the judgments involved in interpreting and evaluating Calabrese and Baldwin's seminal literature studies, because they have been central to establishing claims HG, HP, and HD.

## CHOOSING AND DESIGNING STUDIES

One category of methodological decisions that impinge on scientific research involves the choice of research projects and the design of studies. This section considers three examples of these sorts of judgments in the hormesis case (see figure 2.1): (1) deciding whether to emphasize research on low-dose toxic effects; (2) determining how much to prioritize studies of hormesis relative to MCS, endocrine disruption, or other low-dose phenomena; and (3) choosing whether to employ literature studies or new toxicology experiments to investigate hormesis.

One important judgment is whether to emphasize research on the low-dose effects of toxic chemicals or to focus public-health funding on other topics. During much of the twentieth century, the societal priority of preventing public-health threats pushed the field of toxicology toward the goal of identifying the most obvious harmful effects of chemicals. Consequently, there was much more scientific interest in examining the effects of chemicals at high doses (at which harmful effects became readily apparent) as opposed to low doses.[46] Coupled with this goal of identifying obvious harmful effects was the impracticality of studying low-dose effects. It is very difficult to obtain statistically significant evidence regarding the relatively small effects of toxicants at low-dose levels unless one studies huge numbers of animals. Since the major goal of toxicology was to identify the most apparent harmful effects of chemicals, it is not surprising that few twentieth-century toxicology studies emphasized the low-dose effects of toxicants.

45. For a fairly comprehensive overview of this work see Calabrese, "Paradigm Lost, Paradigm Found."

46. Calabrese and Baldwin, "Marginalization of Hormesis."

**Choosing and Designing Studies**

- Deciding whether to emphasize research on low-dose toxic effects
- Determining whether to prioritize research on hormesis as opposed to MCS, endocrine disruption, or some other low-dose phenomenon
- Deciding whether to perform literature studies rather than new toxicology experiments explicitly designed to test the hormesis hypothesis

**Developing Scientific Language**

- Choosing an appropriate definition for hormesis
- Identifying appropriate terms to describe the hormesis phenomenon
  —deciding whether to distinguish hormesis from other nonmonotonic dose responses
  —deciding whether to describe it as adaptive
  —determining whether it is accurate or helpful to describe it as generalizable

**Evaluating Studies**

- Evaluating the strength of evidence in Calabrese's first literature study, given its failure to clarify the characteristics of the studies that it ignored
- Deciding how much to trust Calabrese's literature studies, given that the original toxicology experiments were not designed to test hypotheses about hormesis
- Determining whether Calabrese's methodologies were too prone to false positive errors
- Weighing both positive and negative strands of evidence concerning hormesis claims
- Evaluating the evidence that the process of carcinogenesis is affected in a beneficial way by hormetic dose-response relationships
- Deciding how to infer from the frequency of inhibitory and stimulatory *data points at low doses* to the frequency of hormetic and threshold *dose-response relationships*
- Weighing the evidence that hormetic effects are beneficial for entire organisms over the long term

**Applying Research**

- Deciding how to disseminate uncertain results
- Deciding whether new policies can be implemented without causing unreasonable harm
- Determining how to address combinations of potential benefits and burdens associated with allowing exposure to hormetic chemicals (e.g., choosing utilitarian as opposed to deontological ethical approaches)

Figure 2.1. Major categories of methodological and interpretive choices in the hormesis case.

Recently, several factors have contributed to much greater interest in low-dose effects. The environmental and public-health communities have become increasingly concerned as it has become possible to identify a wider range of toxic substances present at low concentrations in the human body and the environment. The discovery of endocrine-disruption phenomena, which can be harmful at surprisingly low dose levels, has exacerbated these worries. On the other end of the ideological spectrum, industry groups are interested in studying low-dose effects so that they can more precisely determine thresholds below which toxic substances are no longer harmful. Their goal is to show that the current standards set by regulatory agencies are needlessly strict. Thus, a wide range of groups have become interested in performing more research on low-dose effects, but a second significant judgment is how much to focus these efforts on hormesis as opposed to other phenomena, such as endocrine disruption or MCS. On this subject, there is less agreement. The environmental and public-health communities are especially interested in endocrine disruption. In contrast, the chemical industry and the U.S. Air Force (which faces significant costs for cleaning up chemical spills) have funded recent work on hormesis.[47] In fact, Frederick vom Saal argues that these groups were motivated to study the phenomenon partly because they saw it as a strategy for counteracting growing evidence from endocrine-disruption research that very low doses of toxicants could be more harmful than previously thought.[48]

The attention that powerful interest groups have given to hormesis is noteworthy, because it is often difficult to obtain funds to study controversial phenomena (like hormesis, MCS, or endocrine disruption) until a significant amount of preliminary information about them is available.[49] Unfortunately, a chicken-and-egg scenario arises because it is difficult to obtain this preliminary information without first having a source of research support. In cases like this, the sorts of questions asked and the hypotheses tested are likely to be influenced by the values or concerns of large organizations (e.g., government or industry) with enough money to fund speculative research projects that might serve their interests.[50] As we have seen, the hormesis phenomenon was considered to be of sufficient interest by the U.S. Air Force and the chemical industry to risk significant research funds to investigate it. In contrast, proponents of MCS have worried that few organizations with deep pockets have an interest in funding speculative research on possible physiological causes of MCS (see chapter 7). In fact, because of product liability concerns, industry groups are motivated to collect evidence for the claim that MCS is not primarily physiological at all but is rather a psychological phenomenon akin to posttraumatic stress disorder.[51]

A third decision visible in the hormesis case is whether to investigate the phenomenon with literature studies as opposed to using new in vitro or

47. Kaiser, "Sipping from a Poisoned Chalice."

48. Vom Saal, "Hormesis Controversy."

49. Ashford and Miller, *Chemical Exposures*; Elliott, "Error as Means to Discovery"; Krimsky, *Hormonal Chaos.*

50. For a more extensive discussion of the epistemological implications of this point (namely, that interest groups can have a significant influence on the topics that receive research funding), see Elliott and McKaughan, "How Values in Discovery and Pursuit Alter Theory Appraisal."

51. Ashford and Miller, *Chemical Exposures*; Gots, "Multiple Chemical Sensitivities."

in vivo studies specifically designed to test hypotheses regarding hormesis. Literature studies are relatively inexpensive and quick, and they can uncover evidence from a wide range of previous studies. Nevertheless, multiple authors have worried that this approach, while perhaps advantageous because of funding limitations, is inadequate to provide compelling evidence for claims HG, HP, and HD (i.e., claims about the generalizability, predominance, and default status of hormetic dose-response relationships).[52] Thus, if one wanted to obtain the sorts of information that would be more convincing for making regulatory changes, it would probably be necessary to fund new research studies that test specific hypotheses about the conditions under which hormesis occurs. Kristin Shrader-Frechette has argued, however, that this might be an ethically questionable use of societal resources. Given the evidence that children and other sensitive individuals are already suffering significant health effects as a result of the mixtures of toxic chemicals to which they are exposed, she argues that we should be developing more studies that examine these harmful synergistic effects rather than investigating alleged beneficial effects.[53]

## DEVELOPING SCIENTIFIC LANGUAGE

This section turns to judgments involved in developing scientific categories and terminology, which have received less philosophical attention than many of the other decisions associated with research. Much of the previous work on this topic has focused on the role of scientific language in a few disciplines, especially biology and the social sciences. For example, feminists have famously criticized the "passive egg, active sperm" description of conception.[54] Similarly, environmentalists have examined how values can influence the definitions and usage of terms like 'sustainability' or 'wetlands' or 'climate change.'[55] Philosophers and scientists have also critiqued the use of human social concepts such as "rape" and "slavery" to describe the behavior of other animals.[56]

52. See, for example, Kitchin and Drane, "Critique of the Use of Hormesis"; Mayo and Spanos, "Risks to Health and Risks to Science"; Shrader-Frechette, "Ideological Toxicology"; Thayer et al., "Fundamental Flaws."

53. Shrader-Frechette, "Ideological Toxicology."

54. See, for example, Martin, "Egg and the Sperm."

55. Norton, *Sustainability*; Schiappa, "Towards a Pragmatic Approach"; Schiappa, *Defining Reality*; Gardiner, "Ethics and Global Climate Change." For another analysis of the policy significance of language associated with the environmental sciences, see Harre, Brockmeier, and Muhlhauser, *Greenspeak*. For other work along these lines and covering some of the same material in this chapter, see Elliott, "Novel Account," and Elliott, "Ethical Significance."

56. See, for example, Dupré, "Fact and Value"; Herbers, "Watch Your Language!"

These decisions about categorizing phenomena and choosing terms to describe them might initially appear to be of little significance. On closer inspection, however, it turns out that they can affect society in at least four important ways: (1) by influencing the future course of scientific research; (2) by altering public awareness or attention to socially relevant scientific phenomena; (3) by influencing the attitudes or behavior of key decision makers; and (4) by altering the burden of proof required for taking action in response to public-policy issues.[57] Therefore, numerous scientists and scholars of science communication have argued that more attention should be paid to the ways in which research results are framed for the public.[58] Value-laden terminology might seem to be less of a concern in toxicology than in other areas of science, but this section shows that linguistic decisions in the hormesis case are still socially significant. In the remainder of this section I examine two important kinds of judgments: choosing a definition for the phenomenon and developing terminology to describe it. Chapter 7 provides further examples of how scientific categories and terminology can have important societal ramifications in the cases of endocrine disruption and multiple chemical sensitivity.

It has proven to be quite complicated to develop an adequate definition of the hormesis phenomenon. Some scientists employ the concept of what I call "beneficial hormesis," which can be defined as a beneficial low-dose effect caused by a chemical that produces harmful effects at higher doses.[59] Perhaps part of the motivation for this concept is that it makes the implications of hormesis for public policy particularly clear. If beneficial low-dose effects could be shown to be widely generalizable, the regulation of toxic chemicals might be significantly affected. (Of course, a number of other issues would also need to be considered, including the question of whether sensitive individuals are already exposed to mixtures of chemicals at levels that exceed the hormetic range.) Unfortunately, this concept also has drawbacks. As Calabrese points out, the classification of an effect as a benefit may depend on contextual considerations or particular points of view. For example, hormetic doses of antiviral or antibacterial agents might be beneficial from the perspective of viruses or bacteria but harmful from the perspective of human patients. Calabrese also worries that defining hormesis in terms of benefits might politicize evaluations of the dose-response

57. For further discussion of these four avenues of influence, see Elliott, "Ethical Significance."

58. See, for example, Larson, "War of the Roses"; Larson, "Social Resonance"; Nisbet and Mooney, "Framing Science"; Scheufele and Lewenstein, "Public and Nanotechnology."

59. For authors who employ this concept, see Axelrod et al., " 'Hormesis'—An Inappropriate Extrapolation"; Gerber, Williams, and Gray, "Nutrient-toxin Dosage Continuum"; Poumadere, "Hormesis"; Thayer et al., "Fundamental Flaws"; Zapponi and Marcello, "Low-dose Risk."

relationship.[60] Other researchers have concurred: "The definition of hormesis should not include nonscientific judgments as to beneficial or harmful effects."[61]

Because of these sorts of concerns with the beneficial-hormesis concept, Calabrese encourages definitions that focus primarily on the shape of the hormetic dose-response curve. For example, hormesis was originally defined in 1943 as "the stimulation of biological processes by subinhibitory levels of toxicants."[62] We can call this concept "low-dose-stimulation hormesis."[63] Although researchers frequently refer to hormesis as a phenomenon characterized by low-dose stimulatory effects, a significant disadvantage of this concept is that the notion of low-dose stimulation is vague. Because of biological feedback loops, substances that stimulate one biological endpoint are likely to inhibit other endpoints. One might wonder, therefore, whether instances of low-dose inhibition and high-dose stimulation count as examples of hormesis. For example, Calabrese notes that some antianxiety drugs increase anxiety in the low-dose hormetic zone while decreasing it at higher dose levels, whereas other drugs have the opposite effects.[64] It would be rather odd if U-shaped dose-response curves for one set of drugs (e.g., those that stimulate anxiety at low doses) could be labeled hormetic but not U-shaped dose-response curves for another set of drugs that decrease anxiety at low doses.

An obvious way to solve this problem is to employ the concept of "opposite-effects hormesis," defined as any nonspurious biological effect of a chemical that produces opposite effects on the same endpoint at higher doses.[65] Rather than defining hormesis only in terms of stimulatory low-dose effects and inhibitory high-dose effects, opposite-effects hormesis also includes instances of low-dose inhibition and high-dose stimulation. This concept accords well with Calabrese's literature studies of hormesis insofar as they were designed to identify any cases in which chemicals produced opposite effects at low and high doses.[66]

60. Calabrese and Baldwin, "Defining Hormesis"; Calabrese, "Hormesis: Why It Is Important."

61. Chapman, "Defining Hormesis: Comments"; for further support for removing normative judgments from the definition of hormesis, see Upton, "Comments."

62. Southam and Ehrlich, "Effects of Extracts."

63. For authors who employ this concept, see Calabrese and Baldwin, *Chemical Hormesis*, 1; Stebbing, "Hormesis"; Foran, "Regulatory Implications of Hormesis."

64. Calabrese, "Hormesis: Why It Is Important."

65. Mark Mattson and Edward Calabrese appear to adopt something like this definition for hormesis in their chapter "Hormesis: What It Is and Why It Matters." On p. 1 they claim that "Hormesis describes any process in which a cell, organism, or group of organisms exhibits a biphasic response to exposure to increasing amounts of a substance or condition," although they go on to say that the low-dose effect is *typically* stimulatory or beneficial.

66. Calabrese and Baldwin, "Dose Determines the Stimulation"; Calabrese and Baldwin, *Chemical Hormesis*, III–4.

Unfortunately, some further difficulties apply to both the concepts of opposite-effects and low-dose-stimulation hormesis. One concern is that, if the background level of a particular endpoint is particularly low or high, it may not be possible to observe inhibition or stimulation of the endpoint that occurs at low doses.[67] Nevertheless, even if opposite effects could not easily be observed, one would presumably want to say that hormesis is occurring if the underlying mechanisms that typically produce hormesis were operating in a particular case. A second difficulty is that essential nutrients (e.g., trace metals such as selenium) often produce opposite effects at low and higher doses. Although such phenomena would be included in the scope of the opposite-effects concept of hormesis, many researchers would not consider them to be instances of the phenomenon, in part because they may indirectly exert biphasic effects by influencing many different biological endpoints at once.[68] A final problem is that the concepts of low-dose stimulation and opposite-effects hormesis could include such a wide variety of underlying mechanisms that some researchers might question whether such a diverse range of phenomena should be given a single label.[69] After all, any substance on which organisms depend can be harmful if administered at sufficiently high doses; it might trivialize the phenomenon of hormesis to associate it with every biphasic dose-response relationship, no matter how it is produced.

All three of these difficulties with the concepts of low-dose-stimulation and opposite-effects hormesis arise from the fact that they are operational, and thus they do not specify the mechanisms that produce hormetic effects. By an operational concept, I mean one that is defined in terms of its criteria of application, which in the case of hormesis involves the measurement of some biological endpoint. In contrast, a mechanistic concept requires the identification of an underlying system in which hormetic phenomena are produced by the interaction of parts according to causal laws.[70] One solution to the preceding problems is to define hormesis in terms of a specific mechanism or perhaps a general mechanism schema.[71] For example, the concept of "overcompensation hormesis" can be defined as a biological response in which physiological processes are stimulated to above-normal levels in an

67. Calabrese, "Hormesis: Why It Is Important."

68. Ibid.; Davis and Svendsgaard, "U-shaped Dose-response Curves."

69. Van der Woude, Alink, and Rietjens, "Definition of Hormesis";Weltje, vom Saal, and Oehlmann, "Reproductive Stimulation by Low Doses of Xenoestrogens."

70. For further discussion of operational and mechanistic concepts, see Bridgman, *Logic of Modern Physics*; Bechtel and Richardson, *Discovering Complexity*; Machamer, Darden, and Craver, "Thinking about Mechanisms."

71. For the notion of a mechanism schema see Machamer, Darden, and Craver, "Thinking about Mechanisms."

attempt to restore organismal homeostasis after an initial inhibition by a toxic chemical (see figure 1.2).[72] A. R. D. Stebbing has argued that many U-shaped dose-response relationships could be the result of overcompensation because multiple biological endpoints are monitored and controlled by feedback processes.[73]

Unfortunately, a significant concern with a definition that focuses on overcompensation is that it may not be the only mechanism responsible for hormetic effects. Calabrese, in particular, argues that hormesis may sometimes be the result of what he calls "direct stimulation," in which low doses of a chemical directly stimulate a particular endpoint (such as growth or longevity) without inhibiting it at an earlier time.[74] For example, he suggests that such apparent direct stimulation has been observed on the fermentation rate in yeast exposed to arsenic, the rate of DNA synthesis in chick embryo cells exposed to zinc, the prostate weight of male mice exposed to diethylstilbestrol, and numerous other endpoints.[75]

Calabrese ultimately opted for a definition that incorporates a mixture of the opposite-effects, overcompensation, and direct-stimulation concepts:

> Hormesis should be considered an adaptive response characterized by biphasic [i.e., U-shaped or J-shaped] dose responses of generally similar quantitative features with respect to amplitude and range of the stimulatory response that are either directly induced or the result of compensatory biological processes following an initial disruption in homeostasis.[76]

Unfortunately, even this mixed approach presents difficulties. One problem is that the causal processes underlying direct-stimulation hormesis are not completely understood. Thus, no clear criteria have been developed for identifying cases where a chemical directly stimulates a biological endpoint at low doses (as opposed to producing stimulatory effects via indirect effects on other biological pathways).[77] It is therefore not easy to distinguish instances of direct-stimulation hormesis from biphasic dose responses that are produced by nonhormetic mechanisms. Another difficulty is that it is not clear whether overcompensation and direct stimulation encompass all the mechanisms that researchers would want to label as hormetic. Davis

72. Calabrese, "Evidence that Hormesis Represents an 'Overcompensation' Response."

73. Stebbing, "Hormesis."

74. Calabrese and Baldwin, "Defining Hormesis"; Calabrese, "Hormesis: Why It Is Important."

75. Calabrese and Baldwin, "General Classification of U-shaped Dose-response Relationships."

76. Calabrese and Baldwin, "Defining Hormesis," 91.

77. Calabrese and Baldwin acknowledge that direct-stimulation hormesis actually encompasses an array of mechanisms rather than one particular mechanism; see Calabrese and Baldwin, "General Classification of U-shaped Dose-response Relationships."

and Svendsgaard report a variety of such phenomena.[78] For example, the interactive effects of some metals may inhibit carcinogenesis and produce U-shaped dose-response curves on certain endpoints.

Another problem is that there appears to be "slippage" between the mixed definition of hormesis and the criteria that Calabrese has employed for identifying the phenomenon. This could result in overestimates of the frequency with which hormesis actually occurs. Consider, for example, that the definition is fairly ambitious. It states both that hormesis is adaptive and that it is produced by either of two sorts of mechanisms (namely, overcompensation or direct stimulation). In contrast, the criteria for identifying hormesis in Calabrese's literature studies are fairly loose, in the sense that they merely require that a chemical produce opposite effects on a particular endpoint at low and high doses. However, it is surely plausible that chemicals sometimes produce opposite effects on specific endpoints via mechanisms other than overcompensation or direct stimulation, in which case the literature studies could be identifying alleged instances of hormesis that do not actually fit the definition. Calabrese could perhaps evade this objection by stipulating that any mechanism other than overcompensation that results in opposite effects be labeled "direct stimulation." Unfortunately, the mechanism of direct stimulation would then presumably include a very wide range of phenomena, including instances of endocrine disruption, and it is doubtful that all such phenomena are genuinely adaptive.[79]

Yet another concern related to Calabrese's preferred definition of hormesis is that its avoidance of normative language may in fact be more problematic than it initially appears. His attempt to shield the hormesis concept from being value laden could end up backfiring if it forces value judgments to enter the scientific discussion surreptitiously rather than in a transparent fashion. For example, although Calabrese and his colleagues acknowledge that hormetic effects are not *always* beneficial, they appear to assume that hormetic effects are *frequently* beneficial. Otherwise, it would not make sense for them to frame the hormesis phenomenon as having significant economic implications for chemical regulations and as potentially "turning upside down" current risk-communication messages to the public.[80] Thus, an important strength of a normative concept such as "beneficial hormesis" is that it makes explicit the value judgment that numerous researchers are already making, namely, that many cases of low-dose stimulation are in fact

78. Ibid., 77–78.

79. See van der Woude, Alink, and Rietjens, "Definition of Hormesis"; Weltje, vom Saal, and Oehlmann, "Reproductive Stimulation by Low Doses of Xenoestrogens."

80. Calabrese and Baldwin, "Toxicology Rethinks Its Central Belief."

beneficial. Perhaps partly because of this consideration, a number of scientists continue to define hormesis in terms of beneficial low-dose effects.[81]

Although these debates about how to define hormesis may seem to be rather dry and socially insignificant, critics of claims HG, HD, and HP have pointed out that these linguistic issues should not be ignored. Paul Mushak insists:

> The most recent incarnation of hormesis has been accompanied by a tailored vocabulary for the topic coupled with problems in language precision, yielding ambiguous and potentially misleading terminology. Language matters. Language especially matters with evolving and/or controversial scientific topics where communicating and interpreting new findings must be done free of ambiguity.[82]

Although one might object that conceptual ambiguity can sometimes be fruitful in developing areas of scientific research, it is also surely valuable to recognize when scientific categories or terminology incorporate crucial interpretive judgments that can influence societal perspectives and decisions.

As one example of his concerns about scientific language, Mushak notes that Calabrese and a number of coauthors recently proposed a broadened definition of hormesis.[83] They suggested using the "hormesis" label not only for the biphasic dose-response relationships covered by Calabrese's previous definition but also for similar phenomena involving preconditioning responses to stress. Preconditioning occurs when an organism or cell that is exposed to a stressor (e.g., ionizing radiation, mutagenic chemicals, hypoxia) exhibits an adaptive response, such that it is better able to handle subsequent, more massive exposures to the same stressor. Whether or not this encapsulation of preconditioning phenomena under the hormesis label turns out to be scientifically fruitful, it has intriguing societal ramifications. Associating hormesis with a greater range of phenomena, such as preconditioning, is likely to promote greater familiarity with the concept and more acceptance of it by other scientists, policy makers, and the public. Mark Mattson's efforts to place the beneficial effects of exercise and healthy eating under the hormesis umbrella are likely to foster the same sort of wider social

81. In fact, hormesis is even defined in terms of beneficial effects at the beginning of the edited volume put together by Calabrese and Mattson. See p. v of Mattson, "Preface." See also Axelrod et al., "'Hormesis'—An Inappropriate Extrapolation"; Poumadere, "Hormesis"; Thayer et al., "Fundamental Flaws"; Zapponi and Marcello, "Low-dose Risk."

82. Mushak, "Ad-hoc and Fast Forward." A response to this article is Calabrese, "Hormesis: A Conversation with a Critic." See also Mushak, "Hormesis: A Brief Reply" and Calabrese, "Hormesis: Calabrese Responds."

83. Calabrese et al., "Biological Stress Response Terminology."

recognition and acceptance.[84] These strategies are likely to make the public more open to shifting regulatory practices in response to the hormesis phenomenon, and therefore it is worth scrutinizing them to make sure that they are justified.

Thus, this brief analysis shows that choices about how to define hormesis can have a number of socially relevant effects: making evaluations of it more likely to be politicized, increasing the likelihood of overestimating its frequency, hiding value judgments about the beneficial nature of the phenomenon, and increasing public recognition and acceptance of it. In addition to these definitional questions, at least three other choices about how to describe hormesis deserve attention because of their subtle societal consequences: (1) whether to use the label "hormesis" at all, (2) whether to claim that hormesis is adaptive, and (3) whether to describe hormesis as generalizable.

The first decision involves whether to use the hormesis label or whether to categorize biphasic toxicological phenomena in a different manner. Kristina Thayer and her coauthors argue, for example, that "many examples used to support the widespread frequency of hormesis are better described by the more general term 'nonmonotonic' dose responses. Nonmonotonic is used to describe dose-response relationships in which the direction of a response changes with increasing or decreasing dose."[85] Given the difficulty of arriving at a fully adequate definition of hormesis, it might seem that Calabrese is trying to create a new and unnecessary concept by employing the hormesis label. Moreover, the creation of this new concept is not only scientifically significant but also socially important. Referring to "hormesis" encourages the notion that a potentially significant, new low-dose phenomenon has been uncovered, whereas referring to "nonmonotonic" dose responses merely perpetuates the notion that chemicals can have a variety of different low-dose effects, many of which are difficult to predict based on data at higher doses.

It is no wonder, therefore, that Thayer and her coauthors (who want to downplay the potential significance of hormesis for regulatory practices) would prefer to maintain the terminology of "biphasic" or "nonmonotonic" dose responses. In their view, it is not necessary to employ a new label unless it applies to a specific set of mechanistic phenomena that are distinct from other examples of nonmonotonic responses. Calabrese would argue that the mechanism of overcompensation hormesis is sufficiently distinct to

84. Mattson, "Hormesis Defined."

85. Thayer et al., "Fundamental Flaws," 1271. For another argument that "hormesis" might not be a suitable umbrella term for low-dose stimulatory effects, see Chapman, "Defining Hormesis: Comments."

merit a new label, but it would then seem problematic for him to include the poorly understood mechanism of direct stimulation as part of the definition of hormesis.[86] Moreover, he has acknowledged that data at multiple time points, which are necessary for confirming instances of overcompensation hormesis, are frequently unavailable in the studies that he has inspected.[87] On this basis, Thayer and her coauthors would conclude that we currently have inadequate reason to create a new label of "hormesis." They would insist that Calabrese's literature studies have merely highlighted the prevalence and significance of nonmonotonic dose responses. The goal here is not to settle the argument between Thayer and Calabrese but rather to highlight the presence of these judgments and the fact that they have significant societal, as well as scientific, ramifications.

A second terminological decision is whether to describe hormesis as an adaptive phenomenon. On one hand, it seems plausible that organisms might have greater fitness if they display hormetic responses than if they do not. On this basis, we have seen that Calabrese goes so far as to include the adaptiveness of hormesis as part of its definition.[88] By doing so, however, he is making a controversial judgment, because others question the notion that hormetic effects must be adaptive.[89] It is possible that many seemingly beneficial effects on individual biological endpoints do not increase the fitness of biological organisms over an extended period of time. Moreover, it is difficult to establish criteria for determining whether an alleged instance of hormesis is adaptive. Therefore, some scientists insist that it is unhelpful and possibly misleading to include adaptability as part of the definition or description of hormetic effects.[90] Of course, Calabrese could argue that his definition of the term "adaptive" is broad, such that a response can be adaptive just by being sensitive to environmental conditions (e.g., exhibiting feedback processes), even if it is not always beneficial. However, here again, it is important to consider the social ramifications of this linguistic choice. If people typically think of adaptive phenomena as being beneficial, then

86. Moreover, in some of his recent work, Calabrese returns to operational definitions of hormesis (focusing simply on biphasic dose-response curves) rather than mechanistic ones, so he cannot defend the "hormesis" label by appealing to a unique mechanism to which it refers; see Mattson and Calabrese, "Hormesis: What It Is and Why It Matters." Calabrese would undoubtedly argue, however, that there are at least families of mechanisms that frequently give rise to the hormesis phenomenon.

87. Calabrese, "Hormesis: Why It Is Important."

88. Calabrese and Baldwin, "Defining Hormesis."

89. Axelrod et al., "'Hormesis'—An Inappropriate Extrapolation"; Thayer et al., "Fundamental Flaws."

90. See, for example, Weltje, vom Saal, and Oehlmann, "Reproductive Stimulation by Low Doses of Xenoestrogens."

describing hormesis as adaptive is likely to incline people toward more positive perceptions of the phenomenon, regardless of whether that is justified.

A third terminological question is whether it is appropriate or helpful to refer to hormesis as generalizable, as Calabrese and Baldwin often do.[91] The term "generalizable" is potentially quite ambiguous. It could mean, for example, that for each biological model, endpoint, and chemical class, there is at least one example of a hormetic dose-response relationship. Or it could mean that a particular percentage (say, 50 percent) of toxic chemicals exhibit hormetic dose-response relationships (on at least some endpoints in at least some biological models). It could also mean that, if one were to formulate a comprehensive list of the dose-response relationships for every toxic chemical on every endpoint in every biological model, some percentage of those relationships (again, say 50 percent) would be hormetic. Thus, scientists must decide whether the term "generalizable" has a precise enough meaning to convey useful information or whether it is more likely to serve as a potentially misleading rhetorical device. Moreover, even if it is a sufficiently precise label, some researchers worry that it is too difficult to determine whether hormesis is generalizable unless it is defined in terms of a well-understood mechanistic phenomenon like overcompensation.[92] Nevertheless, despite this ambiguity and potential confusion associated with the concept of "generalizability," it clearly encourages the notion that hormesis might have widespread ramifications. Thus, the term deserves scrutiny not only from a scientific standpoint but also with sensitivity regarding its societal implications.

## EVALUATING AND INTERPRETING STUDIES

Whereas the range of judgments associated with choosing scientific language deserves more attention in the philosophical literature, the role of methodological and interpretive decisions in the evaluation of theories and hypotheses has been extensively discussed.[93] Nevertheless, as we will see in chapter 3, philosophers continue to debate whether the considerations that are allowed to influence these decisions should be limited to those that are constitutive of science (e.g., the value that scientists place on explanatory power or predictive accuracy) or whether they should be broadened to

91. See, for example, Calabrese and Baldwin, *Chemical Hormesis*; Calabrese and Baldwin, "Toxicology Rethinks Its Central Belief."

92. Van der Woude, Alink, and Rietjens, "Definition of Hormesis."

93. See, for example, Kuhn, "Objectivity, Value Judgment, and Theory Choice"; McMullin, "Values in Science," in Newton-Smith.

include contextual factors (e.g., economic or ethical considerations).[94] Much of this work has focused on large-scale choices between opposing theories or paradigms.[95] The hormesis case provides an excellent illustration of the many specific methodological judgments that are associated with small-scale evaluations of particular hypotheses.[96]

One can identify many of the methodological judgments that are present in this case by considering how various scientists have responded to Calabrese's literature studies, which have served as the primary justification for accepting claims HG, HP, and HD. Let us start by examining the basic structure of Calabrese's methodology. He and his coworker Linda Baldwin performed an initial search in which they used keywords associated with hormesis to find relevant articles in computer databases.[97] Their search resulted in 8,500 articles, which they manually narrowed down to 585 "potentially relevant" studies that might provide evidence of the hormesis phenomenon. They examined the evidence for hormesis in each study using a set of a priori qualitative evaluation criteria such as the number of different doses administered, the dose range, the reproducibility of apparent hormetic effects, and the statistical significance of apparent hormetic effects. Based on the evaluation criteria, they found evidence of hormesis in 350 of the 585 studies.

Calabrese and Baldwin subsequently reevaluated the 350 studies using a quantitative scoring system that assigned point values to the studies based on the number of doses in the hormetic range, the magnitude of the hormetic effect, and the number of doses that showed statistically significant effects above control levels. They suggested that the "establishment of highly restrictive, quantitative study design and response criteria permit a more objective assessment of hormetic dose-response relationships."[98] Whereas they judged by the initial *qualitative* criteria that 82 percent of the 350 studies showed moderate or high evidence of hormesis, only 27 percent of the studies showed moderate to high evidence under their *quantitative* evaluative scheme.[99] One should note, of course, that not all of these studies

94. See, for example, Giere, "New Program for Philosophy of Science?"; Kourany, "Philosophy of Science for the Twenty-first Century."

95. See, for example, Kuhn, "Objectivity, Value Judgment, and Theory Choice"; McMullin, "Values in Science," in Asquith.

96. Heather Douglas and Kristin Shrader-Frechette have provided some excellent analyses of methodological value judgments in science. See, for example, Douglas, "Inductive Risk and Values in Science"; Shrader-Frechette and McCoy, "How the Tail Wags the Dog."

97. Calabrese and Baldwin, "Dose Determines the Stimulation"; Calabrese and Baldwin, *Chemical Hormesis.*

98. Calabrese and Baldwin, *Chemical Hormesis*, III-10.

99. Ibid., III-11; see also Elliott, "Case for Caution."

provided statistical significance tests for their results, and the 350 studies that provided evidence for hormesis constituted only a small portion of the 8,500 articles with which they started.

In response to later criticisms that the methodology associated with their first literature study did not provide evidence for the *frequency* at which hormesis actually occurs, Calabrese and Baldwin performed a second literature search.[100] In the second study, they screened 20,385 articles from three journals: *Environmental Pollution* (1970–1998), *Bulletin of Environmental Contamination and Toxicology* (1966–1998), and *Life Sciences* (1962–1998). This time, they used a priori entry criteria to identify studies that had designs adequate to display hormetic effects if those effects occurred. For example, the studies needed to have "a concurrent control, a definable toxicity zone with doses greater than the NOAEL [i.e., the no-observed-adverse-effect level, thus ensuring that the chemical studied was toxic at high dose levels]...and at least two doses below the NOAEL [thus making it possible to detect hormetic effects if they occurred]."[101] They collected 195 articles (out of the 20,385 screened) containing 668 dose-response relationships that met the *entry* criteria for having the *potential* to display hormetic effects.

Of these 668 dose-response relationships, 245 (37 percent) satisfied *evaluative* criteria supporting the *presence* of hormesis. The evaluative criteria required the presence of statistically significant, beneficial low-dose effects if the studies determined statistical significance. In the studies in which the researchers did not determine statistical significance, the evaluative criteria required that at least three doses below the NOAEL displayed a 10 percent increase over controls. Calabrese and Baldwin concluded that their findings "suggest that hormetic responses are quite common and indeed expected if assessed with the appropriate study design criteria."[102]

In subsequent work using the same set of articles and dose-response relationships, Calabrese and Baldwin examined the almost eighteen hundred data points that involved doses below the no-observed-adverse-effect level (NOAEL).[103] They found a 2.5:1 ratio (1171:464) of responses above the control level (indicating stimulation) to those below the control level (indicating inhibition), even though a threshold dose-response model would predict a random 1:1 ratio of responses above and below control values. They also found that the mean response of the doses below the NOAEL was 115 percent of the controls. They claimed that their study "demonstrated that not only was the threshold model unable to adequately account for the data,

100. Calabrese and Baldwin, "Frequency of U-shaped Dose Responses."
101. Ibid.
102. Ibid.
103. Calabrese and Baldwin, "Hormetic Dose-response Model Is More Common."

but also that the responses were consistent with the hormetic model."[104] Calabrese and his colleagues obtained similar results in a subsequent study of a U.S. National Cancer Institute yeast-screening database that included almost fifty-seven thousand dose-response studies.[105]

Although these seminal studies do not exhaust all the literature searches that Calabrese has performed,[106] they illustrate at least seven significant judgments (see figure 2.1) involved in evaluating the strength of the current evidence for claims H, HG, HP, and HD (regarding the existence, generalizability, predominance, and default status of hormesis). An initial methodological decision associated with Calabrese and Baldwin's first literature search is how seriously to discount their findings, given that they failed to clarify the characteristics of the experimental studies that they considered irrelevant to their investigation of hormesis. Their manual review was apparently designed to isolate only articles that *supported* the occurrence of hormesis. Thus, it is possible that some of the roughly seventy-nine hundred articles that they rejected had several doses below the NOAEL and would have provided evidence of a *linear* or *threshold* dose-response curve under the conditions given in the articles. Reviewers thus have to weigh the significance of the roughly 350 studies (less than 5 percent of the 8,500 studies containing keywords related to hormesis) that appeared to show some evidence of occurrence of the hormesis phenomenon. Fortunately, as already noted, Calabrese and Baldwin mitigated this problem in their later work. In their second literature study, they used a screening technique to weed out toxicology studies that were unlikely to provide information about low-dose chemical effects (e.g., because the experiments did not include doses below the no-observed-adverse-effect level).[107] Therefore, it appears that the 20,190 studies that they excluded did not actually provide direct evidence against the occurrence of hormesis.

A second methodological judgment in assessing Calabrese and Baldwin's research has to do with how much to trust the data from the previous studies that they examined, given that the earlier work was not designed specifically to test the occurrence of hormesis.[108] Some commentators have suggested

104. Ibid.

105. Calabrese et al., "Hormesis Outperforms Threshold Model." For a critique of this study, see Crump, "Limitations in the National Cancer Institute," and see also the response in Calabrese et al., "Hormesis and High Throughput Studies."

106. See, for example, Calabrese, "Overcompensation Stimulation."

107. The *no-observed-adverse-effect level* is the dosage below which a toxicant no longer produces statistically significant toxic effects.

108. Jonas, "Critique of 'The Scientific Foundations of Hormesis'"; Mayo and Spanos, "Risks to Health and Risks to Science"; Rodricks, "Hormesis and Toxicological Risk Assessment"; Thayer et al., "Fundamental Flaws."

that, in order to rule out numerous potential random and systematic errors, new studies would ideally need to be designed with rigorous attention to the experimental model, homogeneity and sex of animals, laboratory conditions, nutrition, adaptation period, randomization, diluent, pharmacy and manufacturer of toxicant, details of the toxic exposure (including volume, route, and time of day and month), precautions against contamination, positive and negative controls, and appropriate statistical analysis.[109]

These concerns about the data from previous studies are exacerbated by the fact that they generally provide only weak evidence of hormesis. For example, even though Calabrese and Baldwin claimed that 37 percent of the dose-response relationships in their second literature study were hormetic, less than a third of those alleged hormetic relationships were established with statistical significance tests.[110] To take another example, Calabrese and Baldwin found in an analysis of previous National Toxicology Program data that 31 percent of dose-response relationships appeared to be hormetic. Nevertheless, based on their own ranking scheme, they acknowledged that 78 percent of those dose-response relationships exhibited low evidence of hormesis, whereas only 0.8 percent showed high evidence.[111]

Paul Mushak further emphasizes the tenuous nature of Calabrese and Baldwin's data by highlighting the skewed distribution of the hormetic dose-response relationships found in their second literature search.[112] For example, of the 251 dose-response relationships from the journal *Environmental Pollution* that met Calabrese and Baldwin's entry criteria for having the potential to display hormesis, almost half (116, or 46 percent) appeared in just two years (1985 and 1987). Given that Calabrese and Baldwin screened the journal for twenty-nine years, Mushak worries that this extraordinary clustering of the dose-response relationships in two years could be the consequence of serial publications by relatively few research groups using similar protocols.[113] He found similar, although not quite so dramatic, clustering in the dose-response relationships identified in the *Bulletin of Environmental*

109. Jonas, "Critique of 'The Scientific Foundations of Hormesis,' " 628.

110. Calabrese and Baldwin, "Frequency of U-shaped Dose Responses"; Mushak, "Ad-hoc and Fast Forward." For a response to Mushak, see Calabrese, "Hormesis: A Conversation with a Critic." See also Mushak, "Hormesis: A Brief Reply" and Calabrese, "Hormesis: Calabrese Responds."

111. Calabrese and Baldwin, "Hormesis at the National Toxicology Program."

112. Mushak, "Ad-hoc and Fast Forward."

113. Calabrese has responded to this worry by arguing that the various studies in his database do not appear to involve repetitive publications of the same data by the same groups; see Calabrese, "Hormesis: A Conversation with a Critic." Mushak claims in "Hormesis: A Brief Reply" that his concern was not repetitive publication of the same data but rather repetitive use of the same or similar experimental approaches; see also Calabrese, "Hormesis: Calabrese Responds."

*Contamination and Toxicology* and *Life Sciences*. Moreover, Deborah Axelrod and her coauthors have worried that, even if the data that Calabrese and Baldwin gleaned from previous studies were unproblematic, they may be misinterpreted when reanalyzed for the purposes of defending claims about hormesis. With respect to a classic 1978 study of dioxin, for example, they claim the following:

> The apparent hormetic response drawn from this study is largely an artifact of the evaluation methods applied by the proponents of hormesis. In this study, in no case was an individual tumor response non-monotonic. But by calculating the total number of tumors, an impression can be created that the overall tumor response was hormetic.[114]

A third interpretive judgment in the hormesis case is whether (and, if so, how much) to discount the evidence provided by Calabrese and Baldwin, given that some of their methodologies may have been susceptible to false positives. For example, they considered low doses that increased at least 10 percent from the control in previous studies to provide evidence for hormesis, but Kristina Thayer and her coauthors make the following observation:

> This approach can lead to a large change relative to the control with only a one-count change in response (e.g., the difference between 3 of 20 and 2 of 20 would amount to a 33 percent change). In this manner even small changes in incidence that reflect data variability would be interpreted incorrectly as evidence to support the widespread occurrence of hormesis.[115]

Moreover, Calabrese and Baldwin tended to focus on studies with relatively high incidences of effects among controls, because otherwise it would be difficult to detect the low-dose decrease in effects associated with hormesis. Nevertheless, critics have voiced the concern that, strictly as a matter of chance, control groups may sometimes show higher than normal incidences of effects, thus producing apparent evidence of hormesis that disappears in other trials.[116] Partly because of considerations like these, Paul Mushak is troubled by the fact that Calabrese often depends on just a few studies to indicate that a particular chemical produces hormetic effects, despite the fact that those studies may be a small subset of all the research that has been performed on that substance.[117]

114. Axelrod et al., "'Hormesis'—An Inappropriate Extrapolation."

115. Thayer et al., "Fundamental Flaws," 1272.

116. Mayo and Spanos, "Risks to Health and Risks to Science"; Zapponi and Marcello, "Low-dose Risk"; Mushak, "Ad-hoc and Fast Forward."

117. Mushak, "Hormesis and Its Place." Mushak cites lead as an example; Calabrese appeals to a few dozen studies in a few systems, but thousands of studies have been performed on lead, some of which suggest that lead may have no threshold for its neurotoxic effects.

Proponents of claims HG, HP, and HD have taken pains to respond to these concerns.[118] For example, Calabrese emphasizes that his literature searches revealed the same frequency of hormetic dose-response curves (35–40 percent) regardless of whether he evaluated toxicology studies based on statistical significance tests or alternative criteria. He also argues that, even if studies showed a surprising number of hormetic dose-response relationships in certain years, he subsequently reanalyzed the data and determined that this was not caused by repeated publication of the same data. Moreover, he claims that he and his colleagues typically follow the work of hormesis researchers over several years, confirming that their results are consistent over time and not merely the result of a single experiment. Thus, he claims that his literature studies are much less prone to false positives than his critics suggest.

Calabrese and his collaborators also emphasize that a wide variety of evidence supports the generalizability of hormesis. For example, they argue that evolutionary accounts of the natural history of organisms cohere well with the concept of hormesis, because one would expect biological systems to develop mechanisms that make optimal use of the resources available to them, even including low levels of toxic substances.[119] In fact, they have already identified a range of mechanisms that they believe to be responsible for hormetic effects. Many of these involve pathways for stimulating the expression of protective proteins that prevent and repair oxidative damage.[120] They also emphasize that the breadth of fields (including toxicology, pharmacology, agriculture, experimental psychology, aging research, and biomedicine) in which biphasic dose-response relationships have been observed supports their claims about the generalizability of hormesis.[121]

A fourth judgment in the hormesis case therefore has to do with how much weight to place on these various strands of supporting evidence, given the possibility that they could ultimately be misleading. After all, theories can have extensive explanatory power but ultimately end up being false.[122] Deborah Axelrod and her coauthors also point out cases where the available evidence may challenge claims like HG, HP, and HD: "A number of lines of evidence indicate that mercury, zinc, and other heavy metal pollutants do

118. For the claims in this paragraph, see especially two articles: Cook and Calabrese, "Importance of Hormesis to Public Health," and Calabrese, "Hormesis: A Conversation with a Critic." For further discussion, see Mushak, "Hormesis: A Brief Reply" and Calabrese, "Hormesis: Calabrese Responds."

119. Calabrese, "Hormesis: From Marginalization to Mainstream"; Gerber, Williams, and Gray, "Nutrient-toxin Dosage Continuum"; Parsons, "Hormetic Zone."

120. See, for example, Mattson, "Fundamental Role of Hormesis in Evolution."

121. Calabrese and Baldwin, "Hormesis: The Dose-response Revolution."

122. Douglas, "Science, Hormesis, and Regulation."

not have beneficial effects at environmentally relevant levels when the totality of toxicologic and epidemiologic evidence is considered."[123] Others worry that the U-shaped dose-response curves observed by Calabrese and Baldwin could be the result of many different processes produced by very different mechanisms.[124] Therefore, any claims about the generalizability of hormesis as a single phenomenon could be problematic, because it is not clear exactly what mechanistic phenomena underlie the various U-shaped dose-response curves observed in literature studies. Evaluating claims about hormesis thus requires decisions about how much credence to place in various lines of evidence and counterevidence.

A fifth methodological question concerns the extent to which current evidence indicates that hormetic responses occur on endpoints associated with carcinogenesis and not just on biological endpoints that are unrelated to cancer. In their initial literature study, Calabrese and Baldwin claimed that "the recognition that hormetic responses are widely generalizable with respect to chemical class, animal model, gender and biological endpoint... suggests that the process of carcinogenesis should likewise be an endpoint where hormetic responses could be anticipated."[125] As further support, Calabrese and Baldwin found about twenty instances in which hormesis apparently occurred on endpoints related to some aspect of carcinogenesis (e.g., DNA repair enzyme activity, DNA damage, and cell division). In response to this evidence, they concluded, "That hormetic responses occurred with such a wide range of cancer endpoints argues that the phenomenon is highly generalizable."[126]

Several opposing considerations need to be taken into account. One is that it may be misleading for Calabrese and Baldwin to refer to the *process* of carcinogenesis as an *endpoint*.[127] Biological *endpoints* are typically phenomena that can be quantitatively measured (e.g., longevity, growth, fecundity). *Processes* are developments that take place over a period of time, and they may not be conducive to quantitative measurement. Therefore, it is somewhat unclear whether evidence on *individual endpoints related to carcinogenesis* supports predictions about hormetic effects on *the complex process of carcinogenesis as a whole*. A second concern, following on this first one, is that chemicals can have a variety of effects (some apparently beneficial and

123. Axelrod et al., "'Hormesis'—An Inappropriate Extrapolation," 336; see also Mushak, "Hormesis and Its Place," 502, which emphasizes that there is significant evidence for no-threshold dose-response relationships for radiation, lead, and inorganic arsenic.

124. Menzie, "Hormesis in Ecological Risk Assessment"; Roberts, "Another View of the Scientific Foundations of Hormesis"; Thayer et al., "Fundamental Flaws."

125. Calabrese and Baldwin, *Chemical Hormesis*, VIII-1.

126. Ibid., VIII-34.

127. I thank Kristin Shrader-Frechette for bringing this point to my attention.

others apparently harmful) at any particular dose level. For example, low doses of dioxins may decrease the incidence of breast tumors but increase the incidence of liver tumors.[128] Similarly, cadmium may help prevent some cancers but potentially contribute to increased uterine and breast cancers because of endocrine-disrupting effects.[129] Calabrese and Baldwin cite cadmium as a hormetic agent because it apparently decreases testicular tumors in rats,[130] but Kristina Thayer and her colleagues note that cadmium *increased* the number of prostate tumors in the same study at the same allegedly hormetic doses.[131] Researchers are thus forced to evaluate the significance of multiple lines of evidence when assessing the likelihood of hormetic effects on the process of carcinogenesis.

A sixth judgment concerns the interpretation of Calabrese's literature studies that compare the number of stimulatory low-dose data points with the number of inhibitory low-dose data points in large databases.[132] Because the threshold model predicts a 1:1 ratio between stimulatory and inhibitory data points below the NOAEL, Calabrese and his colleagues interpret their observed 2.5:1 ratio as important evidence for claim HP (i.e., the predominance of the hormetic dose-response model over the threshold model). Nevertheless, the interpretation of these results is not straightforward. For example, Paul Mushak questions the decision by Calabrese and Baldwin to calculate their ratio from only the low-dose data points found in studies that met their entry criteria (i.e., studies that they regarded as having adequate study designs for identifying hormesis).[133] While studies needed to have *two* data points below the NOAEL in order to satisfy the entry criteria, Mushak notes that a variety of other studies identified in Calabrese and Baldwin's literature search had *one* data point below the NOAEL. He suggests that they should have included those data points in their calculated ratio. He also points out that, in a related study by Calabrese and Baldwin, 80 percent of data points below the NOAEL were indistinct from control values (and therefore seemingly supportive of a threshold dose-response model). He

128. Kaiser, "Sipping from a Poisoned Chalice." See Axelrod et al., "'Hormesis'—An Inappropriate Extrapolation," for further discussion of the dioxin case.

129. Kaiser, "Sipping from a Poisoned Chalice."

130. Calabrese and Baldwin, "Toxicology Rethinks Its Central Belief."

131. Thayer et al., "Fundamental Flaws."

132. Calabrese and Baldwin, "Hormetic Dose-response Model Is More Common"; Calabrese et al., "Hormesis Outperforms Threshold Model"; see also Crump, "Limitations in the National Cancer Institute," and Calabrese et al., "Hormesis and High Throughput Studies."

133. Mushak, "Ad-hoc and Fast Forward." For a response to Mushak's article, see Calabrese, "Hormesis: A Conversation with a Critic," and for further discussion see Mushak, "Hormesis: A Brief Reply," and Calabrese, "Hormesis: Calabrese Responds."

emphasizes that it is unclear how to reconcile this finding with Calabrese and Baldwin's claims that their low-dose data support the predominance of hormetic dose-response models over threshold ones.[134]

Another source of difficulty in interpreting Calabrese and Baldwin's ratio is that it was obtained by "stripping hundreds of individual dosing points from lower numbers of intact dose-response curves representing various substances, numbers of points, endpoints, experimental and biological systems, etc."[135] To take just one concern about this methodology, one cannot easily infer the frequency of hormetic *dose-response relationships* from the ratio of stimulatory-to-inhibitory *data points* that have been stripped from those relationships. Consider a highly simplified example: Suppose that every study in a large literature search included two doses below the NOAEL and that the ratio between hormetic and threshold dose-response relationships in the studies was 1:1. For the hormetic relationships, one might expect both doses below the NOAEL to be stimulatory. For the threshold relationships, statistically random variations would tend to result in one stimulatory and one inhibitory data point. One might then expect a roughly 3:1 ratio between stimulatory and inhibitory *doses*, despite the fact that the ratio between hormetic and threshold *dose-response relationships* is 1:1. Therefore, one must employ considerable caution when drawing conclusions about the frequency of the hormetic dose-response model on the basis of a 2.5:1 ratio of stimulatory-to-inhibitory doses.[136] The title of Calabrese and Baldwin's article, "The Hormetic Dose-response Model Is More Common than the Threshold Model in Toxicology," would therefore incorporate fewer controversial judgments if it were worded this way: "Stimulatory Low-dose Data Points Are More Common than Inhibitory Low-dose Data Points in Toxicology."[137]

When researchers turn to judgments associated with claim HD (i.e., that hormesis should be the default model in risk assessment), a seventh set of questions becomes relevant. For example, they need to ascertain whether hormetic effects are likely to remain beneficial for organisms over an extended period of time, how the effects might change when organisms are exposed to multiple chemicals simultaneously, and whether the effects are likely to differ on sensitive subpopulations. Some researchers argue that the evidence for hormetic effects in carefully controlled laboratory settings may have very limited significance for risk management, because humans may already be exposed to background levels of multiple chemicals that exceed

134. Mushak, "Ad-hoc and Fast Forward."

135. Ibid.

136. Calabrese and Baldwin, "Hormetic Dose-response Model Is More Common."

137. Ibid.

the hormetic zone.[138] Others worry that, insofar as hormesis often involves overcompensation responses to disruptions in homeostasis, it might either cause harmful effects that are not fully reversed by the subsequent overcompensation or wear down the organism and result in negative impacts *on the organism as a whole over the long term.*[139] Further evidence for the notion that hormetic effects might be harmful over the long term is the fact that numerous endocrine-disrupting chemicals stimulate endocrine-responsive genes at low doses but inhibit those genes (or others) at high doses. This low-dose stimulation appears to fit many definitions of hormesis, but a growing body of research indicates that it can result in a variety of cancers and other harmful effects in the long run.[140] Calabrese and Baldwin have tried to alleviate some of these concerns by pointing to evidence both that hormesis can occur with mixtures of toxic substances and that it is not always a merely temporary effect.[141] Whether they and other proponents of HD have marshaled convincing evidence is a crucial interpretive judgment.

## APPLYING RESEARCH

Turning to the application of hormesis research to individual and societal decision making, at least three sorts of judgments are particularly salient: (1) decisions about how best to disseminate research results, (2) choices about whether to implement new policies in response to the research, and (3) questions about how to address combinations of harms and benefits when formulating public policy. Because chapter 6 extensively discusses choices associated with the dissemination of research results in the hormesis case, this section focuses on the latter two issues (i.e., implementing new policies and addressing harms and benefits). With regard to implementing new policies, the most obvious judgment involves deciding whether the advantages of regulatory changes in response to hormesis outweigh the

138. Davis and Farland, "Biological Effects of Low-level Exposures"; Shrader-Frechette, "Ideological Toxicology"; Thayer et al., "Fundamental Flaws."

139. For the suggestion that overcompensation responses might not fully reverse initial harmful effects, see Mushak, "Hormesis and Its Place," 503. For the worry that overcompensation responses might wear down the organism or involve trade-offs that are harmful to the organism as a whole, see Shrader-Frechette, "Ideological Toxicology." A specific example comes from Y. Fujiwara et al., "Changes in Egg Size of the Diamondback Moth." They showed that diamondback moths exposed to low doses of the insecticide fenvalerate laid more eggs than control moths, but the eggs were smaller, and the offspring had a lower survival rate.

140. See, for example, S-M. Ho et al., "Developmental Exposure to Estradiol and Bisphenol A"; Alonso-Magdalena et al., "Estrogenic Effect of Bisphenol-A."

141. Calabrese and Baldwin, "Applications of Hormesis."

disadvantages. For example, if regulators institute new policies, a variety of complications could arise as a result of the social, cultural, and political context in which those new regulations are implemented.

Without attempting to give an exhaustive list, I present several potential problems. One is the challenge of distinguishing (given the level of available funding in our society) between chemicals that produce hormetic effects under real-life conditions and those that do not. Very expensive and time-consuming studies would be required to provide convincing evidence that a particular chemical produces hormetic effects under the majority of actual living conditions (taking into account age, diet, behavior, genetics, health, and other chemical exposures). Some commentators argue that, given the variety of toxic chemicals to which humans are currently exposed, many individuals would probably require *less* rather than *more* chemical exposure in order to experience hormetic effects.[142]

Calabrese and Baldwin have appealed to many laboratory studies that provide evidence of hormetic effects in particular organisms with specific chemicals under particular conditions. Nevertheless, it is not clear that these same chemicals would produce hormetic effects in human beings under the usual array of real-life conditions to which the public is typically exposed. For example, some researchers have observed that chemicals cause hormetic effects when cells are exposed to suboptimal nutrient levels.[143] Further studies would be needed to verify that those same effects could occur under the wider range of environmental and nutritional conditions found in human societies.

Given the difficulty of obtaining reliable information about hormetic effects in the human population, another potential problem with changing regulatory policies is that powerful interest groups would likely try to justify public exposures to toxic chemicals even if there were inadequate information about their effects. Numerous authors have documented that industry groups have withheld information, produced and appealed to biased (and even fraudulent) scientific results, and used powerful public relations strategies to weaken regulatory policy for toxic chemicals without adequate scientific justification (see chapter 4).[144] Therefore, despite inadequate evidence of the actual number of toxic substances that would provide beneficial health effects for the public, the representatives of powerful interest groups are likely to call for

142. Shrader-Frechette, "Ideological Toxicology."

143. Vichi and Tritton, "Stimulation of Growth in Human and Murine Cells by Adriamycin."

144. Beder, *Global Spin*; Fagin, Lavelle, and the Center for Public Integrity, *Toxic Deception*; Markowitz and Rosner, *Deceit and Denial*; Shrader-Frechette, *Taking Action, Saving Lives*; Wargo, *Our Children's Toxic Legacy*.

public exposure to greater quantities of most toxic chemicals. For example, the Texas Institute for the Advancement of Chemical Technology distributed a flyer citing examples of hormesis and suggesting that this could allow society "to enjoy the benefits of many chemicals that have been banned."[145]

These considerations do not provide conclusive proof, of course, that new regulatory policies will harm the public. One might argue that the mere possibility that powerful interest groups could abuse the system is not an adequate reason to block all efforts to reform risk-assessment practices. After all, steps can be taken to limit such abuses. For example, strict conflict-of-interest disclosures could be required for research related to hormesis (although chapter 4 does raise concerns about the effectiveness of such policies).[146] One could also demand careful federal oversight of laboratory studies on this topic and place the burden of proof on industry to demonstrate that particular toxic chemicals are genuinely beneficial at particular dose levels.[147] Nevertheless, the possibility that policy makers could prevent industry abuses merely highlights the difficult judgments involved in deciding whether new regulatory policies are warranted. One must decide, given a number of contingent social and institutional conditions, whether the potential costs of adopting new policies are likely to be adequately mitigated or outweighed by possible benefits.

The other major judgment involved in applying hormesis research to public policy is how to address the potential for combinations of benefits and harms. Supposing that hormesis were to occur with a particular set of chemicals, it is very possible that some of them might produce beneficial effects for particular individuals at the same dose range that the chemicals produce harmful effects for other, more sensitive individuals.[148] Consequently, a particularly vexing issue is whether regulatory agencies should try to maximize *benefits* for the entire population or merely try to prevent *harm*. There are at least two broad approaches that regulators might take with this issue.[149] A utilitarian strategy would be to maximize the ratio of benefits to harms for the population as a whole. The other, more deontological approach would be to focus on individual members of the population, making sure that no one is exposed to an unacceptable level of risk without appropriate consent and compensation in the event of injury.

145. Kaiser, "Sipping from a Poisoned Chalice," 377.

146. Krimsky, *Science in the Private Interest*; Task Force on Research Accountability, *Report on Institutional and Individual Conflict of Interest*.

147. Fagin, Lavelle, and the Center for Public Integrity, *Toxic Deception*.

148. Thayer et al., "Fundamental Flaws."

149. Douglas, "Science, Hormesis, and Regulation"; Hansson, "Ethical Principles for Hormesis Policies"; Sandin, "Ethics of Hormesis—No Fuss?"

Sven Ove Hansson has provided an intriguing summary of how these two different approaches have been accepted in various social and institutional contexts. He argues that the utilitarian, collectivist approach dominates in fields associated with risk analysis. In contrast, clinical medicine and disciplines influenced by it tend to take a deontological, individualist perspective.[150] Speaking from a descriptive rather than a normative perspective, there are at least three reasons that the latter, individual-focused approach is likely to dominate discussions of hormesis in the near future. First, ethicists have generally placed a higher priority on preventing harm as opposed to providing benefits.[151] Second, the benefits associated with hormesis appear to be relatively small compared to the potential for harm.[152] Third, as illustrated by controversies over the fluoridation of water, the public has not shown much enthusiasm for government risk-management policies that maximize benefits.

## CONCLUSION

As mentioned in the introduction to this chapter, toxicologist Edward Calabrese is of the opinion that "The toxicological community made an error of historic proportions in its formative years (the 1930–40s) in buying into the threshold model."[153] Nevertheless, he insists that times have changed: "Seven years ago, hormesis would not find its way into even informal conversation among toxicologists. Now, we not only know that it exists but accept its dominance over other models."[154] We have seen in this chapter, however, that major methodological and interpretive judgments permeate efforts to evaluate the evidence that Calabrese has marshaled in support of his claims about hormesis. This chapter has organized these issues into four major categories. One goal of this analysis has been to clarify the questions that researchers and policy makers need to consider as they reflect on the societal ramifications of this phenomenon. For example, we have seen that they have to decide: (1) what study designs would be most fruitful for

150. Hansson, "Ethical Principles for Hormesis Policies." Interestingly, although many commentators associated with the public health community have been fairly cautious about applying hormesis to regulatory policy, the discipline of public health has traditionally been more willing than clinical areas of medicine to take a utilitarian ethical perspective; see, for example, Bryan, Call, and Elliott, "Ethics of Infection Control."

151. Hoffmann and Stempsey, "Hormesis Concept and Risk Assessment."

152. Douglas, "Science, Hormesis, and Regulation"; Hoffmann and Stempsey, "Hormesis Concept and Risk Assessment"; and Sandin, "Ethics of Hormesis—No Fuss?"

153. Calabrese and Baldwin, "Toxicology Rethinks Its Central Belief," 691.

154. Ibid., 692.

obtaining the sorts of information that regulators, members of the public, and other scientists desire; (2) what definitions and terminology are most appropriate for describing this information; (3) what conclusions can legitimately be drawn from Calabrese's literature studies; and (4) whether current evidence justifies altering regulatory policy. Reflecting on the judgments associated with this case should also contribute to a more general understanding of the ways that scientific practice incorporates significant methodological and interpretive choices. In the next chapter I consider how societal values ought to inform these sorts of judgments.

# 3

# An Argument for Societal Values in Policy-Relevant Research

Is science value free? As one introduction to the relationship between science and values says, "The claim that values influence science is much like the claim that genes influence behavior. At this level of vagueness, almost no one will disagree, but there are underlying deep disagreements about how, how much, and with what ramifications they do so, once more specific theses are asserted."[1] Historians, philosophers, and sociologists of science have recently put a good deal of effort into uncovering the range of avenues through which values *do* in fact influence scientific practice. Nevertheless, these scholars continue to disagree about the normative question of which (if any) values *ought* to influence scientific reasoning, especially the evaluation of evidence for particular theories or hypotheses.

In this chapter I argue that, in cases of policy-relevant research such as hormesis, none of the four categories of methodological and interpretive decisions identified in chapter 2 should be entirely insulated from societal values. This argument is based on three major principles. First, the "ethics" principle is that scientists have ethical responsibilities to consider the major societal consequences of their work and to take reasonable steps to mitigate harmful effects that it might have. Second, the "uncertainty" principle is that those researching policy-relevant topics often face situations in which scientific information is uncertain and incomplete, and they have to decide what standard of proof to demand before drawing conclusions. Third, the "no-passing-the-buck" principle is that it is frequently socially harmful or impracticable for scientists to respond to uncertainty by withholding their judgment or providing uninterpreted data to decision makers. The upshot of this third principle is that scientists cannot always leave difficult choices about interpreting uncertain evidence up to policy makers. When these three principles apply to a case, there are ethical reasons for scientists to factor societal considerations into their responses to uncertainty.

1. Kincaid, Dupré, and Wylie, "Introduction," 10.

This argument is important to consider, because it might be tempting to respond to the range of choices encountered in chapter 2 by trying to shield research completely from societal influences that could skew those decisions. By pursuing such a policy, one might think that scientists would be able to address those difficult methodological and interpretive judgments without being biased by outside concerns. This approach is likely to seem even more appealing after considering, in chapter 4, the myriad strategies that interest groups have developed for manipulating scientific findings in order to promote their own concerns. The present chapter cuts off this seemingly appealing position by arguing that societal values should not simply be excluded across the board from the decisions associated with scientific research, especially when it is relevant to public policy. By blocking the easy route of completely eliminating societal influences, this analysis shows why the book's subsequent chapters are needed. They discuss *how* to incorporate societal considerations in a manner that is responsive to a wide range of perspectives and concerns rather than one that serves primarily the interests of deep pockets with extensive resources.

It is crucial to emphasize that the claims in this chapter do not imply that societal influences on science can never be criticized or regarded as illegitimate. For example, it is clearly unacceptable to falsify or fabricate results in order to advance one's political agenda. There are many other methodological norms that constrain what counts as acceptable scientific practice. For example, it would be unacceptable to design a toxicology study with very low power (i.e., with very little likelihood of identifying harmful effects) and then appeal to the study as compelling evidence that a chemical is harmless. The point of this chapter is that, in contrast to these relatively clear-cut cases, other situations provide significant leeway in making interpretive judgments. These might include choices about how to categorize or describe phenomena, what terms to use, what topics to study, what questions to ask, what study design to employ, how to characterize data, and how to interpret ambiguous evidence. I argue that in some cases it is appropriate for societal values to play a role in making all these decisions.

Presenting a systematic evaluation of the literature on the proper role of values in science would be an overwhelming task, so I circumscribe the argument in this chapter in several respects. First, I do not provide a detailed discussion of all the contexts in which societal values should or should not be allowed to influence scientific practice. Rather, I identify a single set of conditions that is sufficient to justify incorporating societal values in scientific practice. I then show that, in policy-relevant areas of research like hormesis, all four categories of judgments identified in chapter 2 meet those conditions at least sometimes. A second limitation is that this analysis does not establish a way to prioritize conflicts among various societal values or between these values and other sorts of considerations. Nevertheless, it does show that societal matters should be among the factors that play a role in scientific judgment.

Despite these limitations, the argument in this chapter is a significant one, because it challenges some widespread assumptions about research. Heather Douglas provides an excellent summary of those common misconceptions:

> [W]e remain under the grip of a post-positivist hangover that all (non-epistemic) values in the (internal stages of the) scientific reasoning process are bad. We fear that any role for values (which some positivists defined as inherently meaningless) in epistemic processes will "distort" knowledge. We train scientists to believe that values are not allowed in science and they must ward off any appearance of personal values or personal judgments playing a role in their doing of science.[2]

By arguing that societal values sometimes have a legitimate role to play, even in the internal stages of scientific reasoning (such as the interpretation of evidence in support of hypotheses), this chapter provides a starting point for the remainder of the book.

The next section provides an introduction to the philosophical literature on the role of values in scientific research. The following section argues for incorporating societal values in "easy cases": judgments associated with the choice of research projects or the application of research to public policy (namely, the first and fourth categories discussed in chapter 2). It is relatively uncontroversial to claim that societal values should influence these sorts of decisions. The last two sections of the chapter address more controversial categories of judgments: decisions about scientific language and the interpretation of results. It is less obvious that societal values have a legitimate role to play in such internal aspects of scientific practice, but we will see that there are convincing reasons for allowing societal considerations to influence even those categories of judgments in some cases.

## BACKGROUND ON VALUES IN SCIENCE

This book does not use the term "values" solely to refer to ethical and political considerations but instead uses it in the way that most philosophers of science do to refer to any quality that scientists regard as desirable, meritorious, or worthy in a theory or hypothesis.[3] Thus, the term "value judgments"

2. Douglas, "Irreducible Complexity of Objectivity," 459.

3. McMullin, "Values in Science," in Newton-Smith; Scriven, "Exact Role of Value Judgments in Science."

refers here to decisions that require weighing the multiple strengths and weaknesses of debated scientific claims or methodologies.[4] In a seminal paper, Michael Scriven helpfully distinguished four different categories of value judgments.[5] First is a group that he called "value-base claims," which consist of assertions like "I value X." A second group involves "market-value claims," which refer to the perspective of a "hypothetical population of prospective purchasers" toward an object.[6] The third category consists of "real-value claims," which are statements about the real value or worth of something. Fourth are "valued-performance claims," which are descriptive claims about the qualities of an object but which, given particular contexts, are value laden because the described qualities are clearly considered valuable.

As Thomas Kuhn famously pointed out, scientific choices of the sort discussed in the previous chapter frequently involve something like what Scriven called "valued-performance claims" and "real-value claims."[7] First, even when researchers agree that qualities like explanatory power, predictive power, or simplicity are desirable, they have to make valued-performance claims about the extent to which a particular theory or hypothesis actually embodies one or more of those valued qualities. Second, when competing theories, hypotheses, or methodologies possess different qualities, scientists have to make real-value claims about which characteristics are most desirable. Thus, we can see that the methodological and interpretive decisions discussed throughout chapter 2 (e.g., choices about which research topics, study designs, or descriptions of hormesis are best to pursue) constitute what this chapter calls "value judgments." Because of the prevalence of these sorts of decisions, Kuhn emphasized that scientific practice cannot be reduced entirely to rule-governed, algorithmic reasoning; good scientists can come to different conclusions when making these choices.[8]

In an effort to clarify the roles that various sorts of values should play in these scientific choices, philosophers have attempted to categorize them. Some analysts contrast epistemic values with nonepistemic ones.[9] They describe the former as those "that are usually taken as constitutive of the knowledge- and truth-seeking goals of the enterprise of science" or that

4. Kuhn, "Objectivity, Value Judgment, and Theory Choice"; see also Brown, *Perception, Theory, and Commitment*.

5. Scriven, "Exact Role of Value Judgments."

6. Ibid., 225. Italics in the original text were removed from the quotation.

7. Kuhn, "Objectivity, Value Judgment, and Theory Choice."

8. See, for example, Brown, *Perception, Theory, and Commitment*; Kuhn, "Objectivity, Value Judgment, and Theory Choice"; McMullin, "Values in Science," in Asquith and Nickles.

9. See, for example, McMullin, "Values in Science," in Asquith and Nickles; McMullin, "Values in Science," in Newton-Smith.

"promote the truth-like character of science."[10] In contrast, nonepistemic values constitute a wide range of considerations (e.g., political, religious, personal, social) that do not reliably promote epistemic goals. Helen Longino has suggested a similar distinction between constitutive and contextual values. According to Longino, constitutive values are those that promote the goals of science, such as developing good explanations, whereas contextual values promote other goods.[11] On either account, the epistemic or constitutive values typically include considerations like accuracy, consistency, scope, fruitfulness, and unifying power.[12]

Nevertheless, the distinction between epistemic (or constitutive) and nonepistemic (or contextual) values has come under attack for at least two reasons. First, it is challenging to decide whether some values, such as unifying power, count as epistemic or nonepistemic. Second, some authors question whether it is even possible to maintain a legitimate conceptual distinction between epistemic and nonepistemic considerations.[13] In order to give proponents of the value-free ideal the benefit of the doubt, this chapter assumes both that it is possible to maintain a clear distinction between epistemic and nonepistemic values and that societal values constitute paradigmatic examples of nonepistemic considerations.

For the purposes of this work, societal values are qualities or states of affairs that societies or social groups hold to be good or desirable. Typical examples include fairness, justice, diversity, efficiency, liberty, stability, privacy, and community. Different groups within a nation or a community may accept differing values or prioritize them differently. Many of these societal values are ethical ones, but some values of social groups could also be challenged from an ethical perspective. The extent to which these societal considerations should play a role in scientific practice continues to be a heavily debated issue. The *descriptive* claim that societal values *have*, as a matter of fact, historically influenced scientific judgments is uncontroversial. The science-studies literature is replete with discussions of how a wide variety of nonepistemic considerations have influenced scientific research.[14] The crucial issue is the *normative* question of what role these nonepistemic values ideally *ought* to play in scientific reasoning.

10. Rooney, "On Values in Science." See also Steel, "Epistemic Values."

11. Longino, *Science as Social Knowledge.*

12. See Kuhn, "Objectivity, Value Judgment, and Theory Choice"; Longino, *Science as Social Knowledge*; McMullin, "Values in Science," in Asquith and Nickles.

13. Longino, "Gender, Politics, and the Theoretical Virtues"; Rooney, "On Values in Science."

14. Koertge, *House Built on Sand*; Jasanoff et al., eds., *Handbook of Science and Technology Studies.*

To address the normative issue, Longino and others have distinguished between four general ways in which values can intersect with scientific work.[15] First, values can channel scientific inquiry in particular directions, such as when funding agencies encourage researchers to pursue socially important lines of investigation. Second, values can influence the way in which scientific research is applied in the realm of public policy or technology development, as when citizens and policy makers debate the pros and cons of pursuing nuclear power as opposed to other sources of energy. Third, values can affect the behavior of scientists as they carry out research, such as the manner in which they treat their colleagues, their research subjects, and their laboratory animals. Fourth, values can influence the internal aspects of scientific reasoning, including inferences from experimental data to theories or hypotheses.

Despite the common aphorism that science should be value free, most analysts believe that nonepistemic values have a legitimate role to play in three of these four aspects of science. It is relatively uncontroversial to claim that contextual considerations can justifiably affect research in the first way (i.e., influencing the choice of projects). For example, societal priorities, individual interests, and ethical concerns can appropriately influence whether scientists put more effort into finding cures for a disease like breast cancer as opposed to heart disease, AIDS, or tuberculosis.[16] Ethical and societal values are also relevant to the second aspect, namely, applying research to policy making or technological development. An example is deciding, on the basis of information about the likelihood that nuclear waste will leak out of a proposed repository such as Yucca Mountain, whether it is advisable to build the proposed facility.[17]

Nonepistemic considerations are also relevant to the third aspect of scientific practice, the behavior of scientists. Ethical constraints on scientific methodology provide an example of these nonepistemic values. For example, scientists are expected to obtain informed consent from human research

15. See, for example, Longino, *Science as Social Knowledge*, 83–86; Douglas, "Inductive Risk and Values in Science"; Kincaid, Dupré, and Wylie, "Introduction"; Machamer and Wolters, "Introduction." One should note that, although it may be helpful for organizational purposes to distinguish these four categories, they are arguably not mutually exclusive.

16. See, for example, Sunstein, *Laws of Fear*. Although Sunstein questions the ability of the public to understand and to make decisions related to narrowly scientific matters, he argues that it would be inappropriate to use solely scientific considerations (such as probability of fatality) to decide what risks to prioritize. He emphasizes that the public might legitimately decide to spend more money (including research funds) to reduce risks of dreaded diseases such as cancer, even if there is a greater chance of dying from something else, like heart disease.

17. Ibid. Whereas Sunstein thinks that scientists alone should evaluate the probability of hazards associated with nuclear power and other technologies, he would readily acknowledge that societal values should play a role in deciding which technologies are most important to develop.

participants before including them in their studies. Other ethical norms or values that guide the relationships of scientists with one another and with society include credit, education, honesty, openness, freedom, social responsibility, and efficiency.[18] The sixth chapter of this book reflects further on the ethical responsibilities of scientists as experts who provide information to the public and to policy makers.

It is the fourth aspect of science (namely, the internal elements of scientific reasoning) that scientists and philosophers are most likely to try to keep free of contextual values.[19] However, even within this fourth category, it is important to keep in mind the variety of ways in which these values can intersect with science. Longino identifies five of them.[20] First, she points out that values can influence the practices of science, such as when biologists pursue more reductionistic as opposed to more holistic methods of analyzing living organisms. Second, she notes that values can alter the questions that scientists ask, as when some of the first researchers investigating the birth control pill allegedly focused on investigating its potential benefits rather than its risks. Third, she argues that values can affect the description or interpretation of data, such as when scientists attempt to make sense of differing average IQ scores among racial groups. Fourth, she suggests that values can influence specific assumptions, such as the long-held anthropological view that males' hunting activities were central to hominid behavioral evolution. Fifth, she suggests that values can alter global scientific assumptions, such as that dichotomies between relatively passive and active components (e.g., cytoplasm vs. genes or egg vs. sperm) are central to much of biological life.

When one considers the breadth of these sorts of interactions, the exclusion of contextual values from all internal aspects of scientific reasoning appears to be a dubious position. After all, nonepistemic values can make a seemingly justifiable contribution to science by helping researchers to recognize crucial theoretical or empirical weaknesses in hypotheses or assumptions that conflict with their values. For example, feminist values famously helped some scientists and philosophers to identify problems with the "active sperm/passive egg" model of fertilization and the "man-the-hunter" account of human evolution.[21] Similarly, Elizabeth Anderson has argued

18. For example, Merton, *Sociology of Science*; Resnik, *Ethics of Science*.

19. See, for example, Dorato, "Epistemic and Nonepistemic Values in Science"; Giere, "New Program for Philosophy of Science?"; McMullin, "Values in Science," in Asquith and Nickles; Mitchell, "Prescribed and Proscribed Values in Science Policy"; Ruphy, " 'Empiricism All the Way Down.' "

20. See Longino, *Science as Social Knowledge*, 86ff, and Longino, "Gender and Racial Biases in Scientific Research."

21. See, for example, Anderson, "Feminist Epistemology"; Longino, *Science as Social Knowledge*; Martin, "Egg and the Sperm."

that nonepistemic values can sometimes help researchers to provide a more comprehensive evaluation of scientific claims.[22] For example, she notes that some scientists have conceived of divorce primarily as a loss, which prevents them from collecting information about the positive consequences of divorce. She claims that "a value-laden conception of divorce as involving both loss and opportunities for growth is more epistemically fruitful, relative to controversies about the *overall* value of divorce, in that it allows us to uncover evidence bearing on both the pros and the cons of divorce."[23]

Proponents of the value-free ideal still insist that their claims are reasonable when they are interpreted narrowly. A modest formulation of their position is that they want to exclude contextual values only from very specific aspects of scientific reasoning. For example, they would claim that, when one is faced with a particular body of evidence and a particular theory or hypothesis, societal values do not have a legitimate role to play in evaluating the evidential support for the hypothesis.[24] Narrow positions of this sort have significant appeal, but there are still two prominent strategies for challenging them: a "gap" argument and an "error" argument. Each argument draws on the three principles mentioned in the introduction to this chapter: (1) the ethical responsibility to consider societal consequences; (2) uncertainty in available information; and (3) social or practical problems associated with withholding judgment.

## The Gap Argument

According to the "gap" argument, there is always a logical gap or underdetermination between theory and evidence. In other words, logic and evidence alone are not sufficient to justify a theory; a wide variety of background beliefs, assumptions, and auxiliary hypotheses are necessary in order to link evidence with theory.[25] Proponents of the gap argument also maintain that epistemic or constitutive values are insufficient to determine which background beliefs should be accepted. Thus, they suggest that other considerations, including societal values, play an unavoidable role in scientific practice, insofar as they fill the evidential gaps left by constitutive values, evidence, and logic. These thinkers argue that the appropriate way to

22. Anderson, "Uses of Value Judgments in Science."

23. Ibid., 20.

24. Giere, "New Program for Philosophy of Science?"; Mitchell, "Prescribed and Proscribed Values in Science Policy."

25. For proponents of the "gap" argument, see Howard, "Lost Wanderers in the Forest of Knowledge"; Howard, "Two Left Turns Make a Right"; Kourany, "Philosophy of Science for the Twenty-first Century"; Longino, *Science as Social Knowledge.*

maintain objectivity in science is not to try to exclude values (therefore driving them underground) but rather to identify the contextual considerations that play a role in one's scientific conclusions and subject them to open evaluation and criticism.[26]

There are three related criticisms of the gap argument. First, one must examine the aims of science in particular research contexts before deciding what sorts of values can appropriately be used for addressing gaps in scientific evidence. It makes sense to appeal to nonepistemic values only if they promote the aims of research in a specific context.[27] A second criticism is that it may be unnecessary to appeal to nonepistemic considerations, because the extent to which theories remain underdetermined by logic, evidence, and constitutive values remains disputed.[28] A third objection is that, in cases in which epistemic considerations are clearly insufficient to determine the evidence for a hypothesis, scientists could merely suspend their judgment rather than appealing to contextual values in support of a conclusion. Because of considerations like these, many critics continue to hold that only epistemic considerations should play a role in evaluating the evidential relationship between hypotheses and evidence.[29] In contrast, proponents of the gap argument would likely respond that the three objections continue to rely on a questionable distinction between epistemic (or constitutive) and nonepistemic (or contextual) considerations.[30]

Fortunately, it is not necessary to settle these complex disputes over the gap argument in order to address the cases of policy-relevant research discussed in the present book. Based on the preceding objections to the gap argument, three conditions appear to be jointly sufficient to justify its application to a particular area of scientific research. These conditions correspond to the three fundamental principles of my argument for incorporating societal values in policy-relevant research. First, regarding the aims of science, there must be ethical (or other contextual) considerations that are applicable to the area of research because of its context—this corresponds to the "ethics" principle. Second, scientific conclusions must be genuinely underdetermined by epistemic factors in the case under consideration—in accordance with the "uncertainty" principle. Third, the context of research must be such

26. Longino, *Fate of Knowledge.*

27. For example, Intemann, "Feminism, Underdetermination, and Values in Science." For discussions of the aims of science and how to evaluate them, see, for example, Laudan, *Science and Values,* and van Fraassen, *Scientific Image.*

28. Giere, "New Program for Philosophy of Science?"; Dorato, "Epistemic and Nonepistemic Values in Science."

29. Giere, "New Program for Philosophy of Science?"

30. See, for example, Longino, "Cognitive and Non-cognitive Values in Science"; Rooney, "On Values in Science."

that scientists are forced to accept one hypothesis rather than another, as opposed to suspending judgment—this corresponds to the "no-passing-the-buck" principle. The later sections of this chapter argue that, whether or not the gap argument applies to all areas of science, the major categories of judgments in the hormesis case (and in much policy-relevant research) do meet these three conditions in some cases.

Critics of the gap argument might still formulate an objection to the third of these conditions. They are likely to emphasize a crucial distinction between two different senses in which researchers might be forced to *accept* a hypothesis. On one hand, scientists might have to make a *practical judgment* about which hypothesis should serve as a *basis for action* by policy makers or citizens. On the other hand, they might be forced to make an *epistemic judgment* about which hypothesis to *believe*. Proponents of a value-free ideal for science are likely to argue that researchers are rarely (if ever) forced to make epistemic judgments.[31] Instead, those proponents would insist that researchers who need to make claims under uncertainty based on societal values should regard their conclusions as merely practical decisions about how to act. Therefore, by employing this distinction between epistemic and practical judgments, one can allow societal considerations to play a role in scientific reasoning while maintaining that the epistemic judgments of science should remain untainted by contextual factors.

One might develop a variety of responses to this distinction between epistemic and practical judgments, but the simplest rebuttal is that it does not challenge the goals of the present book. The thesis developed here is that societal values should not be excluded from any of the four major categories of judgments identified in chapter 2. This thesis is compatible with the claim that, when societal values do influence particular scientific judgments, they should be categorized as practical rather than epistemic. Nonetheless, some critics of the value-free ideal might insist that my seemingly appealing response is too simple. They would argue that, if I allow all judgments that are influenced by societal values to be labeled as practical rather than epistemic, my position becomes trivial. This "triviality" objection could take at least two specific forms. First, one might think that no one would deny my thesis that societal values have a legitimate role to play in scientific choices, as long as I admit that these judgments should be classified as practical decisions. A second way to advance the triviality objection would be to contend that my thesis has minimal consequences for how we think about science.

31. Giere, "New Program for Philosophy of Science?"; McMullin, "Values in Science," in Asquith and Nickles; Mitchell, "Prescribed and Proscribed Values in Science Policy." For more discussion of the distinction between belief and acceptance, see Cohen, *Essay on Belief and Acceptance*, and McKaughan, "Toward a Richer Vocabulary".

According to this form of the objection, it is relatively uninteresting to claim that societal values can affect scientists' practical decisions. After all, the objection goes, as long as we can preserve epistemic judgments that are kept distinct from societal considerations, it is of little interest whether scientists also make practical judgments that incorporate contextual values.

I believe that both forms of this triviality objection are too quick. First, it is not the case that everyone supports allowing scientists to incorporate societal values into their practical judgments. When we evaluate the error argument later in this section, we will encounter the view that scientists should leave the consideration of societal values to those (such as policy makers) who have been expressly given this task. Proponents of this view would insist that, when they are faced with uncertainty, scientists should merely present the evidence available to them in as value free a fashion as possible. According to this suggestion, it is the role of policy makers and the public, not the scientific community, to apply societal values to scientific research. The thesis of this chapter is therefore not trivial, because many analysts would reject even the suggestion that societal values should influence scientists' practical judgments.

According to the second form of the triviality objection, it is uninteresting to claim that societal values should influence practical judgments about which hypotheses to accept. This form of the objection rests on the assumption that scientists can maintain a pure set of epistemic judgments, so it matters little whether they also make practical decisions about which hypotheses to accept for policy purposes. However, we will see in the remainder of this chapter that it is dubious to think that scientists can always maintain a set of pure epistemic judgments in addition to their practical ones. Once one allows societal values to influence a range of decisions that are interspersed throughout scientific practice (including choices about study design, statistical methodologies, data characterization, and interpretation of results), it is sometimes difficult to get back to pure epistemic judgments.[32] Perhaps, with extensive analysis, one might be able to disentangle practical from epistemic claims, but scientists do not always make such complex distinctions in practice.[33] Therefore, if one makes a sharp distinc-

32. Douglas, "Inductive Risk and Values in Science."

33. My claim that scientists cannot always distinguish their epistemic and practical judgments is compatible with the notion that they *should* distinguish these kinds of judgments wherever possible. My point is that this task is frequently very difficult, especially when one considers the full range of ways that methodological and interpretive judgments intersect with scientific research. For an argument in defense of distinguishing epistemic and practical claims whenever possible in the case of hormesis research, see Hoffmann, "Perspective on the Scientific, Philosophical, and Policy Dimensions," especially 23–24.

tion between epistemic and practical judgments, fields of policy-relevant research that are heavily influenced by societal values may fall largely on the practical side of the divide. In effect, the price of keeping epistemic judgments from being affected by societal values may be to admit that some policy-relevant areas of research do not involve many purely epistemic judgments. Contrary to the triviality objection, this appears to be a significant claim about the nature of policy-relevant science.

## The Error Argument

The "error" argument provides a second prominent strategy for arguing against the value-free ideal of science. Whenever researchers draw a conclusion on the basis of available evidence, they run the risk of either accepting a claim that turns out to be false (a false positive or Type I error) or rejecting a claim that turns out to be true (a false negative or Type II error).[34] Numerous philosophers have claimed that the societal consequences of making a false positive as opposed to a false negative error are relevant to deciding how much evidence to demand when accepting a scientific hypothesis.[35] For example, Philip Kitcher has argued, based on ethical considerations, that scientists should demand particularly high standards of proof before accepting conclusions that could cause harm to disadvantaged groups in society.[36] Similarly, Carl Cranor has shown that researchers need to consider the societal consequences of Type I or Type II errors when evaluating health risks from pollution.[37] In the context of pollution, Type I (false positive) errors generally involve the claim that a particular chemical is harmful at a particular dose level (whereas it really is not). Type II (false negative) errors involve the conclusion that a chemical is not a hazard (when, in fact, it is). Type I errors create costs for industry groups and some segments of the economy, whereas Type II errors create costs for public health and the environment.[38]

There are several major objections to incorporating societal values in decisions about how to respond to the potential for false positive or false negative errors. One is that the potential for error merely justifies the use of *some* values in choosing standards for hypothesis acceptance. It is not

34. Douglas, "Inductive Risk and Values in Science."

35. See, for example, Churchman, "Statistics, Pragmatics, and Induction"; Churchman, "Science and Decision-making"; Rudner, "Scientist qua Scientist"; Shrader-Frechette, *Ethics of Scientific Research*.

36. Kitcher, *Science, Truth, and Democracy*.

37. Cranor, *Regulating Toxic Substances*; see also Douglas, "Inductive Risk and Values in Science."

38. See, for example, Cranor, "Social Benefits of Expedited Risk Assessment"; Shrader-Frechette, *Ethics of Scientific Research*.

immediately obvious that *societal* values have a legitimate role to play. For example, Carl Hempel has argued that, in many contexts, scientists could decide on the standards for hypothesis acceptance by appealing to epistemic considerations such as reliability, extensiveness, and systematization.[39] Nevertheless, one way to respond to this objection is to show, as in the case of the gap argument, that scientists sometimes have ethical responsibilities to consider the societal ramifications of their work. If this is the case, then in certain situations they need to examine societal, as well as epistemic, considerations when deciding which errors are most important to avoid.

A second objection to the error argument is that, even if societal values do have a legitimate role to play in setting the standards for accepting hypotheses, perhaps scientists should merely describe the amount of evidence available and let the users of information decide whether or not to accept the hypotheses.[40] In the context of pollution research, for example, the objector might think that scientists should merely report, in a relatively value-neutral fashion, the amount of evidence in favor of the conclusion that a chemical is harmful. On this view, it is a policy maker's responsibility to decide whether that evidence is sufficient to justify the acceptance of particular hypotheses.

According to Cranor, we can refer to the second objection as the "clean-hands-science, dirty-hands-public-policy" doctrine.[41] Cranor acknowledges that scientists could try to keep their hands "clean" of ethical or societal value judgments by presenting their results in a neutral fashion. For example, he notes that epidemiologists could provide a table showing how one might draw varying conclusions from a body of empirical evidence, depending on how one sets the study's statistical variables, such as alpha (false positive rates) and beta (false negative rates). Nevertheless, he provides an excellent summary of the problems with this approach:

> For one thing, considerable anecdotal evidence suggests that risk managers may have considerable difficulty interpreting the most objective presentations of data, for they are complicated and somewhat difficult to understand. In addition, there is some evidence that courts which review regulatory decisions may invalidate agency decisions, if the data on which agencies act present too many alternative views or exhibit too much uncertainty.... If the failure of risk managers or courts to understand the presentation of the objective data will frustrate more effective regulation, this is a consideration for not shifting the interpretive discretion from scientists to risk managers.[42]

39. Hempel, "Science and Human Values."

40. Jeffrey, "Valuation and Acceptance of Scientific Hypotheses." See also McMullin, "Values in Science," in Asquith and Nickles.

41. Cranor, "Some Moral Issues in Risk Assessment."

42. Ibid., 139.

In other words, scientists face a difficult trade-off when communicating with policy makers. On one hand, the more scientists avoid allowing societal values to influence their interpretation of data, the more likely they are to present a mass of complex evidence that confuses decision makers and leads to erroneous conclusions. On the other hand, the more scientists try to present conclusions to policy makers in a straightforward fashion, the more likely they are, in accordance with the error argument, to allow (either explicitly or implicitly) societal values to influence their standards of evidence.

Another problem for the clean-hands-science, dirty-hands-public-policy approach is that decisions about how stringently to avoid false positive or false negative errors become relevant not just at the final point when one decides whether to accept or reject a theory; these decisions also affect the entire process of research. For example, in a case study of research on the health effects of dioxin, Heather Douglas shows how methodological decisions about the statistical analysis of data, the characterization of evidence, and the interpretation of results are all influenced by the errors that one sets out to avoid.[43] Therefore, scientists cannot just provide a straightforward body of evidence to policy makers and let them decide whether the evidence is sufficient to take action. The scientists also have to incorporate societal values about what errors to avoid in the course of collecting and interpreting the evidence.

A third way to object to the error argument is to insist that it does not actually challenge the value freedom of science when that doctrine is interpreted narrowly. According to this objection, the error argument establishes a role for nonepistemic values only in formulating the precise question at stake (i.e., deciding *how much evidence is required* for hypothesis acceptance), not in answering the question (i.e., determining whether the required level of evidence is met).[44] Therefore, the objection goes, one can accept the error argument while continuing to insist that science should be, in an important sense, value free. To put the objection in Bayesian terms, the error argument shows only that one's societal context determines how high the probability of a hypothesis, H, must be relative to a body of evidence, E, in order to accept it. The error argument does not show that the actual value of the probability of H (relative to E) is affected by societal values.

My response to the clean-hands-science-dirty-hands-public-policy doctrine also raises some problems for this third objection against the error argument. According to the objection, nonepistemic values merely determine the question at stake; they set the standard of evidence required in

43. Douglas, "Inductive Risk and Values in Science."
44. I thank Michael Dickson for emphasizing this objection.

order to accept a hypothesis. The process of determining whether that standard of evidence is met is then supposed to remain value free. As we saw in Douglas's dioxin example, however, if nonepistemic values help to determine standards of evidence, they can end up permeating the entire research endeavor. For example, she showed that scientists could legitimately disagree about whether particular rats displayed benign or malignant tumors. Their decisions about how to interpret the ambiguous data depended on whether they were more concerned about avoiding false positives or false negatives. Thus, sophisticated versions of the error argument appear to show that nonepistemic values can legitimately affect not only the standards of evidence but also whether those standards are met.

Nevertheless, those who propound the third objection to the error argument could insist that I have not addressed the most sophisticated forms of their objection. I have shown that there is often no unambiguous evidence, E, available to scientists. For example, scientists could end up with evidence $E_1$ or $E_2$ or $E_3$, depending on how they interpret and statistically analyze the data available to them. Nevertheless, proponents of the objection could still argue that, once one chooses a particular interpretation for the available evidence (say, $E_1$), the probability of H relative to $E_1$ should be independent of societal values. For example, the proponents could acknowledge that societal values are relevant not only to choosing the level of evidence required for accepting that a chemical is toxic but also for deciding how to characterize available data, which statistical analyses to use, and how to interpret the findings. They would just insist that, once one makes all of these elements of scientific practice explicit and specifies how to perform them in order to maintain the proper balance between false positives and false negatives, the remaining analysis should remain independent of societal considerations.

Fortunately, this third objection to the error argument does not challenge the thesis developed in the present chapter. The goal here is to show that, in the context of much policy-relevant research, nonepistemic values have a legitimate role to play throughout scientific practice, including in the interpretation and evaluation of evidence. However, the third objection does not challenge the notion that nonepistemic values have a legitimate role to play in the evaluation of evidence for a hypothesis. The objection merely attempts to show that, in principle, one could disentangle the interpretive process into some components that involve societal values and other components that do not. For the argument in this chapter, it does not matter whether the objector is correct. It is still clearly the case that the error argument establishes a role for societal values throughout scientific practice.

Thus, setting aside the third objection, two conditions appear to be jointly sufficient for justifying an appeal to societal values based on the error argument. In response to the first objection against it, scientists must have ethical reasons for considering the societal ramifications of their work (rather than focusing only on epistemic considerations). Second, the relationship between researchers and those receiving information must be such that it would be socially disadvantageous for scientists to pursue the clean-hands-science-dirty-hands-public-policy strategy (i.e., providing relatively value-free information to policy makers). One should keep in mind that these two conditions for applying the error argument are jointly *sufficient* but not *necessary*. There may be other conditions beyond those identified in this chapter that justify the incorporation of societal values in scientific research. For example, if the critics of the value-free ideal could successfully argue against any significant conceptual distinction between epistemic and nonepistemic values, they might be able to show that societal values should rarely (if ever) be excluded from scientific research. I argue that, even on the basis of more minimal assumptions, societal values have a legitimate role to play in many policy-relevant areas of science.

It is worth noting that the two conditions for applying the error argument correspond to the "ethics" and the "no-passing-the-buck" principles that ground this chapter's arguments for incorporating societal values in policy-relevant science. According to those principles, ethical considerations are applicable to the area of research under scrutiny, and it would be socially harmful for scientists to avoid making value judgments. Nevertheless, the "uncertainty" principle might appear to be absent in the case of the error argument. This absence is merely illusory, however, because a precondition for appealing to the error argument is that one faces a situation of inductive risk. In these sorts of situations, the available evidence does not determine which hypothesis to accept, so one must decide (in response to this uncertainty) how much evidence to demand. Therefore, all three principles that ground the application of societal values to scientific research are visible in the application of the error argument as well as the gap argument.

## THE EASY CASES

As we saw in the previous section, most commentators who insist that science should be value free nevertheless believe it is obvious that societal values can legitimately influence the first category of judgments discussed in chapter 2. In other words, it is uncontroversial that research projects and study designs can be appropriately steered toward questions that are significant, at least in part, for nonepistemic reasons. For instance, Mauro Dorato discusses how nonepistemic values influence the problems that scientists investigate:

> What is essential is that this form of science's dependence on nonepistemic values—which is undeniable and omnipresent... is clearly *not* sufficient, by itself, to deprive the social or the natural sciences of their value-free character from a *cognitive* point of view.[45]

He therefore acknowledges that it would be impossible and unnecessary to exclude contextual values from these sorts of judgments, but he insists that this does not jeopardize the important ways in which science should remain value free.

Those who remain skeptical about allowing nonepistemic values to influence the choice of research projects and the design of studies are likely to appeal to a (rather controversial) distinction between "basic" and "applied" science. Although it is difficult to deny that contextual values should play a role in choosing applied topics, some analysts have questioned whether they are appropriate in the process of choosing basic research areas.[46] Even if one were to grant the distinction between basic and applied science, however, two considerations support a role for nonepistemic values in directing the course of policy-relevant research on topics like hormesis, endocrine disruption, and multiple chemical sensitivity. First, because policy-relevant research falls on or near the applied side of the division, the choice of research projects should be at least partially subject to considerations about which research questions society finds most pressing. Second, even if this area of science were regarded as an example of basic science, societal values would still be relevant in deciding how much money to invest in the pursuit of basic research as opposed to other endeavors.[47] It is therefore relatively uncontroversial to claim that societal values should not be entirely excluded from the first category of judgments discussed in chapter 2.

The fourth category of judgments (i.e., those associated with applying research to decision making) constitute another relatively easy case. In this domain virtually all commentators accept the appropriateness of a role for societal considerations. Consider, for example, the two major judgments in this category that chapter 2 highlights: deciding whether new regulatory policies are justified in response to hormesis and determining how to address combinations of benefits and harms that new policies might create. Assuming for the sake of argument that epistemic considerations could resolve the *factual* question of *whether* particular harms are likely to occur as a result of new regulations, policy makers must also address the *normative* question of whether there is *adequate* evidence that new policies will not

45. Dorato, "Epistemic and Nonepistemic Values in Science."

46. For discussions of the distinction between basic and applied science, as well as its significance, see Kitcher, *Science, Truth, and Democracy*; Stokes, *Pasteur's Quadrant*.

47. Kitcher, *Science, Truth, and Democracy*.

cause an *unreasonable* amount of harm. There will always be some small chance that new policies might have unexpected, harmful side effects, but these concerns do not provide reason to block the regulations unless they exceed some threshold level of significance. Societal values are clearly relevant in deciding how much evidence for potential harms justifies the abandonment of innovative policies.[48]

Similarly, nonepistemic values are clearly crucial in determining whether a utilitarian or a deontological model is more appropriate for deciding how to address benefits and harms associated with the hormesis phenomenon. For example, in the process of raising concerns about narrowly utilitarian approaches to regulation, commentators have previously highlighted at least three considerations that should play a role in these decisions:[49] (1) concerns about justice and fairness, given that disadvantaged groups and children might bear a greater proportion of the risks associated with easing chemical regulations, (2) concerns about whether those exposed to potential risks associated with hormesis could (or would) provide informed consent, and (3) concerns about the difficulty of compensating individuals who might be harmed by hormetic exposures. These sorts of societal considerations clearly have a legitimate role to play in applying scientific knowledge about hormesis to public policy.

## VALUES IN THE DEVELOPMENT OF SCIENTIFIC LANGUAGE

It is much less obvious that societal values should affect the second category of judgments discussed in chapter 2 (namely, developing scientific categories and choosing terminology). Although these linguistic choices are distinct from the group of judgments that analysts have been most concerned to keep free of societal values (namely, judgments associated with the interpretation and evaluation of evidence), they are nevertheless quite internal to scientific practice. Therefore, many analysts are likely to believe that contextual considerations should be excluded from judgments about scientific language. Nevertheless, in this section I argue that this second category of judgments meets the three conditions that justify an appeal to the gap argument, as discussed earlier in this chapter: (1) the presence of good reasons for scientists to consider societal, as well as scientific, goals; (2) the underdetermination of linguistic choices by epistemic considerations; and (3) the fact that scientists cannot plausibly suspend their judgment. Let us consider in turn how each condition is met in the hormesis case.

48. Douglas, "Inductive Risk and Values in Science"; Rudner, "Scientist qua Scientist."

49. Douglas, "Science, Hormesis, and Regulation"; Renn, "Ethical Appraisal of Hormesis"; Shrader-Frechette, "Ideological Toxicology."

First, researchers who address policy-relevant topics arguably have ethical responsibilities to consider the major impacts of their conclusions on society. One could defend this claim by appealing to unique ethical responsibilities associated with the scientific profession, but it is even less controversial to appeal to the moral expectations that we place on all agents.[50] For example, we all have responsibilities not to harm others intentionally. Moreover, even if we do not intend to hurt others, we are blameworthy if we harm them as a result of reckless or negligent acts. Therefore, scientists, like other moral agents, are responsible for considering whether accepting particular conclusions could contribute to causing negligent harm to others.

One might object that accepting specific societal roles can alter one's typical moral duties in some cases, such as when lawyers invoke attorney-client privileges.[51] Nevertheless, we have good reasons for thinking that the social role of being a scientist does not entirely exempt one from typical moral responsibilities. Although special professional obligations may sometimes override standard ethical duties, there need to be strong reasons for thinking that this is the case.[52] It is clear, however, that the social costs of allowing scientists to ignore the broader consequences of their work are much higher than those of requiring at least some attention to these considerations.[53] Thus, like all moral agents, scientists arguably have responsibilities to consider major ways in which their actions might harm others. Because those studying policy-relevant topics are more likely than many other scientists to formulate conclusions that could affect people's health and welfare, they are also more likely to run into cases in which their ethical responsibilities to others impinge on their research. Therefore, those who are performing policy-relevant studies arguably have prima facie ethical responsibilities to consider the major consequences of the conclusions that they draw, which means that the first condition for justifying an appeal to the gap argument is met.

50. For an example of the first avenue, see Shrader-Frechette, *Ethics of Scientific Research*. For an example of the second avenue, see Douglas, *Science, Policy, and the Value-free Ideal*.

51. For a defense of the notion that the members of a profession may be exempted from typical moral responsibilities because of their social role, see Gewirth, "Professional Ethics." For the notion that professional ethics should not diverge from social ethics in general, see Goldman, *Moral Foundations of Professional Ethics*. Further discussion of these issues can be found in Maker, "Scientific Autonomy, Scientific Responsibility," and in Wueste, "Role Moralities and the Problem of Conflicting Obligations."

52. For example, Resnik, "Social Epistemology and the Ethics of Research."

53. Ibid. For recent work on this issue, see Douglas, "Moral Responsibilities of Scientists"; Douglas, "Role of Values in Expert Reasoning"; Douglas, *Science, Policy, and the Value-free Ideal*.

The second condition for applying the gap argument can be met by showing that linguistic choices are sometimes underdetermined by epistemic considerations. Recall from chapter 2 that the hormesis case requires at least two important decisions of this sort to be made. First, researchers have to decide how to define the hormesis phenomenon. Second, they have to choose among a range of potential descriptions for it. These descriptive choices include whether to use the term "hormesis" at all, whether to refer to it as "adaptive," and whether to call it "generalizable." Some philosophers might argue that these sorts of choices about how to categorize and describe phenomena are always underdetermined by epistemic considerations. Whether or not they are correct, it seems relatively obvious that many of these judgments are underdetermined in the hormesis case.

Consider, for example, the definition of the phenomenon. Chapter 2 recounts a litany of problems that plague current concepts of hormesis. Calabrese criticizes the notion of "beneficial hormesis" because the classification of an effect as a benefit may depend on contextual considerations and particular points of view. Moreover, he worries that defining hormesis in terms of benefits might politicize evaluations of the dose-response relationship.[54] Unfortunately, we have seen that operational concepts such as "low-dose-stimulation" or "opposite-effects" hormesis do not identify instances of hormesis very precisely, because they do not refer to specific mechanisms responsible for hormetic effects. Nevertheless, there is currently insufficient information to identify a complete list of these mechanisms, to characterize them precisely, or to determine how common they are. Thus, there do not appear to be decisive epistemic reasons for choosing one definition of hormesis rather than another; they all present significant difficulties.

The third condition for justifying the application of the gap argument to linguistic decisions is that scientists cannot easily suspend their judgment. This condition is especially easy to meet in the case of judgments about scientific categories and terminology. For example, researchers are forced to choose a definition of the hormesis phenomenon, despite the fact that they do not have decisive reasons for accepting one rather than another. Perhaps they could attempt to avoid the decision by not talking about hormesis at all. Nonetheless, chapter 2 points out that even the decision whether or not to use this term, which subdivides the class of nonmonotonic dose responses (into hormetic and nonhormetic ones), is itself a significant choice. Thus, scientists cannot take the easy route of suspending judgment when dealing with some of these linguistic decisions.

Because the three conditions for applying the gap argument are met in the case of linguistic judgments associated with policy-relevant areas of

54. Calabrese, "Hormesis: Why It Is Important," 1453.

research, it appears that societal values should not be systematically excluded from this category of judgments. We have seen that scientists are forced to make decisions that cannot be settled by epistemic considerations alone. Moreover, they have ethical responsibilities with respect to the public (e.g., not to harm others negligently). Therefore, when making judgments that go beyond the available evidence, they have reason to take societal values into account, insofar as they have ethical responsibilities not to cause negligent harm to society. In other words, they need to consider, when filling the gaps left by epistemic considerations, whether particular linguistic choices might violate their ethical responsibilities to society.

At this point in the argument, it might be tempting to argue that scientific language (even in policy-relevant areas of research) rarely has the potential to affect the public. That would be a mistake. As chapter 2 points out, scientists and communication scholars have become increasingly concerned about the "framing" effects of language on the views of other researchers and the public.[55] Recent litigation over an advertising campaign for the artificial sweetener Splenda provides a vivid and entertaining illustration of the power of scientific or pseudoscientific terminology to affect the public. Based on recommendations from an advertising agency, Splenda had captured 62 percent of the U.S. artificial sweetener market by 2007 by using the marketing line "Made from sugar, so it tastes like sugar." This strategy gave their product the impression of being "natural," even though it bears little resemblance to an actual sugar molecule. When the makers of Splenda added the clarification "but it's not sugar" for a period of time, the *New York Times* reported that its sales "fizzled."[56] The significance of terminology is also widely recognized in the medical field; Leonard Jason, a professor of community psychology, notes that "You can change people's attributions of the seriousness of [an] illness if you have a more medical-sounding name."[57] This effect is especially vivid when popular terms for an illness incorporate obvious biases or stereotypes. The difference between referring to "career women's disease" versus "endometriosis" or "yuppie flu" as opposed to "myalgic encephalopathy" is obviously dramatic.[58]

In the hormesis case, referring to a unique phenomenon that is adaptive and highly generalizable strongly encourages the notion that it is a significant

55. For concerns about the power of terminology and framing to influence public opinion about topics such as racism, sexism, global warming, evolution, stem cell research, and emerging technologies, see Herbers, "Watch Your Language!"; Nisbet and Mooney, "Framing Science"; Scheufele and Lewenstein, "Public and Nanotechnology."

56. Browning, "Makers of Artificial Sweeteners Go to Court."

57. Tuller, "Chronic Fatigue No Longer Seen as 'Yuppie Flu.' "

58. Ibid.; Capek, "Reframing Endometriosis."

challenge to current risk-assessment policies. In contrast, avoiding these descriptions of hormesis and referring only to the general category of nonmonotonic dose responses dramatically downplays the notion that regulatory policies need to be altered. Speaking only of nonmonotonic dose responses encourages the notion that the low-dose effects of toxic substances are likely to be variable, difficult to predict, and unlikely to be uniformly beneficial. Chapter 2 notes that it may be partly because of this linguistic effect that critics of hormesis, such as Kristina Thayer, would prefer not to use the term "hormesis" at all.[59] Chapter 7 highlights similarly striking linguistic choices in the MCS and ED cases. Stakeholder groups were sufficiently convinced by the potential societal effects of the language employed in those areas of research that they worked hard to promote specific sorts of terminology. I do not argue in this book that particular linguistic choices in the hormesis, MCS, or ED cases are so far beyond the pale that they would violate researchers' ethical responsibilities. Nevertheless, I have shown in this section that stakeholders' concerns about scientific language should not be excluded across the board as inappropriate influences on scientific practice.

## VALUES IN THE EVALUATION AND INTERPRETATION OF STUDIES

As the earlier sections of this chapter point out, the evaluation and interpretation of evidence are precisely the points at which many analysts are most concerned to restrict the role of nonepistemic considerations. Nevertheless, both the gap and the error arguments provide good reasons for rejecting the exclusion of societal values from this category of judgments, at least in many cases of policy-relevant research. The previous section shows that the three jointly sufficient conditions for applying the gap argument are sometimes met in the case of linguistic judgments associated with hormesis. Those conditions are also sometimes met in the case of judgments about the evaluation and interpretation of evidence.

First, the previous section mentions that scientists have ethical responsibilities to consider the societal ramifications of their work. Even if scientists had no special professional responsibilities, they would still have the basic duties that all moral agents do. Moreover, we have seen that these responsibilities are especially relevant to scientists who study policy-relevant topics that could significantly affect the welfare of other people. Therefore, as long as judgments about how to interpret and evaluate evidence have the potential

59. Thayer et al., "Fundamental Flaws."

to cause negligent or intentional harms, scientists have responsibilities to consider the major societal effects of this category of judgments.

The second condition for applying the gap argument is that the judgments under consideration must be underdetermined by epistemic values. This condition is often met by decisions associated with the interpretation of evidence regarding claims HG, HP, and HD. For example, as chapter 2 emphasizes, some researchers have concluded that endpoints associated with the process of carcinogenesis (e.g., cancer-related death rates) are likely to follow hormetic dose-response relationships. Nevertheless, this judgment depends on the assumption that the evidence of hormetic effects on specific endpoints *related to* carcinogenesis (e.g., the activity of DNA-repair enzymes) constitutes evidence of hormetic effects on endpoints associated with the *entire process* of carcinogenesis (e.g., cancer-related death rates). Epistemic considerations are insufficient at present to determine whether this assumption is true or false. These underdetermined conclusions abound in hormesis research. To take another example, the judgment whether the hormetic effects produced by a specific chemical will be beneficial for human beings over extended periods of time is generally underdetermined by epistemic considerations.

Finally, the third condition for applying the gap argument is that scientists be forced to make practical decisions despite their epistemic uncertainty. This condition also applies in the case of many judgments about the interpretation and evaluation of policy-relevant topics. The scientists who inform policy makers frequently do not have the luxury of suspending judgment. For example, Pamela Franklin argues that the EPA demands both good science and usable science. One of the characteristics of usable science is that it is expedient. As she puts it, "Expediency is critical because research timelines are often incompatible with regulatory deadlines, which typically do not allow time for a comprehensive, definitive scientific study."[60] A classic example of the need for regulatory scientists to make decisions in the absence of compelling evidence has to do with the choices made by government agencies about how to estimate the low-dose effects of toxic chemicals based on their observed effects at higher doses. Researchers regularly acknowledge that the decision by U.S. regulatory agencies to use linear, no-threshold dose-response models for extrapolating the low-dose effects of carcinogens incorporates both a consideration of all the available evidence and the desire to make decisions that protect public health.[61]

In the case of hormesis, scientists who want to provide usable information for regulatory policy are forced to recommend either maintaining

60. Franklin, "EPA's Drinking Water Standards."
61. See, for example, Silbergeld, "Risk Assessment and Risk Management."

current policies (with the risk of harming economic growth and possibly reducing people's well-being) or altering policies to account for hormetic effects (with the risk of harming people from exposure to toxic chemicals). Scientists might be tempted to avoid this predicament by claiming that the available evidence is insufficient for policy makers to draw a conclusion one way or the other. Nevertheless, deciding whether there is adequate evidence to draw a conclusion merely creates a new value judgment. In other words, researchers are then forced to decide how much evidence to demand before being willing to draw a conclusion, given the potential societal consequences of doing so or refraining from doing so.

We can see, therefore, that the gap argument applies to numerous judgments associated with the interpretation and evaluation of policy-relevant research. For example, researchers have to address evidential gaps in order to determine which hormetic dose-response curves observed in other organisms are also likely to occur in humans, including sensitive human subpopulations. Another gap occurs when researchers evaluate whether hormetic dose-response curves are likely to be observed on endpoints associated with the entire process of carcinogenesis, such as cancer-related death rates. A whole range of other evidential gaps applies to questions about whether hormetic responses to one chemical will be significantly altered by the presence of other chemicals and whether hormetic effects will be beneficial over an extended period of time.[62]

The error argument is also applicable to a range of judgments associated with the interpretation and evaluation of evidence. It is not difficult to see that this category of judgments sometimes meets the two conditions that are jointly sufficient for applying the error argument. The first condition is that scientists have good reason to take nonepistemic considerations into account in addition to epistemic ones. The second condition is that the clean-hands-science-dirty-hands-public-policy approach (namely, providing minimally interpreted evidence and expecting the recipients to decide what conclusions to draw) have problematic social consequences in the case under consideration.

With respect to the first condition, we have seen that scientists have ethical reasons not to ignore societal considerations when responding to uncertainty, such as when choosing the standards of evidence required for hypothesis acceptance. With regard to the second condition, it is precisely in the area of toxic-chemical regulations that Carl Cranor has questioned the clean-hands-science-dirty-hands-public-policy doctrine. He has pointed out

62. As chapter 2 notes, researchers have provided some evidence regarding these questions, but the evidence is still fairly minimal and inconclusive; see Cook and Calabrese, "Importance of Hormesis to Public Health."

that regulators are not good at interpreting complicated scientific evidence about these matters and that courts often misunderstand the evidence. We have also seen that decisions about how stringently to avoid particular errors permeate toxicology research. Thus, if societal values are relevant to deciding what sorts of errors are most important to avoid, those values often have to be incorporated by scientists in the analysis and interpretation of evidence.

The interpretation of Calabrese's literature studies provides an excellent example of how the error argument applies to judgments associated with the evaluation of evidence. As chapter 2 emphasizes, critics like Kristina Thayer have argued that some features of the studies inclined them toward false positives. Specifically, Thayer and her coauthors have argued that it was inappropriate for Calabrese to count low doses that increased 10 percent from the control as evidence for hormesis, even when those data points had not been shown to be statistically significant.[63] To take another example from chapter 2, many of Calabrese's literature studies depended on a point system in which varying numbers of points were assigned to previously published dose-response data, depending on the amount of evidence that they provided for hormesis. Numerous judgments are involved in determining how many points to assign to particular sorts of evidence and deciding how high a point value should be required in order to conclude that hormesis occurred in a previous study. These are precisely the sorts of cases where the error argument justifies consideration of societal values about how carefully to avoid false positive as opposed to false negative errors.

## CONCLUSION

Albert Einstein wrote that "science can only ascertain what *is*, but not what *should* be, and outside of its domain value judgments of all kinds remain necessary."[64] His intent was to mitigate conflicts between science and religion by insisting both that science does not address questions about values and that values are still crucial outside of science. Einstein seems to have conceded too much, however. This chapter argues that, at least with respect to policy-relevant research, value judgments are sometimes necessary *within* the domain of science, as well as *outside* it. It is particularly easy to justify the inclusion of societal considerations when deciding what research projects to pursue or how to apply scientific results in the policy sphere. However, we have seen that the gap and error arguments also appear to justify the application of contextual values to judgments that are central to scientific

63. Thayer et al., "Fundamental Flaws."

64. Einstein, "Science and Religion."

practice, including linguistic decisions and judgments about the interpretation of evidence. These arguments depend especially on three principles: (1) that scientists have ethical responsibilities to consider the major societal ramifications of their work; (2) that the evidence available to them is frequently not sufficient to determine their conclusions; and (3) that it is often socially harmful or impracticable for scientists to withhold judgment or to provide uninterpreted, allegedly value-free information to decision makers.

The chapter has focused on the claim that societal values are relevant to *practical judgments* about which hypotheses to accept as a basis of action. This is a more modest thesis than the claim that societal values should influence *epistemic judgments* about which hypotheses to believe, but it is still far from trivial. Many thinkers have tried to preserve the value freedom of science by insisting that value-laden decisions, even about how to act, should be left to policy makers rather than scientists. Moreover, the incorporation of societal values throughout scientific practice, even for the purposes of practical decision making, makes purely epistemic judgments elusive in some areas of policy-relevant science. Once societal values influence the collection, analysis, and interpretation of data, scientists can find it difficult to keep their epistemic and practical judgments distinct in practice. In effect, the price of keeping epistemic judgments from being affected by societal values may be to abandon the attempt to make purely epistemic judgments in some policy-relevant areas of research.

If the arguments developed throughout this chapter are convincing, they raise significant questions about *how* to incorporate societal considerations effectively throughout scientific activity. One might worry, for example, that scientists are not properly trained (or in a legitimate position) to make ethical decisions that affect society at large. The following three chapters take up this challenge by considering, in turn, the three "bodies" that Sheila Jasanoff emphasizes as central to integrating scientific expertise with political decision making: bodies of scientific knowledge (in chapter 4), advisory bodies (in chapter 5), and the bodies of the experts themselves (in chapter 6).[65] These chapters show that scientists do not need to decide by themselves what values should influence the crucial judgments that they need to make. Chapter 5 especially emphasizes that advisory bodies (consisting, in part, of representatives from stakeholder groups) can help guide scientific judgments.

65. Jasanoff, "Judgment under Siege."

# 4

# Lesson #1

## Safeguarding Science

In a striking investigation of studies that analyzed new biomedical drugs, researchers found that only 5 percent of those funded by companies that developed the drugs gave unfavorable evaluations of the new products.[1] In contrast, 38 percent of those funded by independent sources gave unfavorable evaluations *when analyzing the same drugs*. Findings of this sort, which indicate that research results tend to be correlated with funding sources, have become common.[2] For example, a classic study in the *Journal of the American Medical Association* examined 106 review articles on the health effects of passive smoking and found that 63 percent of the articles concluded that it was harmful, while 37 percent disagreed. A multiple regression analysis that controlled for factors such as article quality, topic, year of publication, and peer review found that the only factor associated with the reviews' conclusions was whether the authors were affiliated with the tobacco industry.[3] Three-fourths of the articles that rejected the existence of health effects from passive smoking were funded by industry groups, but few of those articles revealed their funding sources.

In response to these sorts of worrisome findings, the present chapter provides an important lesson for those who want to keep policy-relevant science responsive to societal values. It argues that current university financial conflict-of-interest (COI) policies are not sufficient to keep academic science from being hijacked by powerful interest groups, especially those associated with industry. Rather, a range of other strategies, such as increased government funding for policy-relevant topics, is needed in order to safeguard university science from being overly influenced by "deep pockets." This is not to say that government-funded science is completely value free. Furthermore,

1. Friedberg et al., "Evaluation of Conflict of Interest."

2. See, for example, Als-Nielsen et al., "Association of Funding and Conclusions"; Bekelman, Lee, and Gross, "Scope and Impact of Financial Conflicts"; Davidson, "Source of Funding and Outcomes"; Stelfox et al., "Conflict of Interest."

3. Barnes and Bero, "Why Review Articles on the Health Effects of Passive Smoking."

environmental and public-health groups are not immune from influencing academic research to promote their own agendas. I also emphasize that industry-funded research is not always problematic.

Nevertheless, there are good reasons for focusing on the problematic influences of corporate and military deep pockets in this chapter. First, there is vastly more money available to them than to environmental organizations or to nonmilitary government research projects, so they are able to have an inordinate impact on the information available to the public. Together, industry and military research expenditures constitute about 80 percent of annual U.S. research and development funding.[4] Second, even if the majority of this work is unproblematic, we will see that, in some fields of study (such as the pharmaceutical and public-health research discussed in this chapter), a host of egregious practices have been uncovered in industry-funded research.[5] Even though science funded by agencies such as the National Science Foundation (NSF) and the National Institutes of Health (NIH) is not free of contextual influences, it is more commonly (though still not always) free of such flagrant abuses.

One might object that, even if it is appropriate to focus on the worrisome influences associated with industry-funded research, trying to address these problems in an academic setting constitutes a case of barking up the wrong tree. After all, most of the problematic scientific activities are associated with industrial laboratories or medical communications companies rather than with academia.[6] My response, however, is that if a significant body of public-interest science can be preserved in the university setting, the public can appeal to this work when it needs to challenge or scrutinize special-interest research. Therefore, it is crucial to ensure that academic work remains responsive to an adequate array of societal values. Moreover, because most universities accept the mission of serving the public good, it is easier to defend restrictive policies or reforms in the academic context than in other settings. Finally, some of the suggestions proposed here for improving university research can also be applied to work performed outside of an

4. As I point out in chapter 1, an estimated 65 percent of the money spent on research and development in the United States in 2006 came from industry, whereas 28 percent came from the federal government; see Koizumi, "Federal R&D in the FY 2009 Budget," accessed on 11/24/08. And, in the same year, defense spending accounted for more than 55 percent of the federal R&D budget; see Intersociety Working Group, *Congressional Action on Research and Development*, accessed on 11/24/08.

5. For a discussion of some of the reasons that industry research is more likely to be problematic in certain fields of science than in others, see Wilholt, "Bias and Values in Scientific Research."

6. For example, only about 5 percent of academic research funding comes from industry; see Greenberg, *Science for Sale*. Nevertheless, as we will see in this chapter, in some areas of research, such as the biomedical field, relatively few professors are free of links to industry.

academic setting. This chapter therefore contributes to the goal of making our *bodies of scientific knowledge* more responsive to societal concerns. The following two chapters examine the other bodies emphasized by Jasanoff: *deliberative bodies*, which interpret scientific findings and provide advice to policy makers, as well as the bodies of the *scientific experts* themselves.

The next section of this chapter summarizes a variety of reasons for thinking that policy-relevant science in general, and university research in particular, has become overly influenced by vested interest groups. The following section examines current university policies for addressing financial conflicts of interest. These approaches typically revolve around three major elements: disclosure, management, and elimination of conflicts. Careful consideration of these three strategies indicates that they are likely to be insufficient for ensuring that university research remains responsive to an adequate range of societal values other than those of powerful interest groups. The chapter's final section suggests several options for policy makers and universities to consider: providing more independent funding for policy-relevant topics, eliminating particularly egregious institutional conflicts of interest, creating trial registries, developing adversarial deliberative proceedings, and promoting consensual deliberative forums.

## SPECIAL-INTEREST SCIENCE

A growing body of evidence indicates that special-interest groups are exerting significant influences on contemporary policy-relevant research. It is difficult to precisely document this impact on science, because interested parties generally try to conceal it as much as possible. Nevertheless, this section briefly presents a range of findings that paints a worrisome picture of the state of contemporary policy-relevant science, especially in areas such as pharmaceutical and public-health research. The evidence includes (1) correlations between funding sources and research results, (2) systematic strategies used by interest groups to obtain favorable results, and (3) the finding that influential experts are being co-opted to support the perspectives of deep pockets.

One significant category of evidence consists of empirical studies, such as the work presented in the introduction to this chapter, documenting correlations between funding sources and scientific results. For example, a review of eleven different studies that compared industry-funded biomedical research with independent work revealed that the industry-sponsored research was found to be more likely to favor industry in *every one* of the studies. Pooling the results of all eleven analyses yielded the conclusion that industry-funded research projects were almost four times more likely than independent studies to yield results favorable to industry.[7] These findings should be interpreted with care, because the *correlations* that they reveal between funding sources and research results may reflect a range of *causal* factors. For example, many industry-funded studies could be particularly likely to yield favorable conclusions for the sponsors not because of bias in the interpretation of results but rather because private sponsors purposely choose to perform research on their products primarily when they already appear to be better than those of their competitors. This strategic choice of topics may be part of the explanation, but other data indicate that some of the favorable results obtained by industry are also probably the result of deliberate manipulation of experimental designs. For example, a 2005 survey of more than thirty-two hundred U.S. scientists found that 15 percent of the respondents admitted to changing the design, methodology, or results of a study under pressure from a study sponsor.[8]

The possibility that research sponsors frequently manipulate experimental designs or other features of a study in order to obtain favorable results receives further support from a second body of evidence, which consists of strategies that deep pockets have developed for promoting their interests. For example, Kristin Shrader-Frechette has analyzed a variety of approaches that the purveyors of special-interest science employ in order to obtain results that support their values: (1) using problematic tests, models, or data; (2) employing small samples and short-term studies that decrease the likelihood of uncovering hazards; (3) depending on theoretical estimates rather than empirical measures of harm; (4) failing to do uncertainty analysis; and (5) developing diversionary arguments, such as insisting on human experiments (which are typically unethical) before regarding pollutants as harmful.[9]

As we will see in chapter 7, a good example of these sorts of strategies comes from research on the endocrine-disrupting effects of bisphenol A (BPA), a substance found in plastic products such as baby bottles. After University of Missouri scientist Frederick vom Saal first uncovered preliminary evidence of harmful effects, industry groups developed opposing scientific findings and ultimately forced a National Toxicology Program review of the issue.[10] Subsequent analyses of the industry studies suggest that they were systematically designed in a manner that minimized the likelihood of finding any endocrine-disrupting properties. For government-funded studies, 94 out of 104 reported significant biological effects of BPA, whereas

7. Bekelman, Lee, and Gross, "Scope and Impact of Financial Conflicts."

8. See Weiss, "Many Scientists Admit to Misconduct."

9. Shrader-Frechette, *Taking Action, Saving Lives.*

10. National Toxicology Program, *National Toxicology Program's Report,* accessed on 11/29/08.

0 out of 11 industry-funded studies reported significant effects at the same dose levels. The discrepancy between the studies appeared to be the result of design features associated with the choice of animal strains and feed, the endpoints examined, and the interpretation of data.[11]

Shockingly, in their deliberations about the safety of BPA, the U.S. Food and Drug Administration (FDA) and the European Food Safety Authority (EFSA) prioritized the findings of several industry-funded studies over the many opposing NIH-funded and peer-reviewed academic studies. The apparent reason is that the industry studies were conducted using good laboratory practices (GLP) standards, despite the fact that these standards are primarily concerned with record keeping and do little to ensure that the research employs adequate study designs or methodologies.[12] Unfortunately, these sorts of problems are not isolated. For example, an analysis of studies on alachlor, atrazine, formaldehyde, and perchloroethylene revealed that only 6 out of 43 studies funded by industry organizations yielded evidence that the chemicals were problematic, whereas 71 out of 118 studies funded by organizations without a major stake in the outcome provided evidence of harm.[13] Moreover, as in the BPA case, industry groups successfully used their studies, along with a range of other strategies, to slow the regulation of these chemicals to a standstill.[14]

In their 2008 book *Bending Science,* Tom McGarity and Wendy Wagner provide another fascinating analysis of strategies used by interest groups to manipulate policy-relevant science.[15] They conceptualize the production of policy-relevant information in terms of a multistage pipeline, in which scientists conduct research, interpret data, provide peer review, scrutinize published work, and provide opinions through expert panels. McGarity and Wagner document a range of approaches (at every stage of this pipeline) that interest groups employ in order to promote their values. First, the initial production of

11. Vom Saal and Hughes, "Extensive New Literature."

12. Myers et al., "Why Public Health Agencies Cannot Depend on Good Laboratory Practices."

13. Fagin, Lavelle, and the Center for Public Integrity, *Toxic Deception,* 51. One should note that two of the 118 studies reportedly funded by organizations "without a major stake in the outcome" were actually produced by the Amalgamated Clothing and Textile Workers Union, which should probably be qualified as an organization that does have a significant stake in the results.

14. Ibid.

15. McGarity and Wagner, *Bending Science.* For other presentations of many of the strategies discussed by McGarity and Wagner (as well as by Shrader-Frechette), see Michaels, *Doubt Is Their Product,* and Bailar, "How to Distort the Scientific Record." Bailar points out that these strategies are not unique to industry, even though industry has an exceptionally large amount of money available to implement these approaches; a variety of entities, including federal agencies, have resorted to such strategies.

research can be shaped by manipulating study designs, skewing data collection, strategically framing questions and interpreting results, and funding "friendly" researchers. Second, if problematic findings arise, this material can be hidden by means of gag contracts, concealment, trade secrets, and sealed court settlements. Third, if findings that conflict with the interests of deep pockets are revealed, they can be attacked by "manufacturing uncertainty,"[16] writing letters, lobbying editors, and using legal tools such as the Daubert Supreme Court ruling or the Data Quality Act.[17] Fourth, scientists who produce unwelcome results can be silenced and discouraged from pursuing similar research in the future through the use of defamation suits, data subpoenas, scientific-misconduct allegations, congressional requests, and media circuses. Fifth, research that promotes the concerns of interest groups can be emphasized by stacking government panels, creating specially designed blue-ribbon panels, and commissioning articles or books. Finally, interest groups can influence public opinion regarding the overall state of research using powerful PR firms, front groups, and "truth squads."[18] McGarity and Wagner provide numerous examples of these strategies in action.

A third body of evidence that illustrates interest-group influences on policy-relevant science involves the co-optation of university scientists, especially by the pharmaceutical industry.[19] By some estimates, only about 5 percent of the research performed in an academic setting is directly funded by corporate sources,[20] but industry uses this funding very strategically, along with a range of other avenues for influencing university researchers. For example, growing evidence indicates that a number of biomedical articles and reviews are being ghostwritten. Prominent university researchers are paid to put their names on studies that are designed, performed, and written by medical education companies funded by the pharmaceutical industry. Although it is difficult to uncover evidence about such practices, one study found that more than 50 percent of the articles published on the antidepressant Zoloft between 1998 and 2000 were ghostwritten. Moreover, the ghostwritten articles were published in far more prestigious journals than "normal" articles, were cited significantly more often than others, and were characterized by more favorable evaluations of Zoloft than the others.[21]

16. Michaels, *Doubt Is Their Product.*

17. For information on the Daubert ruling, including ways in which it can be employed to serve the interests of industry groups, see Cranor, *Toxic Torts.*

18. Many of these strategies are also described in Beder, *Global Spin*; Fagin, Lavelle, and the Center for Public Integrity, *Toxic Deception*; and Markowitz and Rosner, *Deceit and Denial.*

19. See, for example, C. Elliott, "Pharma Goes to the Laundry," and Kassirer, *On the Take.*

20. Greenberg, *Science for Sale.*

21. Healy and Cattell, "Interface between Authorship, Industry, and Science." For further information about ghost authorship, see Elliott, "Pharma Goes to the Laundry," and Kassirer, *On the Take.*

One academic familiar with these practices has estimated that up to 90 percent of industry-sponsored pharmaceutical studies that list a prominent academic as lead author may be ghostwritten.[22] Moreover, even when there is not direct evidence of ghostwriting, university researchers have been commissioned to write letters to the editor, editorials, and even textbooks for tens of thousands of dollars.[23]

Other examples of industry influence on academic scientists come from the interpretation of scientific findings by expert panels. For example, many members of FDA expert-advisory committees typically have financial conflicts of interest.[24] In a particularly infamous case, an FDA committee failed to take the highly controversial pain medications Vioxx and Bextra off the market in February 2005. Reporters for the *New York Times* subsequently found that 10 of the 32 committee members had consulted in recent years for the drugs' makers. Moreover, "If the 10 advisers had not cast their votes, the committee would have voted 12 to 8 that Bextra should be withdrawn and 14 to 8 that Vioxx should not return to the market. The 10 advisers with company ties voted 9 to 1 to keep Bextra on the market and 9 to 1 for Vioxx's return."[25]

The hormesis case also illustrates how interested groups become heavily involved in research that intersects with their concerns. Most likely because of the potential significance of hormesis for risk assessment, the Texas Institute for the Advancement of Chemical Technology (TIACT), the Nuclear Regulatory Commission (NRC), and the U.S. Air Force have provided research grants for Edward Calabrese to study hormesis.[26] In addition, he leads an organization called Biological Effects of Low Level Exposures

22. This estimate comes from Dr. John Davis, quoted by Shankar Vedantam, "Comparison of Schizophrenia Drugs."

23. Elliott, "Pharma Goes to the Laundry." Note that these pharmaceutical industry strategies (including ghostwriting and paying academic scientists to produce questionable studies or commentaries) are also used by polluting companies who want to defend their products against accusations that they are harmful; see, for example, Shabecoff and Shabecoff, *Poisoned Profits*, ch. 9; Fagin, Lavelle, and the Center for Public Integrity, *Toxic Deception*, ch. 3; Michaels, *Doubt Is Their Product*; Hardell et al., "Secret Ties to Industry"; Wilholt, "Bias and Values in Scientific Research."

24. Shrader-Frechette, *Taking Action, Saving Lives*.

25. Harris and Berenson, "10 Voters on Panel."

26. The information about Calabrese's funding in this paragraph comes from several sources: Kaiser, "Sipping from a Poisoned Chalice"; Calabrese's 2002 curriculum vitae, http://people.umass.edu/nrephc/EJCCVApril02.pdf, accessed November 2003; personal communication from Calabrese by email on April 29, 2010; and corporate giving reports from ExxonMobil for 2003 through 2008, obtained through personal communication by email from Paul Mushak on April 2, 2010. Some of this information is ambiguous. For example, ExxonMobil's statements from 2003 through 2008 report that a total of roughly $700,000 was provided to BELLE for what it calls the "Chemical Hormesis Database." Nevertheless, Calabrese claims in his personal communication that ExxonMobil funds provided only "general support" for the hormesis initiative and that his actual research on the hormesis database was funded only with TIACT, NRC, and Air Force money.

(BELLE), which funds activities such as workshops, conferences, and newsletters that promote the study of low-dose biological responses to chemicals and radiation.[27] To be fair, it is important to emphasize that Calabrese has sponsored a range of work, including some perspectives critical of hormesis, under the auspices of BELLE.[28] Nevertheless, the organization is partly funded by industry groups (including Canadian Electric Utilities, Dow-Corning, the Electric Power Research Institute, ExxonMobil, the GE Foundation, Gillette, Ontario Hydro, and RJReynolds) that have a significant stake in the outcome of hormesis research. In fact, Frederick vom Saal claims that much of the motivation for studying hormesis came from these industry groups, because they were concerned to counteract the policy ramifications of research on endocrine disruption.[29]

I do not claim that these financial ties have resulted in deliberate bias by researchers in the hormesis case. Moreover, there are a host of factors in addition to financial ones that could have influenced the scientists studying hormesis. For example, even if some researchers have made questionable methodological or interpretive judgments, this could be caused either by the desire to make an important new discovery or by the availability heuristic, which can make the data that researchers collect more salient to them than opposing data with which they are less familiar.[30] Nevertheless, given the extensive evidence that vested interests are currently using a variety of strategies to produce policy-relevant science that serves their interests, it would be unwise to ignore the funding sources for hormesis research. As more university scientists enter into complex institutional and financial relationships, it is important to consider how research on hormesis and other policy-relevant topics can be kept responsive to an array of societal values other than those of powerful stakeholders like industry and the military. The following sections embark on that challenge.

## UNIVERSITY CONFLICT-OF-INTEREST POLICIES

The remainder of this chapter focuses on how to prevent the interests of deep pockets from exerting too much control over university research. As

27. For more information about BELLE, see its website, http://www.belleonline.com/, accessed on June 29, 2007.

28. See, for example, the *BELLE Newsletter* 14(1), on "Hormesis and Ethics," http://www.belleonline.com/newsletters.htm.

29. Vom Saal, "Hormesis Controversy."

30. For discussion of numerous influences on scientific research, see for example, Jasanoff et al., *Handbook of Science*, and Solomon, *Social Empiricism*, which examines the availability heuristic.

the introduction notes, the present book has good reasons for focusing on academic science. Sheldon Krimsky has emphasized that one of the important missions of academic research is to serve the public good.[31] Therefore, it is relatively easy to justify reforms in the university setting in order to promote societal concerns, whereas it is more difficult to alter the research performed by interest groups. Moreover, many of the abuses associated with industry behavior could be mitigated if universities effectively fulfilled their public-interest role. Independent university scientists can challenge questionable claims made by interest groups and can serve as relatively neutral sources of scientific advice. Nevertheless, in at least some areas of policy-relevant science, it is becoming difficult to find academic experts that do not have conflicting interests. For example, the *New England Journal of Medicine* adopted a particularly strict COI policy in the 1990s for editorials and reviews, requiring "that authors of such articles will not have any financial interest in a company (or its competitor) that makes a product discussed in the article."[32] Unfortunately, the editors had to weaken their strict policy because they could find almost no well-credentialed authors who were not conflicted. The revised policy prohibits only "significant" financial interests, thus allowing, for example, honorariums or consulting fees of less than $10,000 per year.[33]

As in the case of the *New England Journal of Medicine*, most universities and journals have responded to corporate influences on scientific research by developing financial COI policies.[34] In this section I examine those policies and argue that they are insufficient to ensure that university research is informed by a representative range of societal values and concerns. In response to this pessimistic lesson, the next section offers some alternative solutions.

One common definition of a conflict of interest is "a set of conditions in which professional judgment concerning a primary interest (such as patients' welfare or the validity of research) tends to be unduly influenced by a secondary interest (such as financial gain)."[35] This definition has several strengths. First, it refers to a set of *conditions* rather than a particular *behavior*, and thus it emphasizes the fact that there can be justifiable concerns about the potential results of conflicted situations even if they do not always result in

31. Krimsky, *Science in the Private Interest.*

32. Drazen and Curfman, "Financial Associations of Authors."

33. Ibid., 1901.

34. See Task Force on Research Accountability, *Report on Institutional and Individual Conflict of Interest*; Task Force on Financial Conflicts of Interest in Clinical Research, *Protecting Subjects, Preserving Trust, Promoting Progress.*

35. Thompson, "Understanding Financial Conflicts of Interest."

problematic actions. Similarly, it refers to conditions that *tend* to influence the judgment of scientists, again because a COI could be a legitimate source of concern even if it does not produce problematic effects in every single instance. Finally, it refers to *undue* influences caused by particular situations. It is admittedly difficult to decide what constitutes an undue influence, but conflicting interests are so widespread that there must plausibly be some threshold below which they are not taken to be a matter of serious concern. It is also important to note that, although the definition acknowledges that different types of secondary influences can exist, this chapter focuses on secondary interests of a financial nature. A complex mixture of interests has always affected scientific practice in both appropriate and inappropriate ways. A major subject of contemporary debate, however, is whether appropriate mechanisms are in place to prevent financial interests in particular from having inappropriate influences on scientific judgment.

Policies for addressing these financial COIs in academic settings currently focus on three major options: removal of the conflict (through divestiture or recusal), disclosure, or management.[36] First, in cases of particularly serious financial COIs, one option is to require that researchers eliminate the conflict, either by recusing themselves from particular research projects or by divesting themselves of the financial ties that create the conflict. A second option is to require researchers to disclose their conflicts to one or more of the following groups: university COI committees, institutional review boards (IRBs), government funding agencies, attendees at oral presentations, and the readers of publications.[37] The third option is to develop management plans for addressing COIs that merit further action beyond mere disclosure. A potential source of confusion is that the term "management plan" is sometimes applied to an entire COI policy (including requirements for disclosure or removal of conflicts), but it is sometimes also applied to a narrower range of responses. Throughout this chapter, "management" is used in the narrower sense, which refers to various strategies that are distinct from disclosure and removal. For example, in a case where biomedical researchers have a financial interest in the drug that they are studying, one might require that they not be directly involved in recruiting participants for a clinical trial (in order to prevent the possibility that they might exert inordinate pressure in favor of participation). One might also require that an external panel, such as a data safety monitoring board (DSMB), review the research protocol and the final statistical analysis to

36. Task Force on Research Accountability, *Report on Institutional and Individual Conflict of Interest*; Shamoo and Resnik, *Responsible Conduct of Research*.

37. Task Force on Research Accountability, *Report on Institutional and Individual Conflict of Interest*, 4–5.

ensure that they have no obvious flaws. Let us consider, in turn, the merits of each of the three options for addressing financial COIs.

### Divestiture and Recusal

Unfortunately, it appears to be very difficult to implement the first approach (i.e., divestiture or recusal) for addressing financial COIs in university research. There is currently great enthusiasm for university-industry partnerships, and a variety of federal policies have been created over the past thirty years to encourage these relationships.[38] Currently, two-thirds of academic institutions hold equity interests in start-up companies that sponsor research at those institutions.[39] Furthermore, the motivation behind these arrangements is not strictly a matter of self-interest on the part of universities. Besides the obvious goals of bringing in research funds and generating income through the creation of intellectual property, the hope is that these collaborations will provide valuable research expertise for industry and also produce start-up companies, thus boosting local and national economies. As a result, however, the number of cases in which universities and scientists are willing to eliminate financial COIs entirely is likely to be fairly limited. For example, in 2005 the National Institutes of Health instituted a strict policy that prohibited almost all forms of financial COIs. The policy was extremely controversial and resulted in the resignation of several influential researchers.[40] Few universities are likely to risk such losses. This is reflected by the fact that the report on COIs by the influential Association of American Universities (AAU) places the majority of its focus on developing disclosure guidelines and suggests a general prohibition on COIs only in cases involving research on human subjects.[41] Although this might seem to be a narrowly *descriptive* point rather than an *ethical* one, any reasonable evaluation of COI policies needs to take account of the manner in which they are likely to be applied. If universities are likely to be overly cautious in calling for divestiture or recusal in response to conflicts, then this element of COI policies is insufficient unless it can be supplemented with further approaches.

Ethicist David Resnik suggests a much more aggressive policy for eliminating COIs than most universities currently pursue.[42] He claims that one

38. Johnson, "End of Pure Science."

39. Bekelman, Lee, and Gross, "Scope and Impact of Financial Conflicts."

40. Derenzo, "Conflict-of-interest Policy."

41. Task Force on Research Accountability, *Report on Institutional and Individual Conflict of Interest*, especially p. 4.

42. Resnik, *Price of Truth*.

should consider three factors when deciding whether to prohibit a financial COI: the significance of the conflict (e.g., the amount of money at stake), the ability to manage it, and the consequences of prohibiting it. On the basis of these considerations, he proposes a variety of situations in which financial COIs should generally be eliminated, including the following: peer review (both for grants and journal articles), research regulation or oversight (e.g., membership on institutional review boards or institutional animal care and use committees), management or ownership of a private company while performing research for the company, and receipt of payment to enroll patients in clinical trials. In contrast, he argues that it is generally acceptable for university scientists to perform research for companies under other arrangements (e.g., as employees or paid consultants) and to perform research on products while holding intellectual property rights on them.

Resnik's proposal seems more likely than that of the AAU to block problematic influences, but it still faces two problems. On one hand, it may be too ambitious. As already noted, most universities are so interested in developing start-up companies that they are reluctant to prevent researchers from holding management or ownership relationships with companies for which they do research. On the other hand, Resnik's proposal still allows COIs that skew research toward the concerns of deep pockets. In particular, empirical studies on pharmaceuticals and smoking (presented at the beginning of this chapter) suggest that financial COIs can significantly affect research even when the conflicts involve only the provision of funding. Thus, it currently appears rather unlikely that prohibition by itself can prevent most potentially problematic effects of financial COIs. Resnik is aware of this problem, and he appeals to disclosure as an important additional strategy for addressing financial conflicts.

## Disclosure

Disclosure is a particularly popular approach that has become the cornerstone of most current COI policies adopted by universities and academic journals. For example, five of the ten operating guidelines in the AAU report involve responsibilities to disclose financial COIs.[43] The NIH and NSF now require the universities that receive their funding to develop COI policies that require various forms of disclosure. A growing number of professional societies and associations are also starting to recommend disclosure.[44] Despite its growing prevalence as a response to financial COIs, however, it is not clear that disclosure is actually a sufficient strategy. Some commenta-

43. Task Force on Research Accountability, *Report on Institutional and Individual Conflict of Interest*, especially pp. 4–6.

44. See Resnik, *Price of Truth*.

tors worry that disclosure policies are inconsistent among universities, that too few journals require disclosure of conflicts, and that investigators do not comply with them.[45] For example, Sheldon Krimsky and L. S. Rothenberg found in 1997 that, of the 61,134 articles published that year in journals with COI disclosure policies, only 0.5 percent of the articles included the disclosure that an author had a financial conflict.[46] This low disclosure rate flies in the face of common sense and runs counter to an earlier study in 1992 by Krimsky and Rothenberg, who found that 34 percent of the articles published in fourteen prominent scientific journals had a lead author with a financial COI (although none of these conflicts were disclosed in the articles).[47] They concluded that the low disclosure rate of COIs was not caused by the failure of journal editors to publish information supplied to them, because 74 percent of the surveyed editors reported that they "always" or "almost always" published disclosures when they were received. It seems quite plausible, therefore, that many scientists do not comply with disclosure policies.

These problems of non-compliance can be exacerbated by confusion or differing expectations about what sorts of conflicts should be disclosed. The money that Ed Calabrese has received from ExxonMobil during the past decade provides a good example in the hormesis case. According to ExxonMobil's Worldwide Giving Reports from 2003 to 2008, the company gave the University of Massachusetts, Amherst, a total of roughly $700,000 that was designated for "BELLE – Chemical Hormesis Database."[48] However, while Calabrese regularly discloses his Air Force funding in his hormesis publications, he has only rarely mentioned his ExxonMobil funding.[49] The Center for Science in the Public Interest criticized Calabrese for this failure.[50] He maintains, however, that the ExxonMobil funding merely provided "general support" for the BELLE initiative on hormesis. Thus, part of the reason for his failure to disclose this funding may have been his belief that it did not directly support the creation and updating of the hormesis database that he discusses in his publications.[51]

45. General Accounting Office, *University Research*; Krimsky, *Science in the Private Interest.*

46. Krimsky and Rothenberg, "Conflict of Interest Policies."

47. Krimsky et al., "Financial Interests of Authors in Scientific Journals."

48. This funding is listed in ExxonMobil's corporate giving reports for 2003 through 2008, obtained through personal communication by email from Paul Mushak on April 2, 2010.

49. Two articles that mention the ExxonMobil funding are "Hormesis: A Conversation with a Critic" and "Hormesis: Calabrese Responds."

50. See the Integrity in Science Watch for the week of June 6, 2008, available at: http://www.cspinet.org/integrity/watch/200806161.html, accessed on June 9, 2010.

51. Personal communication from Calabrese by email on April 29, 2010. Given that Calabrese typically did not disclose his TIACT funding either, another part of the explanation for his lack of disclosure may be that he held to a policy of not disclosing funding sources unless the source or the journal required it.

Cases like this one suggest that there needs to be more clarity about COI policies and expectations, as well as better standardization and improved compliance with them. Nevertheless, a highly significant but less frequently discussed reason for thinking that disclosure policies are insufficient to address financial COIs is that they may still be ineffective even when they are administered effectively. The assumption behind the recent emphasis on disclosure of financial COIs is that this approach mitigates many of the worrisome effects of COIs while causing minimal disruption of research activity. Ideally, the disclosure requirement allows those who receive the disclosed information to be on the lookout for problematic influences, and it motivates those who provide information to be relatively unbiased. Unfortunately, an intriguing body of psychological research challenges these hopes for the effectiveness of disclosure policies.[52]

Daylian Cain and coworkers have highlighted a variety of reasons for skepticism about the notion that those who receive COI disclosures can successfully discount biased information. A crucial problem is that successful "judgmental correction" requires a sense of the direction *and* the magnitude of a biasing influence. Unfortunately, it is very difficult to estimate the extent to which a particular conflict may have influenced an information source. In fact, the disclosure that an information provider has a conflict of interest may even have the paradoxical impact of *increasing* trust in the source, thereby *decreasing* one's expectation of biasing influences.[53] In general, people underestimate situational influences on the behavior of others, and they overestimate the influence of an individual's character, values, and dispositions.[54] The result is a poor ability to predict the extent to which conflicts of interest affect the judgment of those who provide information. Moreover, those who receive tainted information must overcome anchoring biases, which cause both laypeople and experts to remain influenced by initial information even when they attempt to correct their judgments. It is noteworthy that anchors influence decision makers even when they know that information is being manipulated by a source with conflicts of interest.[55] A further problem related to the anchoring bias is the difficulty of unlearning false information. Humans continue to be influenced by information even after it has been shown to be false, and a "sleeper effect" can cause people to start believing information again after it has been discredited.[56]

52. See especially Cain, Loewenstein, and Moore, "Shortcomings of Disclosure."
53. Cain, Loewenstein, and Moore, "Shortcomings of Disclosure," 117.
54. Ross and Nisbett, *Person and the Situation.*
55. Galinsky and Mussweiler, "First Offers as Anchors."
56. Pratkanis et al., "In Search of Reliable Persuasion Effects."

Despite this disconcerting psychological research, one might still hope that COI disclosures could be somewhat beneficial, even if they are not as effective as initially perceived. The problem with this assumption is that COI disclosures may also cause the sources of information to be more biased than if COIs go undisclosed. First, advisors may engage in "strategic exaggeration," purposely skewing their information to a greater extent than normal in order to counteract the degree to which it is discounted. Second, as a result of "moral licensing," advisors may feel more comfortable providing biased information once they have the moral "cover" of admitting their COI. In addition, even if the sources of information consciously try to be as objective as possible, research indicates that people consistently overemphasize both their own objectivity and the extent to which they deserve any benefits received from conflicted situations.[57] Whether as a result of these or other factors, Cain and coworkers have in fact found through various experiments that information sources provide more biased advice when they have disclosed a COI.[58] Thus, they conclude that disclosures may actually do more harm than good, given that people have such a hard time accurately discounting information that they know to be tainted by COIs. Admittedly, one might question whether these results hold true outside the laboratory, because real-life situations involve higher stakes and allow greater potential for people to learn how to discount biases. Nevertheless, Cain et al. contend that these factors are unlikely to be very helpful in light of current psychological research.[59]

Although more work remains to be done in order to understand the conditions under which COI disclosures are either likely or unlikely to be effective, the current evidence indicates that it would be unwise to depend on disclosure as the fundamental strategy for responding to COIs. If university administrators want to employ more promising approaches, they need to consider the other main elements of COI policies. We have already seen that the elimination of conflicts via divestiture or recusal is likely to be considered only in cases of particularly severe conflicts. (What is more, the psychological literature indicates that divestiture is still not likely to be a completely effective solution because the biasing influences of COIs remain even after the conflicts themselves have been eliminated.)[60] Of the three major options proposed in current COI policies, the only remaining strategy is to develop plans for managing the conflicts.

57. Chugh, Bazerman, and Banaji, "Bounded Ethicality as a Psychological Barrier."

58. Cain, Loewenstein, and Moore, "Shortcomings of Disclosure," 116.

59. See also Abelson and Levi, "Decision Making and Decision Theory"; Camerer and Hogarth, "Effects of Financial Incentives in Experiments."

60. Miller, "Commentary."

## Management

Compared to disclosure, management plans for addressing financial COIs have received relatively little attention in current COI policies. For example, the AAU report on COIs provides two sorts of advice: a set of operating guidelines and a set of promising practices. The operating guidelines are supplied as normative suggestions for adoption by all universities, whereas the promising practices provide helpful ideas that university administrators may wish to consider. The operating guidelines say almost nothing about management practices in the narrow sense discussed in this chapter. The only exception is in guideline #2, which suggests that a possible response to some COIs would be to alter the original experimental protocol.

In the list of promising practices, management approaches receive a bit more, but still minimal, attention. For example, when universities determine how extensive a management plan should be in response to particular COIs, the AAU suggests several considerations: the "phase of clinical trial, whether stock is privately held or publicly traded, the size of company, the kind of intervention (diagnostic vs. therapeutic), whether faculty have any influence in the company, and whether a financial relationship is fixed (e.g., fixed payment) or variable (e.g., equity, stock options)."[61] The report also suggests that monitoring processes for COIs focus on "critical control points," such as "disclosure, grant application, IRB review, any necessary reporting to agencies (such as NIH, NSF, FDA), publication, and technology transfer activities."[62] Finally, the report suggests three specific elements of the research process from which conflicted researchers could be excluded as part of a management plan. These elements involve the enrollment of human participants, obtaining informed consent, and analyzing data.[63]

Although current descriptions of management plans in response to financial COIs are rather imprecise and superficial, the other major components of most COI policies (i.e., disclosure and divestiture or recusal) appear to be severely limited in their effectiveness. Therefore, although it is not clear that many universities are actively employing management plans in response to COIs, it seems valuable to consider whether they could, at least in principle, prove to be as effective as they initially appear. Current suggestions for developing management plans focus on two main approaches. The first is to prevent conflicted investigators from engaging in particular aspects of a research project, such as the enrollment of human participants or the analysis of data. The second approach is to have a committee review various elements of the

61. Task Force on Research Accountability, *Report on Institutional and Individual Conflict of Interest*, 8.

62. Ibid.

63. Ibid.

project to ensure that they are performed appropriately. The remainder of this section argues that, when one considers the wide range of ways in which value judgments impinge on the research process, it is unlikely that these management plans can ensure that an adequate range of societal concerns receives attention. This analysis also supports the present chapter's criticism of disclosure policies, because it seems very unlikely that the recipients of research information can successfully evaluate the extensive range of ways that a scientist's judgment could be influenced by ties to interest groups.

The present argument against the effectiveness of COI management plans rests on the following dilemma. Management efforts (such as supervision by internal or external committees) are likely to be *either* limited in effectiveness *or* extremely bureaucratic and time consuming, because of the diverse range of ways in which scientific research is permeated by value judgments that might be influenced by COIs. On one hand, management plans could focus on blocking a few particularly serious avenues through which financial COIs could influence research. This is by far the more likely approach for universities to adopt, but we will see that a variety of ways that COIs can skew research toward the concerns of wealthy interest groups may well be missed. On the other hand, the plans could provide highly detailed scrutiny of research projects and provide maximal insulation against worrisome influences. Unfortunately, providing scrutiny of this sort would likely produce a bureaucratic nightmare. One might attempt to avoid this dilemma by arguing that relatively few studies or scientists are genuinely likely to be influenced by financial COIs in a manner that harms societal interests. If this argument were convincing, universities could provide very careful management of a few highly problematic studies, thereby blocking the majority of worrisome influences from COIs and avoiding bureaucratic gridlock. The discussion in the preceding section suggests, however, that some scientific fields are sufficiently influenced by interest groups to make it unrealistic to assume that universities could carefully manage all the studies where these influences are present.

To pursue this argument, let us review some of the major ways that value judgments impinge on scientific research, as described in chapter 2, and consider the potential for management plans to prevent financial COIs from exerting too much influence on those judgments. Chapter 2 divides value judgments into four categories, while acknowledging that the fourfold division is helpful primarily for organization and does not reflect sharp distinctions in actual practice.[64] The first category involves judgments associated with the development of research projects, including the choice of research

64. Recall that others have made similar distinctions among different categories of value judgments; see, for example, Douglas, "Inductive Risk and Values in Science"; Longino, *Science as Social Knowledge*; Machamer and Wolters, "Introduction."

topics, proposal of hypotheses, and design of studies. Many analysts have pointed out that financial interests can have troublesome effects on these sorts of value judgments. For example, a common concern is that pharmaceutical research money is disproportionately targeted toward relatively insignificant but lucrative problems of the West (e.g., baldness, impotence, obesity) compared to more serious problems facing developing countries (e.g., malaria, AIDS). It is also well known that agricultural programs at universities tend to be dominated by chemical-based research that is conducive to profits for large agribusiness firms but that may be detrimental to the environment and public health.[65] With respect to experimental design, this chapter has already mentioned Kristin Shrader-Frechette's discussion of the ways that financial concerns have affected many industry-funded studies of public-health threats. She claims that this research often involves problematic models, small sample sizes, short time frames, lack of uncertainty analysis, and theoretical estimates rather than actually measured parameters.[66] All these strategies are designed to minimize false positive results while increasing false negatives. For example, in an analysis of ethical and scientific issues associated with industry studies of pesticides on human subjects, the EPA Science Advisory Board found that the industry studies invariably involved sample sizes that were dramatically too small, allowing for huge rates of false negatives.[67]

Management plans seem unlikely to systematically eliminate these avenues through which financial COIs can influence the judgment of university scientists. Admittedly, management committees could sometimes examine the design of studies to ensure that they are not blatantly biased toward producing results desired by sponsors. It would require a tremendous amount of bureaucratic activity, however, for management committees to inspect in detail the study designs of all university research projects (even just those in particular fields such as public health and biomedical research) sponsored by organizations with vested interests in the results. Nevertheless, this sort of scrutiny appears to be necessary in order to prevent worrisome influences of financial COIs, because current reviews in fields such as medicine and toxicology suggest that a large proportion of studies funded by industry sponsors may be designed in a questionable fashion.[68] Moreover, management committees would almost certainly be in

65. Berry, *Unsettling of America*; Thompson, *Spirit of the Soil*.

66. Shrader-Frechette, *Taking Action, Saving Lives*; U.S. EPA, *Comments on the Use of Data*. See also vom Saal and Hughes, "Extensive New Literature."

67. Oleskey, Fleischman, Goldman, Hirschhorn, Landrigan, Lappé, Marshall et al., "Pesticide Testing in Humans." For other examples of industry strategies to increase the false negative rate of studies, see vom Saal and Hughes, "Extensive New Literature."

68. Barnes and Bero, "Why Review Articles on the Health Effects"; Bekelman, Lee, and Gross, "Scope and Impact of Financial Conflicts"; U.S. EPA, *Comments on the Use of Data*.

no position to encourage scientists to pursue research projects or hypotheses that could serve the public interest but that are difficult to fund. Thus, as Sheldon Krimsky emphasizes in his book *Science in the Private Interest*, current COI management plans are not equipped to ensure that university scientists continue to fill all aspects of their role as sources of "public interest science."[69]

Chapter 2 suggests that a second category of ways in which value judgments impinge on scientific research involves the choice of scientific categories and terminology. Perhaps the best-known example of how financial considerations can affect scientific terminology and concepts is the manner in which pharmaceutical companies have tried to influence concepts of disease. For instance, many commentators have voiced concern that Eli Lilly inappropriately popularized the questionable concept of premenstrual dysphoric disorder (PMDD) largely so that the company could create a new market for fluoxetine hydrochloride (i.e., Prozac) and extend patent protection on it.[70] Although other financial influences on scientific concepts have received less attention, Edward Schiappa has provided fascinating examples of how political interest groups can strategically employ different scientific definitions for environmental phenomena like wetlands.[71]

These linguistic choices are likely to fly under the radar of COI management committees unless they are composed of individuals with significant expertise in the field under investigation and great sensitivity to the role of value judgments in scientific research and public policy. However, creating management committees of this sort to address all financially conflicted research is again likely to be too onerous an undertaking for most universities. In addition, even if a management committee were concerned about particularly biasing choices of language and insisted that they be left out of publications, scientists with financial COIs could still perpetuate potentially problematic linguistic choices in other contexts.

The third category of value judgments discussed in chapter 2 involves the numerous methodological judgments involved in interpreting and evaluating study results. These sorts of choices become even more critical when one formulates a review article, which requires weighing evidence from multiple studies. It is because of this consideration that the *New England Journal of Medicine* embarked on its failed attempt to prevent researchers with any financial COIs from writing these sorts of articles. Another significant way that values play a role in the evaluation of studies

69. Krimsky, *Science in the Private Interest.*

70. See, for example, J. R. Brown, "Funding, Objectivity, and the Socialization of Medical Research," especially 303–304.

71. Schiappa, *Defining Reality.*

is by either encouraging or discouraging the criticism of other work. For instance, Kristin Shrader-Frechette recounts cases in which flawed studies of health threats in local communities received little attention, because the university faculty who might have evaluated those studies had financial relationships with polluters. In contrast, industry-funded organizations like the American Petroleum Institute (API) are known for allocating large funds to aid scientists who challenge research that reflects negatively on industrial interests.[72]

Management committees may be able in some cases to prevent egregious influences of financial COIs on these sorts of value judgments, but they are unlikely to prevent them across the board. In the case of an original investigator performing a study, a management committee could perhaps ensure that the researcher does not make obviously unreasonable methodological value judgments in the evaluation of study data. Nevertheless, the management committee cannot easily prevent other investigators from making questionable judgments in their evaluation of the data produced by the original researcher. For example, a recent paper by Lennart Hardell and colleagues provides several case studies of highly influential epidemiologists who had undisclosed financial ties to industry groups in recent decades.[73] The conflicted researchers not only produced original research that downplayed a variety of cancer risks but also pursued a number of strategies (such as writing review articles and submitting recommendations to government bodies and commissions) to question the scientific claims of those who were reporting risks. Thus, the presence of financial COIs may steer the interpretation of scientific evidence toward the interests of powerful interest groups.

The fourth category of value judgments that impinge on science involves the application of research to decision making in individual or social contexts. This category of value influences feeds back into the other categories in complicated ways. For example, if policy makers recommend a "public-health-friendly" approach to chemical regulation (according to which false negatives would be prevented as much as possible), this approach could have a variety of implications for the design and interpretation of studies. Scientists could alter their statistical analyses of the data, characterize ambiguous data differently, and employ different methodological value judgments when interpreting empirical results.[74] Values associated with the application of research could also affect the way that scientists disseminate information to the public. For instance, industry-affiliated climatologists are

72. Shrader-Frechette, *Taking Action, Saving Lives.*

73. Hardell et al., "Secret Ties to Industry."

74. Cranor, *Regulating Toxic Substances*; Douglas, "Inductive Risk and Values in Science."

notorious for overemphasizing uncertainty associated with climate change and failing to give an adequate representation of the views of the scientific community as a whole.[75] An even more basic way that value judgments affect the dissemination of research results is that studies may be disproportionately more likely to be published if they serve their sponsors' interests rather than if they conflict with those interests. Some of the early scandals associated with financial COIs involved attempts by industry groups to block university researchers from disseminating research results that reflected poorly on their products.[76]

As with the first three categories of value judgments, management committees are unlikely to block all the ways that powerful interest groups manipulate policy-relevant research via this fourth category of judgments. There continue to be numerous reports alleging that industry groups are intimidating scientists who try to disseminate information that conflicts with their interests.[77] Furthermore, scientists with financial COIs may be much less likely to employ "public-health-friendly" methodological value judgments and statistical analyses of their data that decrease the likelihood of false negatives. They might also be more likely to present research results in a manner that furthers the interests of industry. Although it is plausible that COI management committees can help to prevent obvious problems with the interpretation and dissemination of information, it would be a bureaucratic nightmare for them to make detailed inspections of the manner in which all conflicted scientists interpret and disseminate their research results. Moreover, most scientists would probably regard such inspections as an unacceptable exercise in the micromanagement of research.

It appears, therefore, that management plans, like the other two standard elements of COI policies, are unlikely to ensure that university research remains responsive to a range of societal perspectives and concerns. There are so many ways in which value judgments affect the practice of scientific research that any practical management scheme is unlikely to stay abreast of them. To sum up, it is instructive to compare the traditional concerns that management plans have been designed to address with the range of value

75. Beder, *Global Spin.*

76. A particularly important example is the Nancy Olivieri case; see, for example, J. R. Brown, "Funding, Objectivity, and the Socialization of Medical Research."

77. Consider just two recent examples concerning the regulation of pharmaceuticals. First, GlaxoSmithKline allegedly exerted pressure on Dr. John Buse, a diabetes expert at the University of North Carolina, to keep him from raising questions about the safety of Avandia; see Saul, "Doctor Says Drug Maker Tried to Quash His Criticism of Avandia." Second, Merck appears to have applied pressure on several researchers, including Dr. Joan-Ramon Laporte of the Catalan Institute of Pharmacology in Spain, to try to silence criticism of Vioxx; see Matthews and Martinez, "Emails Suggest Merck Knew Vioxx's Dangers at Early Stage."

judgments that this book has highlighted. So far, proposals for management plans (such as those discussed in the AAU report) emphasize the prevention of harm to human subjects and perhaps also some protection against obviously flawed experimental design and interpretation. This section has emphasized that we should also worry about how deep pockets can influence the choice of topics that are pursued, the particular questions that are asked, the design of the studies (including subtle choices based on downstream concerns about the application of research to public policy), the categories and terms employed, the effectiveness and balance of criticism within the scientific community, and the manner in which scientific information is disseminated to policy makers and the public.

## ADDITIONAL RESPONSES

This final section of the chapter argues that, despite the weaknesses of the COI policies currently adopted by most universities, other strategies may promote research that is responsive to a range of societal concerns besides those of powerful interest groups. It describes five approaches: (1) providing more funding for independent research; (2) preventing particularly egregious institutional conflicts; (3) creating trial registries; (4) developing adversarial deliberative forums; and (5) creating consensual deliberative forums. This is by no means an exhaustive list. These five are chosen in order to illustrate some of the most promising strategies that are currently being discussed. University administrators and policy makers can choose individual strategies or combinations of approaches in an effort to develop appropriate responses to particular areas of research. For example, in certain fields the existing COI policies may be largely adequate, because the research is not overly skewed toward the interests of particular stakeholders. In other areas of work, the level of influence from vested interests (as well as significant policy relevance) is so high that multiple approaches are warranted to control the influences of COIs. Based on the examples in this chapter, pharmaceutical and public-health research appear to be two areas that merit extensive scrutiny.

One particularly important strategy for alleviating the effects of financial COIs in highly sensitive areas of research (such as the assessment of pharmaceuticals or toxic chemicals) is to require or encourage independent studies by researchers without significant financial ties to interested parties. For example, James Robert Brown suggests that the best strategy for promoting medical research that genuinely fulfills societal concerns is to socialize it.[78]

78. J. R. Brown, "Funding, Objectivity, and the Socialization of Medical Research."

Nevertheless, one need not go that far in order to arrive at changes that could significantly improve areas of policy-relevant research that are currently overrun by deep pockets. Sheldon Krimsky suggests a system in which any company that wishes to submit data to the FDA for the approval of a drug would be required to work with a national institute for drug testing (NIDT).[79] The NIDT would negotiate with the company to create protocols that conform with uniform quality-control requirements, and the institute would contract out the research projects to relatively independent university researchers or centers. One could develop a similar system for companies that need to submit scientific findings to agencies like the EPA or OSHA. Numerous other prominent intellectuals and associations, including Marcia Angell, Philip Kitcher, Kristin Shrader-Frechette, and the American Public Health Association, are calling for more independent assessment and testing on topics related to medicine, public health, and the environment, including hormesis.[80]

A second approach that might increase the responsiveness of university research to a range of societal concerns is for university administrators to prevent or prohibit COIs in a broader range of cases than they would otherwise consider. We have seen that the practice of divestiture or recusal is likely to be fairly unpopular with most universities, considering that they are engaged in extensive efforts to foster relationships with private industry. Nevertheless, attention to the limitations of disclosure and management might encourage university administrators to consider taking greater steps to prevent COIs, especially at the institutional level. For example, they might question the wisdom of contracts between private companies and entire departments, such as the 1998 deal between Novartis and UC Berkeley's Department of Plant and Microbial Biology.[81] One goal of the present chapter has been to encourage this sort of careful thinking about whether the benefits of particular links between universities and interest groups truly outweigh their drawbacks.

A third strategy for preventing vested interests from manipulating policy-relevant research is to develop trial registries. As McGarity and Wagner point out, one effective way to "bend" science is to conceal findings that do not promote one's interest. This strategy can generate a skewed impression of the effectiveness of drugs or the harmfulness of toxic substances. In order

79. Krimsky, *Science in the Private Interest*, 229.

80. Reiss and Kitcher, "Neglected Diseases and Well-ordered Science"; Angell, *Truth about the Drug Companies*; American Public Health Association (APHA), *Supporting Legislation for Independent Post-marketing Phase IV Comparative Evaluation*; Shrader-Frechette, "Ideological Toxicology"; Shrader-Frechette, "Nanotoxicology and Ethical Conditions for Informed Consent"; Shrader-Frechette, *Taking Action, Saving Lives*.

81. Press and Washburn, "Kept University."

to address this problem, a number of governments and organizations have created registries where clinical trials can be reported. Most prominent medical journals now have the policy of requiring, as a condition for publication, that clinical trials be submitted to a registry at their inception.[82] Therefore, companies have an incentive to make the existence of their studies known when they initiate the research; as a result, they cannot bury them as easily if they generate unfavorable results. Admittedly, this strategy is limited in its effectiveness, because it does not prevent interest groups from designing or interpreting studies in a manner that serves their interests. Nevertheless, it has become an accepted strategy not only for university research but also for pharmaceutical studies performed outside the university setting. Therefore, when conjoined with other approaches, it can serve as an effective tool in the arsenal of those who seek to generate more societally responsive research.

A fourth approach for encouraging greater societal scrutiny of policy-relevant research (both inside and outside the academic setting) is to facilitate adversarial deliberation among various stakeholders. One might object that scientific institutions already incorporate deliberative mechanisms (e.g., peer-review processes for journal articles and grant applications), so there is no need to create additional ones. Unfortunately, we have a variety of reasons for thinking that university administrators and policy makers may need to augment the deliberation that currently occurs within the scientific community. First, it is not clear that scientists do in fact adequately scrutinize each other's work and consistently identify questionable judgments or errors made by their peers. Empirical evidence provides worrying indications that the reproducibility of evaluations provided by peer reviewers is poor and that the review process may not consistently weed out errors or fraud.[83] Researchers studying the peer-review process argue that current evidence is inadequate to evaluate its effectiveness or to predict the characteristics of good reviewers.[84] Moreover, it appears that some areas of policy-relevant work have become so captured by interest groups that existing deliberative mechanisms cannot be trusted. One thinks, for example, of the FDA panels (discussed earlier in this chapter) that approved Vioxx and

82. See, for example, Angell, "Time for a Drug Registry"; DeAngelis et al., "Clinical Trial Registration."

83. Concerning the lack of reproducibility among reviewers see especially Cole, Cole, and Simon, "Chance and Consensus in Peer Review"; Rothwell and Martyn, "Reproducibility of Peer Review in Clinical Neuroscience." For an overview of empirical research on the limitations of peer review, including its spotty record at identifying errors and fraud, see Wager and Jefferson, "Shortcomings of Peer Review in Biomedical Journals."

84. Callahan and Tercier, "Relationship of Previous Training and Experience"; Jefferson, Wager, and Davidoff, "Measuring the Quality of Editorial Peer Review."

Bextra under the influence of numerous conflicted members. One also thinks of the journal articles or letters about drugs like Zoloft that have been ghostwritten by "medical education companies" under the names of prominent academic scientists. Thus, rather than passively relying on existing deliberation within the scientific community to promote societally responsive research, administrators and policy makers would be well advised to consider new adversarial deliberative forums for evaluating some areas of policy-relevant science.

There are several precedents for this suggestion. During the 1950s, Harvard University president James B. Conant argued that quasijudicial adversarial proceedings could improve government decisions about military research and development. In order to alleviate worrisome political influences on these decisions, he suggested that technical experts should be appointed to develop arguments for and against proposed research projects. One or more referees could then hear the arguments of the experts on each side, cross-examine them, and (on the basis of this information) present recommendations to government decision makers.[85] Similarly, in the 1960s and 1970s, Arthur Kantrowitz famously proposed a "science court" that could evaluate debated scientific issues that were relevant to public policy.[86] Roughly along the lines of Kantrowitz's proposal, Justin Biddle recently proposed a system of "adversarial proceedings for the evaluation of pharmaceuticals" (APEP).[87] The result would be an institutionalized system in which a group of relatively impartial scientists hears conflicting perspectives on the safety and effectiveness of particular pharmaceuticals and renders judgments on the debated issues.

Even without instituting these novel adversarial formats, Tom McGarity and Wendy Wagner have argued that many existing adversarial legal institutions could be tweaked in order to assist in the scrutiny of policy-relevant science:

> In advocating increased reliance on adversarial procedures, we are suggesting, perhaps counterintuitively, that the way to reduce the impact advocates have in the realm of science is to enhance the role they play in the legal realm by increasing the range of affected interests that have access to the relevant legal procedures. The goal for this suite of legal reforms is therefore to restructure existing adversarial processes... in ways that catalyze otherwise dormant subgroups of affected parties to engage in effective oversight of policy-relevant science.[88]

85. Conant, *Science and Common Sense.*

86. See Kantrowitz, "Proposal for an Institution for Scientific Judgment"; Kantrowitz, "Science Court Experiment."

87. See Biddle, "Socializing Science."

88. McGarity and Wagner, *Bending Science*, 284.

McGarity and Wagner argue that plaintiffs' attorneys in tort cases have tremendous incentive to uncover questionable scientific research performed by defendants, both because of the large amounts of money invested in litigation and because of the potential for huge damage awards. Moreover, plaintiffs' attorneys have the power to obtain internal documents and testimony that regulators would often not be able to access. Although these materials are frequently not made public, they can sometimes be released as a condition for settling litigation.

Unfortunately, a significant worry at present is that regulated industries have been attempting to weaken the power of the tort system despite evidence that it already fails to provide adequate incentives against marketing unsafe products.[89] McGarity and Wagner argue that these efforts to weaken the tort system should be halted, and they even suggest that evidentiary burdens of proof could be shifted to assist plaintiffs in some cases.[90] Carl Cranor has already shown that one would not need to make dramatic legal changes in order to ease the evidential burden on plaintiffs; regulated industries frequently convince judges to accept evidentiary standards in tort cases that are both legally and scientifically problematic.[91]

Despite their potential for uncovering questionable judgments associated with policy-relevant research, however, adversarial deliberative approaches may be problematic in some contexts. For example, proposals for science courts have traditionally maintained an overly sharp distinction between factual and value-laden issues, and they generally exclude the "lay public" from participating in the consideration of allegedly factual questions.[92] Another worry is that adversarial formats may, under some circumstances, promote gridlock, distrust, and manipulative communication between stakeholders.[93]

In response, numerous authors have proposed *consensual* deliberative forums. For example, in addition to their calls for adversarial proceedings, McGarity and Wagner note that "Science advisory panels, staffed by independent and representative experts and asked to review a specific body of policy-relevant science, can serve as ballast against stakeholder dominance and help to identify and appropriately discount bent science."[94] Moreover, some consensual formats can provide opportunities for nonexpert members

89. Cranor, *Toxic Torts*.

90. McGarity and Wagner, *Bending Science*, 288.

91. Cranor, *Toxic Torts*.

92. Shrader-Frechette, *Science Policy, Ethics, and Economic Methodology*.

93. Busenberg, "Collaborative and Adversarial Analysis in Environmental Policy"; Futrell, "Technical Adversarialism and Participatory Collaboration"; Jasanoff, "Procedural Choices in Regulatory Science."

94. McGarity and Wagner, *Bending Science*, 260.

of the public to add their voices to those of experts.[95] To take one prominent example, the seminal National Research Council report *Understanding Risk* encourages "analytic-deliberative" formats that integrate technical scientific analyses with input from a wide range of "interested and affected" parties.[96] Calls for these sorts of deliberative forums mirror Sheila Jasanoff's contention that democratically and scientifically informed societal decision making requires attention not only to bodies of scientific research but also to deliberative bodies. Therefore, chapter 5 examines consensual deliberative bodies in some detail and argues that the development of such forums might provide a promising avenue for ensuring that judgments associated with hormesis research are responsive to a range of societal concerns.

## CONCLUSION

Many effects of financial conflicts of interest that we have observed throughout this chapter are not accidental. In the 1970s, as environmental regulations grew, advisors to industry offered the following advice:

> Regulatory policy is increasingly made with the participation of experts, especially academics. A regulated firm or industry should be prepared whenever possible to co-opt these experts. This is most effectively done by identifying the leading experts in each relevant field and hiring them as consultants or advisors or giving them research grants and the like. This activity requires a modicum of finesse; it must not be too blatant, for the experts themselves must not recognize that they have lost their objectivity and freedom of action.[97]

Even in the 1960s, the tobacco industry was already setting aside money with the goal "to seed the universities with research money and grow an unassailable crop of advocates."[98] We have seen that these efforts have only become stronger in the ensuing decades.

This chapter has highlighted the weaknesses of current university COI policies for preventing this strategic co-optation of policy-relevant research. It has argued that all three major components of current COI policies will likely be insufficient to promote research that is responsive to an adequate range of societal values. Divestiture and recusal are likely to be unworkable in many cases, and psychological research raises significant questions about the adequacy of disclosure. Moreover, the complex array of judgments asso-

95. Douglas, "Inserting the Public into Science"; Kleinman, *Science, Technology, and Democracy*; Sclove and Scammell, "Practicing the Principle."

96. National Research Council, *Understanding Risk*.

97. Owen and Braeutigam, *Regulation Game*, 7.

98. Zegart, *Civil Warriors*, 290.

ciated with scientific research challenges the effectiveness of management plans.

Some elements of current COI policies may still turn out to be *necessary* components of a more adequate response. The present chapter has focused only on the argument that the elements of current policies are not *sufficient* for protecting the integrity of research. Thus, whether in conjunction with current policies or in place of them, additional strategies are worth pursuing. This is particularly true in areas of science like hormesis research, where large quantities of money are at stake and numerous financial COIs are present. The present chapter has suggested five additional approaches for consideration: (1) providing more funding for independent research; (2) preventing particularly egregious institutional conflicts; (3) creating trial registries; (4) developing adversarial deliberative forums; and (5) creating consensual deliberative forums. The next chapter focuses on the final strategy and discusses how it might apply to the hormesis case.

# 5

# Lesson #2

## Diagnosing Deliberation

Ortwin Renn has identified a significant problem for policy makers:

> We live in a pluralist society with different value systems and worldviews. Who can legitimately claim the right to select the values or preferences that should guide collective decision making, in particular when the health and lives of humans are at stake?[1]

The preceding two chapters make Renn's concerns appear all the more significant. Chapter 3 shows that significant value judgments are present not only in public-policy decisions themselves but also in the scientific research that informs those decisions. Chapter 4 provides evidence that these judgments are all too often guided by deep pockets that have large amounts of money at stake in the outcomes of scientific work. In order to prevent these interest groups from having inordinate effects on academic science, the chapter proposes several responses.

One of the suggestions in chapter 4 is to develop appropriate, broadly based deliberative bodies. These forums would provide avenues for multiple stakeholders to influence the value judgments associated with research. We have already seen that Sheila Jasanoff makes a very similar suggestion. She argues that effectively incorporating science in democratic decision making requires more than just a narrow focus on the body of scientific knowledge.[2] It is also important to have effective deliberative bodies that can influence the collection, interpretation, and application of scientific findings.

The present chapter develops these ideas in more detail. It begins with an overview of previous scholarship on deliberation and public participation in science and technology policy. Drawing on this background, it

1. Renn, "Model for an Analytic-deliberative Process."

2. See Jasanoff, "Judgment under Siege." For more discussion of the three "bodies" that contribute to the successful integration of science with politics, see the introductory chapter of this book.

develops the book's second lesson for integrating societal values with scientific work, namely, that citizens and policy makers need to more effectively "diagnose" whether controversial areas of research would benefit from formal mechanisms for deliberation. Whereas deliberative forums have become increasingly popular approaches for addressing environmental *policy*, they have played less of a role in scientific *research* itself. Moreover, when members of the public have influenced research, their involvement has generally been ad hoc and limited to the study of specific local hazards. Therefore, this chapter proposes a model for examining controversial areas of policy-relevant research to determine whether they merit a formal deliberative response and to consider what role nonscientists should play in the process. Finally, it applies this model to the hormesis case and considers what it might recommend in response to this pressing area of policy-relevant science.

## BACKGROUND ON DELIBERATION

This chapter builds on a growing body of previous scholarship. Interest in deliberative democracy and public participation in science policy has skyrocketed in recent years.[3] Numerous government agencies, nongovernmental organizations (NGOs), and citizens' groups are already experimenting with deliberative processes that integrate stakeholders' perspectives in policy decisions. The U.S. Environmental Protection Agency, the Department of Defense (DOD), the National Institutes of Health, and the Department of Energy (DOE) have all instituted strategies for incorporating public discussion into their decision-making processes. Many authors claim that the nascent field of nanoscale science and technology is providing an ideal opportunity to experiment with deliberative proceedings at the earliest stages of research and development.[4] Meanwhile, local municipalities are experimenting with public participation as a way to defuse conflict over difficult decisions about budgeting, development, water use, and waste

3. For literature on deliberative democracy, see Dryzek, *Deliberative Democracy and Beyond*; Fishkin and Laslett, *Debating Deliberative Democracy*; Macedo, ed., *Deliberative Politics*. For public participation in science policy, see Fiorino, "Citizen Participation and Environmental Risk"; Guston, "Innovation Policy"; Kleinman, *Science, Technology, and Democracy*; Renn, Webler, and Wiedemann, eds., *Fairness and Competence in Citizen Participation*.

4. Arnall and Parr, "Moving the Nanoscience and Technology (NST) Debate Forwards"; Barben et al., "Anticipatory Governance of Nanotechnology"; Guston, "Innovation Policy"; Munn, "Expert's Role in Nanoscience and Technology"; Royal Society and the Royal Academy of Engineering, UK (2004), *Nanoscience and Nanotechnologies*, http://www.nanotec.org.uk/finalReport.htm, accessed on 6/29/07; Rogers-Hayden and Pidgeon, "Reflecting upon the UK's Citizens' Jury on Nanotechnologies"; Toumey, "Science and Democracy."

disposal.[5] An accompanying academic literature is documenting the range of deliberative mechanisms available, the strengths and weaknesses of these approaches, and the range of situations and questions for which various forms of deliberation are particularly appropriate.[6] This section provides an overview of previous studies on deliberation, including a definition of the concept, an introduction to various motivations for pursuing it, and finally a brief introduction to some of the deliberative mechanisms that have already been implemented.

## Defining Deliberation

In many respects this chapter follows the description of deliberation in the influential National Research Council (NRC) report *Understanding Risk,* which analyzes the role that deliberation can play in the characterization of risks.[7] The NRC document is a particularly good starting point, both because it synthesizes a large body of previous literature and because it emphasizes the importance of "diagnosing" deliberation, which is a central theme in the present chapter. The NRC defines deliberation as "any formal or informal process for communication and for raising and collectively considering issues."[8] Moreover, the *Understanding Risk* report calls for *broadly based deliberations,* defined as those that meet the following conditions:

> [I]n addition to the involvement of appropriate policy makers and specialists in risk analysis, participation from across [the spectrum of interested and affected parties must be]...sufficiently diverse to ensure that the important, decision-relevant knowledge enters the process, that the important perspectives are considered, and that the parties' legitimate concerns about the inclusiveness and openness of the process are addressed.[9]

The NRC distinguishes broadly based deliberation from the concept of public participation.[10] Although these concepts are closely related, one of the most important differences is that public participation has often been

5. See, for example, Renn, "Model for an Analytic-deliberative Process"; Irvin and Stansbury, "Citizen Participation in Decision Making"; Weeks, "Practice of Deliberative Democracy"; Douglas, "Inserting the Public into Science."

6. See, for example, Beierle, "Using Social Goals to Evaluate Public Participation"; Kleinman, *Science, Technology, and Democracy*; National Research Council (NRC), *Understanding Risk*; Rowe and Frewer, "Public Participation Methods"; Irvin and Stansbury, "Citizen Participation in Decision Making."

7. NRC, *Understanding Risk.* See also NRC, *Decision Making for the Environment,* a report that advocates analytic-deliberative processes for addressing environmental decisions.

8. NRC, *Understanding Risk,* 73.

9. Ibid., 77.

10. Ibid., 78.

associated with downstream debates about public-policy decisions, whereas the NRC focuses on upstream deliberation about how to frame problems and to direct policy-relevant research, as does this chapter. Also, broadly based deliberation may include scientific experts and representatives of stakeholder groups, not just members of the public.

## Motivations for Deliberation

The motivations for pursuing broadly based deliberation are often divided into three categories: normative, substantive, and instrumental.[11] The normative justification is that it provides citizens an opportunity to exert democratic control over policies and institutions that significantly affect their lives. In doing so, it can highlight the values, assumptions, and preferences of the public.[12] As Kristin Shrader-Frechette puts it, "If my ox is in danger of being gored, I have the right to help determine how to protect it, even if I may be wrong."[13] Admittedly, the strength of this argument depends to some extent on one's views about how much influence laypeople (as opposed to their government representatives) need to have over policy making in order to respect their rights.[14] Whether or not broadly based deliberation is normatively required *in principle*, however, there are at least four reasons for thinking that, given the political context in the United States, it can contribute significantly to making science-policy decisions more legitimate.

First, the members of U.S. administrative agencies (such as the EPA) are not directly elected by the public. Second, many of these agencies have, or at least are suspected by large numbers of the population as having, social and financial ties to vested interest groups that may prevent them from acting as faithful representatives of all citizens' interests. Third, administrative agencies and lawmakers in the United States have such large numbers of constituents (many of whom have extremely different values and priorities) that their ability to consent to policy decisions on behalf of those that they represent is quite limited. Fourth, the deliberative forums proposed in this chapter are not designed to *replace* current representative forms of government but rather to provide an additional source of *input* to assist those who are making decisions on behalf of the public.[15]

11. Fiorino, "Citizen Participation and Environmental Risk"; NRC, *Understanding Risk*; Douglas, "Inserting the Public into Science."

12. Beierle, "Using Social Goals."

13. Shrader-Frechette, "Evaluating the Expertise of Experts," 117.

14. For a defense of more representative approaches to scientific and technical decisions, see Sunstein, *Risk and Reason*, and Sunstein, *Laws of Fear*.

15. See Beder, *Global Spin*; Dietz, "Preface"; Fiorino, "Regulatory Negotiation as a Form of Public Participation"; Shrader-Frechette, *Risk and Rationality*; Shrader-Frechette, *Taking Action, Saving Lives*.

Another motivation for pursuing broadly based deliberation is its potential for yielding substantively better decisions. It is, admittedly, difficult to measure the success of deliberative exercises, in part because specific evaluation methods tend to be controversial.[16] On one hand, those that consider only whether particular groups receive what they want from a deliberative process are not very objective. On the other hand, those that focus only on procedures (e.g., adequate representation, face-to-face interaction, openness of government officials to public input) may not pay sufficient attention to outcomes. Thomas Beierle has evaluated 239 published cases of stakeholder involvement in environmental policy based on four questions that spanned both process and outcome measures: (1) Were the decisions proposed by the deliberators cost effective relative to other plausible options open to them? (2) did the decisions increase joint gains for the stakeholders relative to alternative options? (3) did the participants contribute new ideas or information? (4) did the participants have access to scientific information and expertise? He concluded that the decisions were improved relative to the status quo in the majority of cases, and the cases that incorporated more intensive approaches for integrating stakeholders' perspectives tended to produce the highest-quality decisions.[17]

Because this chapter argues for broadly based deliberation not only in response to policy decisions but also in response to controversial areas of policy-relevant research, it is important to address the objection that judgments internal to the practice of research are not appropriate topics for broadly based deliberation that includes stakeholders. According to this objection, nonscientists cannot productively contribute to technical decisions about matters such as the design of studies, the collection of data, or the interpretation of results. One response is that the concept of broadly based deliberation, as it is defined by the NRC and employed in this chapter, allows leeway for experts to represent citizen groups on deliberative panels when the material under discussion is too complex for nonscientists to handle. The decision-making process just needs to be open and transparent enough to incorporate the knowledge, perspectives, and concerns of major interested and affected parties. Another response is that an extensive body of research has documented the ability of those outside the scientific community to make significant contributions to scientific research projects that have practical ramifications.

One of the most famous examples of this lay expertise comes from Brian Wynne's analysis of the relationships between expert analysts and sheep farmers after the radioactive contamination of British sheep following the

16. Beierle, "Using Social Goals," 79.
17. Beierle, "Quality of Stakeholder-based Decisions."

Chernobyl nuclear accident of 1986.[18] Wynne argues that the experts made serious mistakes because they failed to account for details of sheep behavior and soil type that were well known to the affected farmers. Along similar lines, Alan Irwin has documented how the National Union of Agricultural and Allied Workers (NUAAW) challenged a safety evaluation of the herbicide 2,4,5-T by the British Advisory Committee on Pesticide. Whereas the advisory committee depended on laboratory analyses of 2,4,5-T, the NUAAW appealed to the experiences of agricultural workers and argued that the laboratory studies did not adequately reflect the real-world conditions under which 2,4,5-T was applied in the fields.[19] Other social scientists have examined famous cases in which local community members uncovered public health threats caused by toxic waste dumps, such as Love Canal, New York, or Woburn, Massachusetts. They argue that ordinary citizens have sometimes engaged in a sort of "popular epidemiology" by working with experts to gather and analyze data that vindicated their concerns.[20]

In addition to its normative and substantive advantages, broadly based deliberation may also produce instrumental benefits. Many commentators note that the American public has very little trust in elected officials, and deliberative processes may, in at least some cases, increase that trust. It can also reduce conflict between stakeholders by providing a structured opportunity to settle differences and develop greater understanding of opponents' views. As a result, deliberative processes can decrease the costs of litigating controversial policy issues. For example, Frank Fischer argues that citizen participation in policy making may be one of the few effective avenues for responding to the "Nimby" (not-in-my-backyard) problem. He notes that "Nimby refers to a situation in which people recognize the need for a particular type of unpleasant or hazardous facility but object to having it located anywhere near them."[21] Whereas the "Nimby syndrome" has often resulted in policy gridlock or stalemate, Fischer reports that efforts to site hazardous waste facilities have been more successful when governments engage in a highly transparent and participatory decision-making process.[22] Of course, it is crucial for government agencies to create deliberative processes in good faith and not merely as a ploy to increase public acceptance of their decisions.[23]

18. Wynne, "Sheep Farming after Chernobyl," 11–15, 33–39.

19. Irwin, *Citizen Science*.

20. Brown and Mikkelsen, *No Safe Place*; Couch and Kroll-Smith, "Environmental Movements and Expert Knowledge."

21. Fischer, "Citizen Participation and the Democratization of Policy Expertise."

22. See also Beierle, "Using Social Goals"; Busenberg, "Collaborative and Adversarial Analysis in Environmental Policy"; Fiorino, "Citizen Participation and Environmental Risk"; NRC, *Understanding Risk*.

23. Irvin and Stansbury, "Citizen Participation in Decision Making," 57.

## Mechanisms for Deliberation

Policy makers now have a wide variety of mechanisms available for promoting deliberation.[24] These include public hearings, citizens' advisory committees and task forces, alternative dispute resolution, citizens' juries and panels, surveys, focus groups, and interactive technology-based approaches.[25] Thomas Beierle organizes these approaches along four dimensions: (1) direction of information flow; (2) degree of interaction among opposing interests; (3) type of representation; and (4) decision-making role of the public.[26] Surveys, focus groups, and public comment periods all tend to provide one-way flows of information from the public to the government; they involve relatively little interaction among potentially opposing parties; and they provide the public with little decision-making power. One can also reverse the flow of information so that it moves from government to the public via right-to-know policies, public notice periods, and various forms of public education. These latter, reverse-flow mechanisms are otherwise very similar to the preceding ones, in that they provide little decision-making power for the public and relatively little interaction among opposing parties.

In recent years, novel strategies for broadly based deliberation have incorporated two-way flows of information between the public and the government or other experts. In a public hearing, individual citizens are able to represent themselves. Consensus conferences, citizens' juries or panels, and citizen advisory committees employ a small group of citizens who can provide information about public perspectives on the issue under consideration. These citizens' panels have the advantage of providing the participants with more extensive education about the issues under consideration. They generally bring the selected individuals together for an intensive period of several days or for a series of meetings over weeks or months. Depending on the specific approach, those involved generally read background material about the topic under consideration, listen to and interview experts, and formulate recommendations. Commentators have noted that the reports provided by consensus conferences and citizens' juries generally provide well-informed and thoughtful responses to the issues under debate.[27]

24. For an overview, see Beierle, "Using Social Goals"; NRC, *Understanding Risk*; and Renn, Webler, and Wiedemann, *Fairness and Competence*. Regarding the differences between consensual and adversarial deliberative formats, see Jasanoff, "Procedural Choices in Regulatory Science."

25. NRC, *Understanding Risk*, 199–205.

26. Beierle, "Using Social Goals," 87–88.

27. Kleinman, *Science, Technology, and Democracy*; Sclove and Scammell, "Practicing the Principle."

Of course, there are still legitimate concerns about incorporating greater public participation in policy making. One common worry about citizens' panels is that the outcomes of their deliberation may depend on the framing of the information that the participants receive.[28] Another worry is that, as in the case of the town-hall meetings that accompanied the health-care debates in the United States in 2009, radical groups can polarize the discussion and prevent open-minded deliberation. These problems occurred to some extent during the "GM Nation?" public engagement exercises that were held in the United Kingdom in 2003.[29] Yet another potential weakness of many deliberative mechanisms is that their recommendations are generally advisory and can be largely ignored unless strategic plans are in position for placing them in the public and legislative spotlight.[30] Mediation and regulatory negotiation methods generally incorporate greater decision-making authority, but they may suffer from less democratic legitimacy because of the major role that experts who are associated with interest groups play in the deliberative process.

Although these weaknesses of the various mechanisms for public participation and deliberation are important to keep in mind, the following sections of the chapter argue that they can be addressed, at least in part, by carefully diagnosing and designing deliberative forums that are most appropriate in response to specific issues. For example, it may be helpful in many cases to create deliberative exercises early in the development of a new technological or scientific issue, *before* positions on the issue have become too polarized.[31] If there is a great deal of polarization, then it becomes important to employ highly structured formats that constrain the ability of any one interest group to hijack the proceedings. It is also important, in the case of consensus conferences or citizens' panels, to have an organizing board that is respected and regarded as reasonably neutral. This lessens the worry that the background information provided to the participants will be strongly biased in one direction or another.

## EXTENDING DIAGNOSIS TO SCIENTIFIC RESEARCH

The central lesson of this chapter is that scientists, policy makers, and citizens ought to "diagnose" what sorts of deliberative processes are warranted

28. Joss and Durant, *Public Participation in Science.*

29. See Rogers-Hayden and Pidgeon, "Developments in Nanotechnology Public Engagement in the UK."

30. Guston, "Evaluating the First U.S. Consensus Conference"; Kleinman, *Science, Technology, and Democracy*; Renn, "Model for an Analytic-deliberative Process."

31. Rogers-Hayden and Pidgeon, "Developments in Nanotechnology Public Engagement in the UK."

in response to specific areas of policy-relevant scientific research. Deliberation has previously been emphasized much more heavily in response to science and technology *policy* than in response to *research* itself. Moreover, when members of the public have become involved in specific research projects, their participation has generally been ad hoc and often directed at studying specific local hazards in places like Love Canal or Woburn. Admittedly, the effort to incorporate members of the public in the National Advisory Councils that guide research funding at the NIH constitutes a partial exception to this lack of systematic public involvement in research.[32] Nevertheless, a growing chorus of figures emphasizes that decisions about research funding constitute only a small fraction of the judgments to which the public might fruitfully be able to contribute.[33]

My argument for more systematically diagnosing deliberation in response to scientific research rests on two principles: (1) we sometimes have good reasons to incorporate broadly based deliberation in response to research; however, (2) poorly designed deliberations can be quite problematic. With regard to the first point, the previous section has already presented normative, substantive, and instrumental considerations that support deliberation in response to major decisions associated with science and technology. Moreover, chapters 2 and 3 emphasize that important decisions must be made not only in the areas of technology policy and risk characterization but also in scientific research itself. These decisions or judgments include choosing projects and questions for investigation, designing studies, selecting statistical methodologies, developing appropriate terminology, characterizing and interpreting data, evaluating results, deciding how carefully to avoid Type I (false positive) as opposed to Type II (false negative) errors, and drawing lessons for public policy.[34] In the next section of this chapter, I review a number of these judgments in the hormesis case.

Some readers might still find it counterintuitive that judgments internal to scientific practice, such as the design and interpretation of studies, could constitute an appropriate subject for broadly based deliberation. Nevertheless, there is significant evidence that the normative, substantive, and instrumental arguments for broadly based deliberation apply, in at least some cases, to these sorts of decisions. In addition to the examples associated with

32. Stokes, *Pasteur's Quadrant.*

33. For others who call for broadly based deliberation in response to a wide variety of judgments associated with scientific research, see Douglas, "Inserting the Public into Science"; Kleinman, ed., *Science, Technology, and Democracy*; Kleinman, *Science and Technology in Society*; Wilson and Willis, *See-through Science.*

34. See, for example, Longino, *Science as Social Knowledge*; Kincaid, Dupré, and Wylie, eds., *Value-free Science?* and Machamer and Wolters, eds., *Science, Values, and Objectivity.*

sheep farming, 2,4,5-T hazards, and popular epidemiology discussed in the previous section, Steven Epstein provides an excellent case study of AIDS activists who assisted in the design of clinical drug trials in the 1980s.[35] These activists made an important *normative* contribution by challenging specific trial designs that would have required AIDS patients to receive placebos rather than promising new drugs. They also provided valuable *instrumental* input by working with experts to develop trial designs that were more likely to be accepted by members of the AIDS community. Moreover, the activists pointed out that participants in placebo-based trials would have found ways to obtain experimental drugs even if they were placed in placebo groups, so they also made a *substantive* contribution to the quality of research by proposing study designs that were less likely to be corrupted. Epstein's studies of AIDS activists are in keeping with a good deal of evidence that suggests that ordinary citizens have an impressive ability to bring themselves up to speed with respect to specific areas of science when they become concerned about particular aspects of research or policy.[36]

Skeptics could still argue that many circumstances are likely to arise in which it is neither necessary nor fruitful to involve the public in judgments internal to scientific reasoning. This brings us to the second principle in support of systematically diagnosing deliberation in response to policy-relevant scientific research. While valuable in some circumstances, broadly based deliberation can be problematic if it is not well designed. Some of the potential difficulties associated with poorly planned deliberative processes include increased cost; wasted time; inadequate knowledge on the part of participants; worse decisions if dueling interest groups exert too much control; difficulty providing adequate representation of all stakeholders, especially disadvantaged groups; and creation of increased rather than decreased hostility among stakeholders.[37] Moreover, many of the judgments associated with scientific research can be technical, difficult to identify, and deeply embedded in scientific practice. Because of these sorts of considerations, Renee Irvin and John Stansbury argue that policy makers need to examine the context of specific decisions to determine whether public participation is likely to be helpful or harmful.[38] In other words, the potential weaknesses of broadly based deliberation, coupled with the benefits that it can provide when it is designed well and applied to appropriate cases,

35. Epstein, "Democracy, Expertise, and AIDS Treatment Activism."

36. Kleinman, *Science and Technology in Society*; Toumey, "Science and Democracy."

37. Irvin and Stansbury, "Citizen Participation in Decision Making"; Kleinman, *Science and Technology in Society*, ch. 7.

38. Irvin and Stansbury, "Citizen Participation in Decision Making"; see also NRC, *Understanding Risk*.

supports this chapter's call for more systematic diagnosis of deliberative proceedings in response to specific areas of policy-relevant research.

The notion of "diagnosis" employed in this chapter comes from the NRC *Understanding Risk* report on risk characterization, although others have called for similar processes.[39] The NRC document suggests that those responsible for risk characterizations should develop "a provisional *diagnosis of the decision situation* so that they can better match the analytic-deliberative process leading to the characterization to the needs of the decision, particularly in terms of level and intensity of effort and representation of parties."[40] By an "analytic-deliberative process," the report refers to the integration of formal scientific analysis with deliberative reflection on the crucial judgments associated with the analysis. The NRC provides an eight-step process for diagnosing the sorts of analytic-deliberative processes most appropriate in a particular context:

1. Diagnose the kind of risk and the state of knowledge.
2. Describe the legal mandate.
3. Describe the purpose of the risk decision.
4. Describe the affected parties and likely public reactions.
5. Estimate resource needs and timetable.
6. Plan for organizational needs.
7. Develop a preliminary process design.
8. Summarize and discuss diagnosis within the organization.[41]

These steps are intended to help government agencies determine what forms of analysis and deliberation to pursue, who should be involved, and what questions need to be addressed.

Although the model in the NRC report provides a helpful overview of the elements that could be part of a diagnostic process, this chapter suggests a somewhat simpler three-step approach. Whereas the NRC model is geared especially for government agencies that need to develop risk characterizations, the approach in this book is designed for scientists, policy makers, citizens, or nongovernmental organizations (NGOs) who are concerned about the societal ramifications of particular areas of research. The eight-step NRC process is unwieldy for individual citizens

39. See especially Beierle, "Using Social Goals"; Irvin and Stansbury, "Citizen Participation in Decision Making"; NRC, *Public Participation in Environmental Assessment and Decision Making*. Although the 2008 NRC report is similar to the 1996 report in its emphasis on developing appropriate deliberative forums for integrating multiple stakeholder perspectives in environmental decision making, the concept of "diagnosis" in the 2008 report focuses somewhat narrowly on identifying potential barriers to successful public participation.

40. NRC, *Understanding Risk*, 161.

41. Ibid., 143.

and small groups who aim to develop a rough sense of whether formal deliberative proceedings might be helpful in a particular context. Moreover, the NRC model includes some steps (such as planning for organizational needs) that are clearly geared toward formal diagnostic processes within a government agency. Therefore, the remainder of this section develops a streamlined approach that can assist individuals or groups in developing informal diagnoses in response to policy-relevant areas of scientific research.

The three-step diagnostic model proposed here focuses on three steps:

1. Examine the current status of research in the area of interest and the societal ramifications of the research
2. Consider, based on the characteristics of science and its societal context, the major purposes, benefits, costs, and limitations of various forms of deliberation
3. Suggest (based on the preceding considerations) a specific deliberative process, perhaps including: (a) format; (b) questions that ought to be addressed; (c) individuals or groups to include; and (d) a rough timeline for the procedure

To examine the status of research in a particular area (in accordance with the first step), one might ask questions such as these:

- Are the major principles of the field well established, or are they fairly new and controversial?
- Are there major anomalies or problems that have cast doubt on those principles?
- Are there extensive disagreements among scientists or allegiances of particular scientists to opposing interest groups?
- Are there major judgments about which scientists disagree? If so, what are the sources of the disagreement?

To evaluate the societal context for a body of research (again as part of the first step), one could ask these questions:

- What sorts of effects might the research have? Could it contribute to the development of new products or technologies? Would it have the potential to support particular regulations or public policies?
- Are the effects limited to particular interest groups, or do they extend to all humans, all living organisms, or even future generations? Who might be benefited or harmed?
- How are the effects of the research likely to be distributed geographically? Will they be limited to people or animals in a local area, or could they be more widespread?

- What is the relationship between the research community, the policy makers, and the public? Does the public trust the claims of the scientific community? Do members of the public have values or lay expertise that are relevant to the research?

In the second step of the diagnostic process, when one considers the major purposes, benefits, costs, and limitations of various forms of deliberation, some questions to consider include the following:

- What are the major motivating factors for engaging in deliberation? Is the goal to help members of the public to influence areas of scientific research that could affect their lives? Is the purpose to secure greater objectivity of scientific results? Is the aim of the deliberative process to reassure the public that interest groups are not exerting inappropriate influence over scientific judgments?
- Will citizens be motivated to participate in the deliberative process?
- Does the research topic involve highly technical material that will be difficult for nonexperts to understand?
- Do various segments of the public have very different attitudes toward the research?

With respect to the costs, benefits, and limitations of various forms of deliberation, Irvin and Stansbury provide some valuable generalizations.[42] In particular, they have focused on the consequences of including direct public participation in deliberative proceedings. They suggest that costs are likely to be low when citizens already volunteer for projects that benefit the community, when stakeholders are geographically localized, when citizens have adequate income to participate in deliberations, when the community is relatively homogeneous, and when the topic does not involve highly technical material. The benefits are likely to be high when the issue is gridlocked, when there is significant hostility toward the government, when representatives with significant community influence are willing to participate, when a facilitator with high credibility can be found, and when stakeholders have significant interest in the issue. Admittedly, in many cases it may still be difficult to predict whether it is worth incorporating direct public participation in deliberative proceedings. Those providing a diagnosis may have to take the NRC's advice of erring on the side of being more rather than less inclusive when choosing participants.[43]

42. Irvin and Stansbury, "Citizen Participation in Decision Making."
43. NRC, *Understanding Risk.*

In the third step of my proposed diagnostic model, one appeals to the information collected in the first two stages to justify a specific deliberative process, including at least four elements: (a) a recommended deliberative format (e.g., a consensus conference or a public hearing); (b) crucial questions to address over the course of the deliberations; (c) recommended individuals or groups to include in the deliberations; and (d) a tentative timeline for the deliberative process. It is important to emphasize that, although even this simplified diagnostic process might seem to be complicated and potentially time consuming, it need not be a formal, lengthy affair. It begins when concerned citizens, academics, or interest groups informally scrutinize policy-relevant areas of research to determine whether particular topics merit further attention. If a body of research appears to warrant a formal process of broadly based deliberation, then policy makers or government agencies can pursue a more systematic diagnosis. After all, one or more federal agencies (or other organizations with extensive resources) would probably need to concur with a diagnosis in order to provide funding for deliberative proceedings. The following section illustrates what a diagnosis of the hormesis case might look like.

## DIAGNOSIS OF THE HORMESIS CASE

### Step One: Characteristics of Research and Societal Context

According to the model proposed in the preceding section, the first step in diagnosis is to analyze the characteristics of current research on hormesis and its significance for society. At present, this is a highly disputed area of study. Many researchers associated with regulatory or environmental groups remain unconvinced by claim HD (i.e., that hormesis should be the default model for risk assessment), whereas some scientists with ties to industry are sympathetic to the claim. As we saw in chapter 2, hormesis research incorporates numerous value judgments. Given that organizations affiliated with industry and the U.S. Air Force have provided significant research funding in this area, the public will (understandably) worry that these value judgments may have been influenced by the interests of the groups that provided funding.

Consider some of these judgments (discussed more extensively in chapter 2) that might be important to address in a deliberative forum. A first set of questions involves the choice of research projects and the design of experiments. Few observers are likely to question the value of studying the low-dose effects of toxic chemicals, but some analysts might argue that the hormesis hypothesis itself should not be a major priority.[44] For example, Kristin Shrader-Frechette argues that it is more important to focus on determining the harmful effects of chemicals, especially their synergistic effects on sensitive subpopulations like children.[45] Even some of those who support further research on hormesis might suggest that it is more valuable to study the ramifications of the phenomenon in therapeutic contexts like aging and pharmaceutical research rather than in regulatory contexts. Another crucial judgment involves the choice of study designs for examining the phenomenon. If deliberators set particular goals for future research (e.g., facilitating decisions about altering regulatory policy), then they will need to decide what sorts of study designs are most likely to facilitate those goals.

A second set of questions for deliberators to consider stems from value judgments associated with scientific categories and terms. They may want to consider, for example, the benefits and disadvantages (from both a social and a scientific perspective) of using the term "hormesis" to designate a distinct phenomenon or of discussing nonmonotonic dose-response curves in general. A related issue is whether to define "hormesis" in a relatively neutral manner (e.g., a compensatory biological defense response) or to expose normative judgments explicitly and define it in terms of low-dose beneficial effects. It would also be helpful to clarify whether (and in what senses) it is appropriate to claim that hormesis is generalizable or adaptive.

A third set of issues involves the interpretation and evaluation of previous studies on hormesis. Deliberators need to consider how much significance to give to the literature studies performed by Calabrese, given the concerns raised in chapter 2 (e.g., possible weaknesses in the original toxicological studies, the potential for false positives as a result of the criteria applied in the literature studies identifying hormesis, and the possibility for some alleged hormetic effects to be the result of random variations in control values). Other judgments involve weighing the strength of evidence for claims HG, HP, and HD (regarding the generalizability, predominance, and default status of hormesis) relative to counterevidence.

Finally, deliberators should arguably consider issues associated with the application of hormesis research to policy. One question is how to characterize the current views of the scientific community for the public and how to

44. As chapter 8 emphasizes, another worry about research on low-dose toxic effects is that scientists and policy makers can become overly focused on studying the details of chemical toxicity and fail to perform enough strategic research on novel ways to lessen our use of potentially toxic substances; see, for example, Sarewitz, "Tale of Two Sciences"; Tickner, ed., *Precaution, Environmental Science.*

45. Shrader-Frechette, "Ideological Toxicology."

convey the important areas of uncertainty in an effective fashion. Another value judgment is whether new policies can be implemented, given the current social context, without causing unreasonable harm. This book, like most of the literature on hormesis, has focused on regulatory policies, but one might also consider the ramifications of hormesis research in other contexts, such as setting prescription levels for pharmaceuticals. Finally, deliberators must consider how to weigh potential beneficial effects of hormetic chemicals on some individuals versus possible harmful effects on others. Although these final judgments about weighing harms and benefits would probably be among the most likely to be included in a deliberative process (even if one did not engage in a careful process of diagnosis), we have seen that there are numerous other important judgments to consider as well.

The first step of the diagnostic process involves considering not only the current state of scientific research but also the societal context of hormesis research. Depending on the generalizability of the phenomenon, it could affect many aspects of science and policy. Proponents of claims HG and HP argue that it could have significant ramifications not only for risk assessment but also for ecology, medicine, psychology, and any other discipline that considers the effects of stress, pharmaceuticals, or toxicants on biological systems.[46] Nevertheless, we have already seen that the public is likely to have misgivings about scientific findings on hormesis, given that organizations affiliated with industry and the U.S. Air Force have provided funding for this area of work.[47] These sorts of concerns are not unfounded, given the variety of recent cases in which scientists and government regulatory agencies have been "captured" or inappropriately influenced by industry (see chapter 4). Moreover, even if there were adequate evidence in support of claim HD, a variety of authors have emphasized that it would be difficult to convince the public to take a positive attitude toward pollution.[48] As a result, numerous groups are likely to strenuously oppose any efforts to ease regulations in response to hormesis research.

## Step Two: Purposes, Costs, Benefits, Limits

In the hormesis case, it appears that the typical justifications for engaging in deliberation could eventually support a formal process that includes representatives from a wide variety of stakeholder groups. From a normative

46. Calabrese and Baldwin, "Hormesis: The Dose-response Revolution."

47. Kaiser, "Sipping from a Poisoned Chalice."

48. Elliott, "Hormesis, Ethics, and Public Policy"; Renn, "Implications of the Hormesis Hypothesis."

perspective, a broadly based deliberative process would provide an opportunity for multiple citizens' groups to scrutinize and possibly influence value judgments in an area of science highly relevant to their health and economic well-being. Substantively, a formal process of deliberation might help scientists to pinpoint the sources of their disagreements, and it would alleviate epistemic concerns that vested interest groups might be exerting problematic influences on crucial scientific judgments. Instrumentally, broadly based deliberation would send a signal that any future revisions to regulatory policy in response to hormesis would not be foisted on the public without open discussion of the scientific and political issues involved.

In this case, costs or delays associated with broadly based deliberation are overshadowed by the conflicts that would probably arise if changes to regulatory policy occurred without extensive discussion. At this time, however, one might object that we have insufficient scientific evidence for claim HD to justify extensive deliberative proceedings. The problem with this objection is that much could be gained by creating a simple and inexpensive deliberative forum that would advise decision makers about the conditions under which more extensive deliberative mechanisms would be justified in the future. After all, the hormesis phenomenon has received a good deal of attention in scientific journals, textbooks, and the popular press.[49] Therefore, it would be valuable for the public to have a source of information about hormesis that is trustworthy and transparent. Furthermore, the NRC (1996) encourages policy makers to err on the side of initiating too much deliberation rather than too little. In the hormesis case, early deliberation could be quite valuable in preparing government agencies and stakeholders for a range of future scenarios.

Another potential objection to initiating formal mechanisms to promote broadly based deliberation is that there are already some existing avenues for deliberation in response to phenomena like hormesis. These include typical scientific practices like the submission of journal articles for peer review and the evaluation of previous scientific work in review articles. Nevertheless, depending on deliberation within the scientific community in response to a highly controversial and policy-relevant phenomenon like hormesis is problematic for a number of reasons. First, we saw in chapter 4 that empirical studies of peer review leave its effectiveness in doubt, and evidence indicates that the reproducibility of peer reviews is poor.[50] Second,

49. See, for example, the list of popular presentations of hormesis cited by Ed Calabrese in his article "Hormesis: From Marginalization to Mainstream."

50. Jefferson, Wager, and Davidoff, "Measuring the Quality of Editorial Peer Review"; Wager and Jefferson, "Shortcomings of Peer Review in Biomedical Journals." Sheila Jasanoff also provides a helpful overview of the weaknesses of peer review in her book *The Fifth Branch*.

it is unlikely that the public would trust typical avenues for deliberation within the scientific community, given the concerns about financial conflicts of interest highlighted in chapter 4. Third, the scientific community is likely to focus much more on evaluating factual aspects of research than on considering the full range of societal and policy ramifications that sometimes need to be addressed as part of deliberative proceedings.

Nevertheless, other existing deliberative mechanisms, such as the scientific advisory committees created by government agencies such as the EPA and the FDA, largely evade these objections.[51] These panels, like the EPA Science Advisory Board (SAB), are typically required by law to have fairly balanced representation, and they routinely address questions that are at the interface of science and policy.[52] Thus, they establish a precedent for something very much like what I have suggested here. One could implement many of the suggestions in this chapter by evaluating hormesis research in an EPA advisory panel. The most significant limitation of such an approach is that existing advisory committees generally do not incorporate explicit representatives of particular stakeholder groups. However, such limited deliberation might be adequate in the near term if agencies were disinclined to devote much money to examining the phenomenon.

Thus, it appears that formal deliberative proceedings could be highly beneficial for almost everyone involved in this case: researchers, government agencies, industrial and military groups, environmentalists, and the public. Researchers would benefit by learning both about the kinds of scientific evidence that various groups are looking for and about the crucial (but perhaps implicit and unrecognized) value judgments associated with their work. Government agencies and industry groups would benefit by obtaining a clearer understanding of the current state of research on this phenomenon and the sorts of evidence that might be needed in order to justify new risk assessment practices. Moreover, it seems rather unlikely that any regulatory changes in response to hormesis could be successfully formulated without the legitimacy provided by an extensive and transparent deliberative process. At the very least, the costs of deliberative proceedings are likely to be dwarfed in this case by the potential costs of litigation and wasted effort associated with railroading through new policies without adequate study. Finally, the public would benefit by having earlier and greater opportunities to exert democratic influence on an area of research that could have

51. For an excellent analysis of the scientific advisory boards that serve agencies such as the U.S. EPA or FDA, see Jasanoff, *Fifth Branch*.

52. In *The Fifth Branch*, Sheila Jasanoff has carefully analyzed the ways in which scientific advisory boards strategically address both scientific and policy matters (and negotiate the boundaries between these domains).

significant ramifications for their health and well-being. The biggest problem with deliberation appears to be the danger of its looking like (or turning into) a ploy to ease chemical regulations, particularly if the process is not designed in a sufficiently open fashion.

### Step Three: A Specific Deliberative Process

Based on the considerations raised in the preceding two diagnostic steps, I recommend a varied approach to deliberation in the hormesis case. Initially, it would be advisable for an agency such as the EPA to convene a panel of experts who could reflect on the hormesis issue. The agency could choose an existing scientific advisory committee, or it could create a new focus group and perhaps even include representatives of key stakeholders. The National Academy of Sciences committees that produce the BEIR Reports (on the health effects of low-dose exposure to ionizing radiation) provide at least one model for how this sort of deliberative body could function.[53] The experts could examine a range of questions related to the four categories of judgments that this book has highlighted in the hormesis case:

- Should more funding be allocated to hormesis research? How should we balance the allocation of funding between hormesis and other questions related to low-dose effects (e.g., endocrine disruption, synergistic chemical effects)?
- What sorts of study designs would address societal concerns about hormesis most effectively?
- How should hormesis be defined? Is it justifiable to regard it as adaptive and generalizable?
- Which claims (e.g., H, HG, HP, HD) does current evidence enable us to accept with a good deal of confidence? What are the crucial gaps in our current knowledge? Does the available evidence support the claim that the hormetic dose response is more common than the threshold dose response?
- Should current regulatory standards be altered in response to hormesis? Does the phenomenon have other important practical ramifications that ought to be examined closely in the near future?
- How should regulatory bodies handle cases in which levels of chemical exposure that may be beneficial to some individuals may be harmful to others?

53. See, for example, National Research Council (NRC), *Health Effects from Exposure to Low Levels of Ionizing Radiation.*

I would not recommend instituting new regulatory policies based on the recommendations of this advisory group, partly because I doubt that we have adequate scientific evidence to justify such changes but also because a forum of this sort might have inadequate legitimacy from the public's perspective. Rather, the deliberations of this committee could influence the course of future research on the phenomenon.

An initial deliberative stage of this sort would steer a middle course between two dangers. On one hand, it would not require the level of investment necessary for a larger-scale deliberative exercise. It would be especially inexpensive if the deliberation merely took place in an existing scientific advisory committee. Therefore, even those who doubt that hormetic models should have any ramifications for risk assessment might be able to support this approach as a means of providing reliable information to the public. On the other hand, it would avoid the danger of waiting too long before initiating formal deliberation on hormesis research. Confused citizens and industry groups could benefit significantly from having a balanced source of information about the hormesis hypothesis in the near term. An advisory committee or focus group could clarify the strength of the existing evidence for claims HG, HP, and HD. It could also identify potential ramifications of hormesis and the sorts of information that would be most helpful for guiding future societal responses to the phenomenon.

Ideally, the focus group or advisory committee instituted in the first stage of deliberation would meet periodically to reconsider its earlier judgments on the basis of current research results. At some point, this group might decide either that new regulatory policies would be justified or that the evidence had increased to a level at which new policies could reasonably be considered. This group of experts could formulate a set of recommendations for policy makers, but I also recommend another mechanism for deliberation, such as a consensus conference or a citizens' panel. In order to meet normative and instrumental goals of legitimacy and public acceptance, it would be important at this stage in the deliberative process to include members of the general public, who would be selected in as broadly representative a fashion as possible. A topic as controversial as hormesis, with the potential for widespread effects on the public welfare, arguably merits an intensive deliberative format of this sort. A significant strength of a deliberative tool like a citizens' panel is that it could provide a forum for laypeople to express their perspectives while allowing them to receive expert input. The scientific focus group initially developed in response to hormesis research could help to diagnose the most appropriate format for these subsequent deliberative processes. Many of the questions proposed earlier for the focus group would also be important for the citizens' panel to address.

Some readers might find the proposal of a citizens' panel to be unconvincing and perhaps a bit over the top. It is important to remember, however, that I am suggesting this sort of deliberative proceeding only if a balanced advisory committee or focus group came to the conclusion that regulatory changes might be warranted in response to hormesis. In that sort of highly controversial context, policy makers would need as many avenues for receiving informed public opinion as possible. Moreover, even if a citizens' panel sounded like a more aggressive deliberative format than necessary in response to the hormesis phenomenon, one could expand the focus of the panel to include a broader array of reflections on current regulatory policy. Sheila Jasanoff has argued that the current trend toward incorporating public participation in the governance of science ought to be accompanied by efforts to broaden the *culture* of science policy making so that it moves beyond mere technical methods of predicting risks. She calls for deliberative forums to analyze the *framing* of science-policy decisions, the special *vulnerabilities* that afflict some citizens, the *distribution* of risks and benefits caused by technological advances, and the opportunities for social *learning* in response to specific science-policy issues.[54] In the hormesis context, this broader sort of reflection might require thinking about how to address an array of new and controversial findings, including the endocrine-disruption and the MCS phenomena discussed in chapter 7. It might also require consideration of more systematic concerns about current regulatory policy, such as the need to focus more attention on the synergistic effects of multiple chemical exposures or the desirability of promoting safer alternatives to potentially toxic chemicals rather than fighting interminably over their precise toxicity.[55]

From a democratic perspective, however, the top-down deliberative processes that I have described so far are not a substitute for the sorts of bottom-up, grass-roots deliberation associated with the normal political process.[56] Therefore, scientists and government agencies would do well to regard formal deliberative mechanisms like focus groups or citizens' panels as starting points for further democratic deliberation that cannot be easily engineered or controlled from the top down. Initiating deliberation with a formal mechanism like a focus group has the advantage of promoting broadly based deliberation as early as possible in the research process, with

54. Jasanoff, "Technologies of Humility."

55. On the issue of synergistic effects, see Krimsky, "Environmental Endocrine Hypothesis and Public Policy." On promoting alternatives to potentially toxic substances, see Sarewitz, "Tale of Two Sciences."

56. For discussions of democratic political action in response to public-health threats, see Shrader-Frechette, *Taking Action, Saving Lives.*

maximal opportunity for influencing subsequent research and policy discussions. Nevertheless, one of the goals of these top-down approaches to deliberation should be to highlight crucial societal issues associated with the hormesis phenomenon in order to facilitate subsequent stages of more informal public participation and political action. As we have seen in the earlier sections of this chapter, an intensive deliberative process is not guaranteed to prevent significant conflict or to have a significant impact on the decisions made by government agencies. It seems even less likely, however, that government agencies would be able to avoid major conflicts if they attempted to make regulatory changes without pursuing extensive deliberative proceedings.

## CONCLUSION

In the first chapter of this book, we encountered a worry presented by David Guston: "The delegation of significant authority from political to scientific actors is arguably the central problem in science policy, both analytically and practically."[57] In other words, Guston is concerned that many policy decisions have become so dependent on scientific claims that democratic decision making has been jeopardized. Scientific conclusions that are relevant to the policy sphere frequently depend on significant judgments about how to interpret ambiguous evidence. In this context, the values of scientists can have a significant impact on their conclusions and therefore a surreptitious effect on policy decisions. The present chapter considers one way to address this problem, namely, by creating deliberative forums in which the judgments that influence policy-relevant science can be made explicit and scrutinized. Under some circumstances, these forums can even incorporate ordinary citizens, thus providing a further check against the antidemocratic potential of science-based policy making.

In addition to providing an overview of the recent literature on deliberation in science and technology policy, this chapter has focused on two goals. First, it has argued that it is important to diagnose appropriate deliberative proceedings in response not only to new technologies or risk characterizations but also to policy-relevant areas of scientific research. Second, the chapter has proposed a formal deliberative process in response to hormesis research. In order to facilitate informal diagnoses of topics like hormesis, the chapter has modified the eight-step NRC model into a simplified three-step diagnostic process.

57. Guston, "Institutional Design for Socially Robust Knowledge," 63.

The chapter has recommended a mixed deliberative approach in the hormesis case. An initial stage, which is arguably justified at the present time, would consist of a focus group or an advisory committee composed of scientific experts and perhaps representatives from important stakeholder groups. The committee would formulate recommendations for future research topics and study designs, for defining and describing the phenomenon, for evaluating the evidence provided in previous studies, and for responding to hormesis in policy contexts. If the committee eventually concluded that evidence for the phenomenon might justify changes to regulatory policy, it would be wise to organize further mechanisms for deliberation. At this point, a citizens' panel could add to the perspectives of the expert focus group. The conclusions of these formal deliberative bodies would also undoubtedly be studied, contested, and extended through the informal deliberation of citizens engaged in democratic political action.

Admittedly, the recommendations made by the deliberative bodies proposed in this chapter would generally not be binding on the government agencies that sponsored them. Moreover, the suggestions made by agency-organized deliberative bodies might have very little sway over research funded by private entities. Therefore, the analysis in this chapter supports the call in chapter 4 to maintain an adequate supply of independently funded studies by researchers without significant financial ties to interested parties. These independent scientists would still be under no institutional obligation to adopt, say, the terminology or study designs suggested by an advisory committee or a citizens' panel. Nevertheless, they would be likely to pay significant attention to recommendations made by balanced, well-informed deliberative bodies, especially if those recommendations were associated with government agencies that provide research funding. Therefore, the deliberative forums proposed in this chapter provide another important avenue for integrating societal values into policy-relevant research.

# 6

# Lesson #3

## Ethics for Experts

In at least one test, the dioxin compound 2,3,7,8-TCDD was found to be "the most potent carcinogen ever tested," yet for many years the overall health effects of this chemical have been hotly debated.[1] Unfortunately, these debates illustrate the power of interest groups to manipulate scientific information. Sharon Beder reports that "A handful of studies funded by Monsanto and BASF [a multinational chemical company based in Germany], which purported to show no health effects from dioxin exposure apart from chloracne [a skin condition], proved disproportionately influential, not withstanding their dubious methodology."[2] For example, Monsanto-affiliated scientists published results in major journals such as *Scientific American, Science,* and the *Journal of the American Medical Association,* allegedly clearing dioxin of most ill effects.[3] Subsequent court proceedings revealed crucial falsifications in the studies, but Monsanto continued to exert significant control over the dissemination of information about dioxin.[4] When environmentalists tried to publicize the allegations that these studies were problematic, scientists affiliated with Monsanto sued for libel. Beder claims that "Press coverage in the US and abroad dried up once the libel case was brought."[5] Moreover, congressional hearings and agency documents revealed that the U.S. Centers for Disease Control and the

1. Beder, *Global Spin,* 141.
2. Ibid., 142.
3. Ibid.
4. For another example of potentially misleading scientific data receiving tremendous publicity due to the efforts of industry groups, see Markowitz and Rosner, *Deceit and Denial,* 259ff. Markowitz and Rosner report that questionable reviews of tumor registry data by LSU researcher Vivien Chen enabled government and industry representatives to promote the notion that high cancer death rates in Louisiana were the result of poor medical care rather than environmental pollution.
5. Beder, *Global Spin,* 143. The strategy of using lawsuits to attack citizens and scientists who challenge questionable industry research has been documented extensively in McGarity and Wagner, *Bending Science.* See also Shrader-Frechette, *Taking Action, Saving Lives.*

Environmental Protection Agency inappropriately helped the chlorine industry avoid regulation and lawsuits by manipulating reports, suppressing data, and performing dioxin assessments that were "flawed and perhaps designed to fail."[6]

We saw in chapter 4 that the dioxin case is not unique. Interest groups exert significant control over much policy-relevant research. The chapter suggests several strategies, including maintaining significant support for independently funded research projects, to ensure that our *bodies of scientific knowledge* are informed by a more adequate range of societal values. Chapter 5 argues that it is also important to promote broadly based *deliberative bodies* that incorporate an adequate range of stakeholder perspectives on how to interpret and apply policy-relevant research. This chapter addresses the third body that Jasanoff has identified as crucial for effectively integrating scientific expertise and democratic decision making, namely, the *bodies of experts* themselves.[7] It develops an ethics of expertise (EOE) that can guide researchers in disseminating their findings. Providing scientific information in accordance with a suitable EOE can assist citizens and policy makers in at least three ways: (1) enabling them to better understand the societal ramifications of current research; (2) helping them to challenge findings with which they disagree or that they find questionable; and (3) highlighting crucial value judgments that merit additional scrutiny and reflection.[8]

One might object, however, that an EOE of this sort will be of little practical help in combating the worst influences of interest groups. For example, it is well known that the tobacco and fossil-fuel industries have hired "experts" to present skewed information on their behalf.[9] The worry is that, unless significant sanctions are imposed for violating an ethics of expertise, these sorts of experts are not likely to be motivated to change their behavior. I respond to this objection by noting that an EOE can be helpful to those

6. Shrader-Frechette, *Taking Action, Saving Lives*, 52.

7. Jasanoff, "Judgment under Siege."

8. For previous work aimed at assisting experts in identifying, evaluating, and revealing crucial value judgments that affect their work, see, for example, Douglas, "Role of Values in Expert Reasoning"; Douglas, *Science, Policy, and the Value-free Ideal*; Longino, *Fate of Knowledge*; Longino, *Science as Social Knowledge*; Mayo, "Sociological vs. Metascientific Views of Risk Assessment"; Mayo and Spanos, "Risks to Health and Risks to Science"; Shrader-Frechette, *Ethics of Scientific Research*; Shrader-Frechette, "Radiobiological Hormesis, Methodological Value Judgments, and Metascience." This chapter adds to previous work through its investigation of a general framework (based on the concept of informed consent) for identifying ethical responsibilities to disclose information in particular ways.

9. See Beder, *Global Spin*; McGarity and Wagner, *Bending Science*; Shrader-Frechette, *Taking Action, Saving Lives*.

who *receive* information, as well as to those who *disseminate* it. Those who seek trustworthy sources of information can use an EOE like the one proposed here to help them determine whether they should trust the claims of alleged experts. If one finds that an expert does not follow ethical guidelines for disseminating research findings, significant questions arise about the expert's credibility.[10]

Using the guidelines of an EOE to evaluate experts could also prove valuable for the media. It is well known that news outlets tend to create a distorted impression of scientific disputes, because they try to provide equal time or space for everyone's views. The result is what anthropologist Chris Toumey calls the "pseudosymmetry of scientific authority":

> This habit of the media [of providing equal time for each side of a controversy] leads to a systematic distortion of scientific authority when one scientist representing a small faction of dissidents or insurgents receives as much media attention as another scientist representing the majority of experts in that field, for equal time makes it seem that the scientific community is about equally divided when it is not.[11]

One strategy that the media can use to alleviate this problem is to disclose the important sources of funding and institutional connections of the experts that they cite. As chapter 4 points out, however, disclosing conflicts of interest is not a sufficient solution by itself, partly because the recipients of information frequently do not know how much to discount the claims of those with conflicts of interest.

An additional strategy that might prove helpful to the media is to examine whether alleged experts who supply scientific information follow the basic guidelines of an EOE. Instead of blindly reporting the claims of scientists on both sides of a controversy, it would be less misleading to report the views of a few individuals who disseminate information responsibly. These experts are likely to acknowledge the range of important perspectives within the scientific community without giving the impression that all are equally well supported. Thus, formulating an EOE can serve a valuable social function for citizens and the media, even if not all experts are motivated to follow it.

Consider some of the questions that an EOE might address:

- how to characterize and frame the current state of scientific information on debated questions

10. See Daston and Galison, *Objectivity*, for further discussion of the role that adherence to ethical research standards has historically played in decisions about which experts to trust.

11. Toumey, *Conjuring Science*, 155.

- how (and to what extent) to express the full range of opinions held by different members of the scientific community
- how to present the various sorts of uncertainty associated with scientific information
- whether or not to advocate specific policy responses to controversial matters
- whether to allow societal or ethical values (e.g., the desire to protect vulnerable human or environmental communities) to influence the presentation of scientific information
- how to prevent public misinterpretation of scientists' views
- how to vary the answers to each of the preceding questions based on different contexts in which scientists provide information (e.g., courtroom testimony, newspaper articles, congressional hearings, citizens' gatherings, journal articles)

Although these are difficult questions that might be tempting to avoid, the ability of citizens to influence and respond to scientific information depends crucially on how they are answered.

Given the complexity involved in disseminating scientific findings to the public, it is unfortunate that relatively few analysts have devoted attention to developing an EOE for researchers.[12] For example, Kenneth Pimple suggests that scientists' social responsibilities in general (not to mention their specific responsibilities for disseminating information) have received less analysis than ethical issues internal to scientific practice (e.g., management of data, relationships among researchers, treatment of human and animal research subjects).[13] Moreover, some of the previous efforts to develop an EOE do not appear to be entirely satisfactory as they currently stand. For instance, based on the need for trust between experts and laypersons, John Hardwig has proposed a promising EOE that includes twenty-one ethical maxims.[14] Nevertheless, he does not show in detail whether the concept of trust is rich enough to provide a basis for adjudicating conflicts among the maxims. He also fails to specify how the maxims should be applied in particular cases.

In an effort to address some of the gaps in previous work on the ethics of expertise, and in order to promote better societal awareness of the value judgments associated with policy-relevant research, this chapter suggests a

12. For previous work in this area, see, for example, Douglas, "Role of Values in Expert Reasoning"; Hardwig, "Toward an Ethics of Expertise"; Jamieson, "Scientific Uncertainty"; Pielke Jr., *Honest Broker*; Resnik, *Ethics of Science*; Shrader-Frechette, *Ethics of Scientific Research*; Thompson, "Ethics of Truth Telling and the Problem of Risk."

13. Pimple, "Six Domains of Research Ethics."

14. Hardwig, "Toward an Ethics of Expertise," 92 ff.

new theoretical framework.[15] It proposes that one might build a promising EOE based on the notion that the scientific community should promote the self-determination of those who use its findings. In other words, researchers should strive to enable decision makers to formulate choices that accord with their own beliefs and values. On this basis, the chapter argues for its fundamental lesson, namely, that the concept of informed consent (as previously analyzed by biomedical ethicists) may provide a set of criteria and guidelines that can help scientists to fulfill their ethical responsibilities. In other words, the scientific community's responsibilities to promote self-determination can be conceptualized as responsibilities to enable members of the public (and their political representatives) to give informed consent to personal and political decisions that affect their well-being.

Others have previously appealed to the concept of informed consent in order to guide science-policy decisions.[16] Nevertheless, this previous work has focused primarily on determining whether particular decision-making procedures (such as broadly based deliberation) enable the *public* to provide consent rather than on elucidating the responsibilities of the scientific *experts* who provide the information that facilitates public consent. The present chapter builds on a much smaller body of previous work, which suggests that expert scientists and engineers might find guidance regarding their moral responsibilities by considering how to promote the informed consent of those who use their findings.[17]

The next section justifies my use of the informed-consent concept as the basis for an EOE. It also draws on previous studies of the concept from the biomedical-ethics literature in order to suggest a series of ethical guidelines for scientific experts. The following section considers how this EOE might prove valuable to those performing research on hormesis. Thus, the chapter

15. Although the theoretical framework proposed in this chapter is relatively new, it may be compatible with much of the previous work on the ethics of expertise. For example, it is plausible that one of the best ways for experts to maintain the trust of decision makers who depend on them for information is to promote the ability of those decision makers to provide informed consent to societal decisions. Thus, one could potentially regard an EOE based on informed consent as a way to flesh out and specify Hardwig's EOE based on trust. At the very least, the EOE proposed in this chapter would presumably support most of the maxims that Hardwig proposed in his earlier work.

16. See, for example, Fiorino, "Citizen Participation and Environmental Risk"; Shrader-Frechette, *Risk and Rationality*; Shrader-Frechette, "Consent and Nuclear Waste Disposal"; Wigley and Shrader-Frechette, "Environmental Justice."

17. Mike Martin and Roland Schinzinger have suggested that engineers could find ethical guidance by conceptualizing their work as social experimentation on members of the public, which requires some form of informed consent; see their *Ethics in Engineering*. David Resnik provides an ethics of expertise that is even more parallel to my own in his article "Ethical Dilemmas in Communicating Medical Information to the Public."

both sketches a theoretical framework for an EOE based on informed consent and demonstrates how it can provide practical ethical advice to working scientists. It does not aspire to provide an *exhaustive* account of the social responsibilities of scientists. Experts have other duties (e.g., choosing appropriate research projects, maintaining fidelity to employers, whistle-blowing under some circumstances) besides those associated with disseminating information. Nevertheless, the EOE developed here provides a coherent framework for organizing a number of ethical considerations for scientists so that they can enhance citizens' ability to evaluate, influence, and respond to scientific research.

## AN ETHICS OF EXPERTISE BASED ON INFORMED CONSENT

### The Plausibility of Informed Consent as a Theoretical Framework

The principle of informed consent became a central feature of biomedical ethics during the twentieth century. In the context of the professional-patient relationship, obtaining informed consent provides a method of ensuring that patients receive adequate information about the range of treatment options available, as well as the risks and benefits associated with them. In the context of medical research, obtaining informed consent promotes people's ability to make a carefully considered decision about whether to participate in potentially risky studies. In both contexts, ethicists such as Tom Beauchamp and James Childress argue that obtaining informed consent helps to ensure that two necessary conditions for autonomous decision making are met: "Virtually all theories of autonomy agree that two conditions are essential for autonomy: (1) *liberty* (independence from controlling influences) and (2) *agency* (capacity for intentional action)."[18]

Insofar as the principle of informed consent has been designed to promote the self-determination of decision makers, it appears to provide a promising theoretical basis for developing an EOE. One of the main justifications for proposing an EOE in this book is to prevent experts from taking undue license in providing information to the public. Specifically, to the extent that experts seek to respect a range of societal values, they cannot disseminate information in a manner that serves only the beliefs and values of individual clients. Rather, they must aspire to provide information in such a way that all members of society, with their diverse beliefs and values, can consider how the experts' information relates to their own projects and perspectives. As we have seen in the preceding chapters, there is a danger that

18. Beauchamp and Childress, *Principles of Biomedical Ethics*, 58; italics in original.

scientific experts may (consciously or unconsciously) smuggle significant and controversial value judgments into their work. This leads to a covert weakening of democratic participation in decision making, because the values of scientific experts (many of whom are tied to interest groups) surreptitiously replace those of citizens.[19] Therefore, the goals in biomedical ethics of obtaining informed consent appear to overlap with the goals of formulating an EOE for scientific researchers; both processes are designed to help the recipients of information to engage in intentional actions that accord with their own values.[20] Because the concept of informed consent has already been extensively analyzed by biomedical ethicists,[21] it provides a ready-made theoretical framework for guiding scientific experts who disseminate information to the public.

The EOE developed here does not incorporate all the actual details of the consent process that plays a role in biomedical contexts. For example, I am obviously not proposing that scientists ask those who receive information from them to read and sign a consent form. Like Beauchamp and Childress, this chapter does not treat "informed consent" as an event or a signature but rather as an autonomous authorization of personal or societal decisions.[22] Thus, to say that the scientific community has a responsibility to promote the informed consent of decision makers is merely to say that scientists should provide information in a way that promotes the recipients' self-determination. Because biomedical ethicists have suggested guidelines and criteria that are likely to facilitate self-determination in a medical context, those guidelines and criteria appear to provide a promising framework for other contexts that also involve scientific information. At the very least, examining the framework used to promote informed consent in biomedical situations may spur further reflection on the similarities and differences between those contexts and other situations where scientific experts disseminate information.

19. National Research Council, *Understanding Risk*; Shrader-Frechette, *Risk and Rationality*; Turner, *Liberal Democracy 3.0*.

20. If one took the view that scientists could legitimately decide what is in the best interests of society as a whole, one could argue that they should disseminate information in a manner that directly promotes those societal interests rather than promoting the self-determination of society's individual members. In this chapter, I presume that, in general, the best way for scientists to serve society is to promote the self-determination of individuals. This does not preclude, however, the occurrence of some cases (such as in public-health contexts) in which scientists have additional ethical responsibilities based on fiduciary duties to society as a whole.

21. Beauchamp and Childress, *Principles of Biomedical Ethics*; Faden and Beauchamp, *History and Theory of Informed Consent*; May, *Bioethics in a Liberal Society*; Mazur, *New Medical Conversation*; Wear, *Informed Consent*.

22. Beauchamp and Childress, *Principles of Biomedical Ethics*.

One might worry, however, that an EOE based on informed consent might demand too much from scientists. This EOE would clearly be socially valuable, because it would promote the ability of citizens with diverse values to use, analyze, and even challenge policy-relevant scientific information. Nevertheless, critics might question whether the scientific community truly has ethical responsibilities to promote the informed consent of citizens and policy makers. To respond to this objection, one might appeal either to special professional duties of scientists or to responsibilities that apply to all moral agents.[23] As in chapter 3, I want to focus on ethical principles that apply to all moral agents, because it is less controversial and still quite effective in this case.

In order to justify the duties of the scientific community to promote the informed consent of those who make decisions based on scientific information, one can appeal to a general moral standard that T. M. Scanlon calls the "Principle of Helpfulness."[24] It is noteworthy that he even illustrates the principle using a case in which an individual is supplying information:

> Suppose I learn, in the course of conversation with a person, that I have a piece of information that would be of great help to her because it would save her a great deal of time and effort in pursuing her life's project. It would surely be wrong of me to fail (simply out of indifference) to give her this information when there is no compelling reason not to do so. It would be unreasonable to reject a principle requiring us to help others in this way (even when they are not in desperate need), since such a principle would involve no significant sacrifice on our part.[25]

The central element of this principle is that, in situations where one can significantly help another individual by engaging in an action that requires little sacrifice, it is morally unacceptable not to help. This obligation is easy to justify using a utilitarian framework that seeks to maximize the common good, and Scanlon argues that deontological or contractualist thinkers should accept it as well.

Despite the apparent modesty of this principle, critics might claim that it is still too demanding, because it could (to take a famously discussed example) establish obligations to change our Western lifestyles in order to give more money to suffering populations around the world.[26] Nevertheless, this

23. My reflections on this point have been significantly influenced by Heather Douglas, Travis Rieder, and Justin Weinberg.

24. I thank Travis Rieder for highlighting the relevance of Scanlon's principle.

25. Scanlon, *What We Owe to Each Other*, 224.

26. For the obligation to help suffering people based on something like the Principle of Helpfulness, see Singer, "Famine, Affluence, and Morality." For criticisms of his claims in this and other work, see Jamieson, ed., *Singer and His Critics*.

criticism is directed at cases in which seemingly small sacrifices aggregate into significant and counterintuitive demands. The objection does not threaten instances in which the sacrifices involved in helping others are clearly minimal. It is doubtful that anyone would want to challenge the moral obligation to provide a piece of information to someone who could greatly benefit from it, if the only barriers to supplying it were minor concerns such as indifference.

Consider how the Principle of Helpfulness applies to scientific experts. They have extensive knowledge of research findings, including the major value judgments associated with them. Because of their expert knowledge, it is generally extremely easy for them to promote the self-determination of information recipients by highlighting crucial weaknesses, ambiguities, limitations, or interpretive judgments associated with available research. This information can be extremely valuable to concerned citizens and policy makers who are trying to decide how to respond to socially relevant scientific results. Nevertheless, whereas it is easy for experts to provide this information, it can be very difficult for citizens to obtain it if experts do not clarify it for them. This does not preclude scientists from taking sides on debated policy-relevant matters; it merely requires that they acknowledge the crucial points at which their judgments are controversial or worth considering further.[27]

Based on these considerations, experts have prima facie ethical obligations under the Principle of Helpfulness to disseminate information in a manner that promotes the informed consent of policy makers and citizens who make decisions based on scientific findings. Of course, the precise conditions under which these obligations demand large enough sacrifices to be overridden are a matter of debate. Moreover, if one were to justify this EOE based on scientists' professional obligations, it might be reasonable to demand greater sacrifices from them before excusing them from their responsibilities. Despite these matters of debate, the minimal claim that experts should promote the informed consent of information recipients (in the absence of countervailing factors) seems uncontroversial.

## The Details of an EOE Based on Informed Consent

The basic principle of an EOE based on informed consent might run something like the following:

27. Here again, it is helpful to draw comparisons to medical contexts, in which physicians obtain informed consent from patients. Physicians often make recommendations regarding what they take to be the best course of treatment, but they also (ideally) acknowledge alternative options and the risks associated with their preferred approach. In principle, this helps patients to make decisions that accord with their own beliefs and values.

> *Consent Principle:* Scientists have prima facie duties, in contexts in which their findings are likely to be used for particular individual or group decisions, to disseminate that information in a manner that promotes the ability of those affected by the decisions to provide some form of informed consent to them.

It is important to note that this principle requires only that the scientific community promote *some form* of informed consent. In principle, individuals affected by a decision might provide their consent via a number of more or less direct ways, including electing government representatives, making consumer decisions in the marketplace, participating in a consensus conference, or engaging in some form of activism.[28] The important point for the purposes of this chapter is that, no matter how the public provides consent to personal or societal decisions, consent cannot be obtained unless the decision makers have adequate scientific information on which to base their decision.

Most biomedical ethicists suggest that the concept of informed consent can be broken down into several components that serve as necessary conditions for promoting self-determination. Thus, one can identify scientists' responsibilities in specific cases under the Consent Principle by considering what they would need to accomplish in order to achieve these components of informed consent. This chapter employs the analysis of five components (disclosure, understanding, voluntariness, competence, and actual authorization or consent) elaborated in Beauchamp and Childress's fifth edition of their *Principles of Biomedical Ethics*.[29] Their work is a good reference, both because they base their analysis on the particularly extensive earlier study of informed consent by Faden and Beauchamp[30] and because their book is one of the most widely respected biomedical-ethics texts. The rest of this section examines how the first three components (disclosure, understanding, and voluntariness) could yield a list of ethical considerations for scientists who disseminate information to policy makers or to the public at large. (Figure 6.1 summarizes a list of these guidelines.)

The first component identified by Beauchamp and Childress is *disclosure*.[31] In biomedical contexts, this component reflects the fact that physicians and researchers need to disclose particular sorts of information about proposed clinical procedures and research projects in order for patients and research subjects to provide informed consent. In the context of a general EOE for scientists, this component reflects the notion that those who make decisions based on scientific information cannot provide adequate informed consent

28. See, for example, Rowe and Frewer, "Public Participation Methods."
29. Beauchamp and Childress, *Principles of Biomedical Ethics*.
30. Faden and Beauchamp, *History and Theory of Informed Consent*.
31. Beauchamp and Childress, *Principles of Biomedical Ethics*.

Considerations based on disclosure:

- The dissemination of information should arguably meet the *reasonable-person standard* of disclosure, which should be augmented by the *subjective standard* when groups of users with particular informational needs can be identified.

- Disclosed information should generally include particular *categories* of information that can be justified on the basis of the reasonable-person standard of disclosure, perhaps including the following:
  - major *uncertainties* and *value judgments* associated with current scientific information
  - major *disagreements* within the scientific community
  - major *conflicts of interest* that might influence the judgment of experts
  - the *benefits* of proposed actions (when particular actions are under consideration)
  - the *risks* of proposed actions (when particular actions are under consideration)
  - major *alternatives* to proposed actions (when particular actions are under consideration)

- Using an analogy to the therapeutic privilege, experts who deal with information that could significantly diminish the autonomy of particular individuals or groups (especially those that are already disadvantaged) should explore one or more of the following options, depending on the details of the situation:
  - disclosing the information in a manner that will cause the least damage to the autonomy of those who are at risk
  - contributing to societal initiatives that would diminish the harmful impact of the disclosed information
  - refraining from disclosing the information
  - avoiding obtaining the information

Considerations based on understanding:

- Information should be presented in such a way as to promote the substantial understanding of decision makers, where substantial understanding involves having justified, relevant beliefs about all the information that is *material* or *important* to assessing the nature and consequences of one's actions.

- Information should be presented in such a way as to avoid common sources of *misunderstanding:*
  - information overload
  - misleading framing of information
  - false beliefs that result in unjustified inferences

Considerations based on voluntariness:

- When providing information that may influence people's decisions, experts should arguably engage in *persuasion* rather than *coercion* or informational *manipulation* (at least when the manipulation is sufficiently serious to be incompatible with substantial understanding), with these terms having the following meanings (see Beauchamp and Childress 2001, 94–95):
  - Coercion involves the intentional use of credible and severe threats of harm.
  - Persuasion involves convincing others by the use of reasons.
  - Manipulation involves influencing others by means other than coercion or persuasion.

- Interpretations of research results should promote the substantial understanding of those receiving the information, and interpretations should definitely not involve informational manipulation that prevents substantial understanding.

**Figure 6.1.** A list of ethical considerations for disseminating information based on the Consent Principle.

to those decisions unless they receive the right sorts of information. As Beauchamp and Childress explain, ethicists and legal scholars have typically worked with three potential standards of disclosure: professional practice, subjective, and reasonable-person standards.[32] Let us consider each of these in turn.

According to the professional practice standard, a professional community's typical practices count as the criteria for adequate disclosure. Although this approach may be helpful in legal contexts, it is arguably too weak for developing an *ethics* of expertise, because the field of ethics is concerned with *evaluating* professional practices rather than merely preserving them.[33] The subjective standard holds that the adequacy of disclosed information should be judged on the basis of the specific informational needs of the individual giving consent. Although this may be an excellent guide for some cases in the clinical setting,[34] it is probably impractical as a general standard for an EOE, because scientific experts generally disclose information to many people (who may have somewhat different informational needs) rather than to individuals.

According to the reasonable-person standard, the criteria for adequate disclosure are based on the information that a reasonable person would wish to receive when faced with a particular decision. Although this standard faces at least two problems of its own, it appears likely that it can still provide valuable guidance about disclosure for the purposes of an EOE. The first problem is that the standard may not require adequate consideration of the differing needs of individuals. One can respond, however, that even if *meeting* the reasonable-person standard is not always a sufficient condition for *achieving* adequate disclosure, *failure* to meet the reasonable-person standard might be a sufficient condition for *preventing* adequate disclosure. Thus, one can at least use the reasonable-person standard to identify information that, if left undisclosed, would be problematic under the Consent Principle. One could then supplement the reasonable-person standard with the subjective standard by claiming that, when it is possible to identify a particular group of people who will make significant use of the information that a scientific expert provides, that expert should try to meet the group's special informational needs.

A second problem with the reasonable-person standard is that the notion of a "reasonable person" may be difficult to specify. One might respond, however, that there are likely to be many situations in which, under any

32. Ibid.

33. May, *Bioethics in a Liberal Society*, 17ff.

34. Ibid.

justifiable definition of a "reasonable person," that person would want a particular set of information. In particular, biomedical ethicists have argued that physicians should disclose all information that is *material* to the action under consideration (from the perspective of both the professional and the individual giving consent). Material information is defined as that which is relevant to deciding whether to take a particular action or to take an alternative action.[35] In the biomedical context, this information generally includes the purpose of consent, its nature and limits, the professional's recommended course of action, the risks and benefits of the proposed procedure, alternative courses of action, and perhaps the professional's conflicts of interest.[36]

Admittedly, the contexts in which scientific researchers disclose information may sometimes be quite different from those in which clinicians or researchers obtain informed consent. Nevertheless, it seems likely that the reasonable-person standard of disclosure could be employed to develop a comparable list of material information that decision makers would wish to receive from scientific experts. For example, this information might include major uncertainties and value judgments associated with current scientific information, major disagreements within the scientific community, major conflicts of interest that might influence the experts' judgment, the benefits of proposed actions (when particular actions are under consideration), the risks of proposed actions, and the major alternatives to proposed actions (see figure 6.1).

In their reflections on the disclosure component of informed consent, biomedical ethicists have also considered the conditions under which it is justifiable for professionals to withhold information intentionally. Beauchamp and Childress list these situations under three categories: the therapeutic privilege, the therapeutic use of placebos, and the performance of research.[37] The therapeutic privilege involves withholding information if one judges that a depressed, emotionally drained, or unstable patient would be harmed by it. The other two categories (therapeutic use of placebos and performance of research) involve withholding information from patients for the sake of producing a placebo effect or obtaining valid research data that require subjects to be unaware of the details of the procedure. Not all these categories seem applicable to the case of scientific experts. One might argue, however, that the guidelines for allowing physicians to withhold information based on the therapeutic privilege might also be applicable to scientists

35. Faden and Beauchamp, *History and Theory of Informed Consent*, 302ff.

36. See, for example, Beauchamp and Childress, *Principles of Biomedical Ethics*; Wear, *Informed Consent*; Wilkinson, "Research, Informed Consent, and the Limits of Disclosure."

37. Beauchamp and Childress, *Principles of Biomedical Ethics*.

who must decide whether to withhold (or refrain from gathering) information that might be socially harmful.[38]

In particular, Beauchamp and Childress suggest that one way to justify withholding information based on the therapeutic privilege is to show that the information would actually *hinder* a patient's autonomy rather than *promoting* it.[39] Thus, the Consent Principle suggests that experts should also consider withholding (or at least be very circumspect about disseminating) information that would be likely to challenge the self-determination of particular individuals. In this respect, the EOE proposed in this chapter might accord closely with some of Philip Kitcher's proposals in his book *Science, Truth, and Democracy*.[40] Kitcher argues that scientists may have a responsibility to avoid collecting particular forms of information (or to exercise great care about disseminating it) if it would detract from the autonomy of already disadvantaged members of society.[41] For example, he argues that those who study whether particular racial, ethnic, or gender groups have lower than average levels of intelligence must be aware of their responsibilities to disseminate the findings with special care. Based on the disclosure component of informed consent (and the therapeutic privilege in particular), the Consent Principle would arguably support many of Kitcher's suggestions.

The second component of informed consent (after disclosure) is understanding. According to Beauchamp and Childress, substantial understanding requires the acquisition of pertinent information and justified, relevant beliefs about the nature and consequences of one's actions.[42] Several aspects of this component could yield ethical considerations for an EOE. First, Faden and Beauchamp have emphasized the plausibility that those making a decision do not need *perfect* understanding of the information relevant to their decision in order to provide adequate informed consent; they merely need *substantial* understanding.[43] This point is important, because a number of philosophers and sociologists of science have worried that incommensurability between the perspectives of experts and laypeople might create a serious impediment to democratic decision making on scientific issues.[44] The Consent Principle suggests that informed consent (and thus reasonable, democratic decision making) is still possible if the laypeople making a decision can develop enough justified, relevant beliefs based on their communication with scientists. For

38. Kitcher, *Science, Truth, and Democracy*; Kitcher, *Vaulting Ambition*.
39. Beauchamp and Childress, *Principles of Biomedical Ethics*.
40. Kitcher, *Science, Truth, and Democracy*.
41. Ibid., 93ff.
42. Beauchamp and Childress, *Principles of Biomedical Ethics*.
43. Faden and Beauchamp, *History and Theory of Informed Consent*.
44. See, for example, Turner, *Liberal Democracy 3.0*.

example, Faden and Beauchamp argue that substantial understanding merely requires that decision makers understand all the information that is *material* or *important* for their decisions.[45]

A second and particularly crucial issue that biomedical ethicists have emphasized concerning the component of understanding is the cluster of common ways in which disclosed information may be *misunderstood* by those who receive it. These sources of misunderstanding might be a particularly important area of consideration for scientists who disseminate information to the public. One source of misunderstanding is "information overload." Thus, it might be advisable in some contexts for scientists to withhold unimportant information, especially if it involves unfamiliar terms or is difficult to organize in a meaningful fashion.[46] Another very important source of misunderstanding is the *framing* of disclosed information. For example, in the medical context, Beauchamp and Childress emphasize that "choices between risky alternatives can be heavily influenced by whether the same risk information is presented as providing a gain or an opportunity for a patient, or as constituting a loss or a reduction of opportunity."[47] Framing is likely to be an important issue for scientific experts to consider under the Consent Principle as well, because philosophers and sociologists of science have argued that framing can play an important role in disputes that draw on scientific information.[48]

A third source of misunderstanding is the possibility that those receiving information have false beliefs that invalidate decisions made on the basis of technically correct disclosed information. For example, let us say that scientific experts were to disclose that environmental factors are more important than genetic factors in causing the current worldwide increase in obesity rates. Decision makers might still be unable to provide adequate informed consent to policy decisions if they have false beliefs about the most appropriate ways to address those environmental factors. Thus, the Consent Principle would encourage scientists to anticipate and counteract false beliefs, misleading framing, and other forms of misunderstanding that might prevent members of the public from making autonomous decisions in response to scientific information.

A third component of informed consent, voluntariness, may also yield guidelines for scientists who disseminate information. In order to analyze

45. Faden and Beauchamp, *History and Theory of Informed Consent.*
46. Beauchamp and Childress, *Principles of Biomedical Ethics,* 90.
47. Ibid.
48. See, for example, Nisbet and Mooney, "Framing Science"; Roth, Dunsby, and Bero, "Framing Processes in Public Commentary"; Shrader-Frechette, "Hydrogeology and Framing Questions."

this component, Beauchamp and Childress describe three ways in which people can be influenced when making decisions: (1) coercion (deliberate and successful influence by a credible threat of harm that the influenced person cannot resist), (2) persuasion (deliberate and successful influence by appeals to reason), and (3) manipulation (any deliberate and successful influence that is neither coercive nor persuasive).[49] They claim that consent is not voluntary if it is the result of coercion or informational manipulation that prevents substantial understanding of a decision situation. In other words, voluntary consent must involve only persuasion or informational manipulation that is sufficiently minor to be compatible with substantial understanding. In the medical context, physicians have responsibilities under this component to minimize informational manipulation that could be produced by selective presentation of information, tone of voice, or framing.[50]

Scientific experts arguably have similar responsibilities under the Consent Principle suggested here. Chapter 4 presents empirical evidence indicating that pharmaceutical studies sponsored by corporations with financial interests in the results tend to produce results that favor the interested corporations.[51] If scientific experts deliberately and effectively manipulate the design or interpretation of studies in order to obtain those misleading results, their behavior would be ethically problematic under the voluntariness component (and, presumably, the understanding component) of informed consent. The voluntariness and understanding components might also provide guidance for scientists who want to determine how much to interpret their results for information recipients. One would arguably need to consider, in particular cases, whether the interpretation of information could qualify as a manipulation that prevents substantial understanding of the decision situation or whether the interpretation actually promotes the understanding of those making the decision.

## Objections and Clarifications

Despite the potential guidance provided by the theoretical framework suggested in this section, one might raise several objections to it. First, one might worry that the Consent Principle is too demanding. For example, it might seem unrealistic to expect scientists, who are preoccupied with

49. Beauchamp and Childress, *Principles of Biomedical Ethics*; see also Donnelly, *Consent*; Gert, Culver, and Clouser, *Bioethics*.

50. Beauchamp and Childress, *Principles of Biomedical Ethics*, 95.

51. See, for example, Friedberg et al., "Evaluation of Conflict of Interest"; Krimsky, *Science in the Private Interest*.

research, to spend time worrying about how the public might misunderstand the information that they disclose. One might even argue that the work of scientists as "knowledge generators" is so valuable that they should not be bothered by ethical concerns about the societal ramifications of their work.[52] One response is to reiterate that the Consent Principle states only that the scientific community has prima facie responsibilities to promote informed consent. Thus, if these duties required significant sacrifices or threatened other significant responsibilities, they could be overridden. Another response is that scholars in related disciplines, such as ethics or the philosophy of science, can assist scientists in fulfilling their ethical responsibilities. As this book illustrates, one of the important contributions that philosophers can make to environmental disputes is to help identify crucial value judgments and to highlight ways in which scientific experts can make their claims more useful to policy makers and members of the public. Thus, even if it would normally be too demanding for scientists to promote the informed consent of information recipients in a particular context, ethicists could provide them with advice that makes it relatively easy.

A second possible objection to an EOE based on informed consent is that there are significant *differences* between the contexts in which clinicians obtain informed consent from patients and the situations in which the Consent Principle would apply. Thus, one might question the attempt in this chapter to glean insights from the biomedical literature on informed consent and to use them to guide scientific experts who disseminate information to the public or to policy makers. For example, one important difference between these two contexts is that, whereas clinicians address their disclosures to particular patients, it may be somewhat unclear as to whom scientific experts should be directing their disclosures of information. The information provided by scientific experts may be relevant to a variety of different decisions, and it is often not just one person or even one group providing informed consent to each decision. Another difference is that, whereas a single physician might be the primary source of information for the informed consent of his or her patients, social decisions are generally based on information disseminated by many different scientists. Thus, the responsibilities of individual scientists might be somewhat different from those of individual clinicians. A third difference is that, whereas physicians provide information to their patients via a fairly standardized process (e.g., discussing a consent form with a patient), scientists disseminate information to the public in a very wide variety of situations. These contexts might include public testimony before government policy makers, legal testimony

52. For a formulation of the argument that professionals (such as scientists) sometimes have unique responsibilities because of their social roles, see Gewirth, "Professional Ethics."

in court cases, journal articles, commentaries, review articles, taped interviews for television news, interviews for newspaper articles, and presentations for citizens' gatherings.

In response to all these differences, I argue that they do not provide any direct reason to deny that scientific experts have a responsibility to promote the informed consent of decision makers who draw on scientific information. Rather, the differences suggest that one must apply the Consent Principle in a manner that is sensitive to the particular situations in which scientists find themselves, which may be significantly different in some cases from those of medical researchers or clinicians. For example, the Consent Principle generally encourages experts to play the role of what Roger Pielke Jr. calls an honest broker rather than an issue advocate.[53] In other words, experts who provide information about policy-relevant science should generally offer some sense of the range of options or conclusions available to decision makers, even if they defend one option as preferable to others. Nevertheless, in certain instances (most notably judicial proceedings), we expect individual scientists to be more aggressive advocates for one side of a controversy, because institutional structures are present to ensure that we hear from experts with an adequate range of opposing perspectives. Under those unique sorts of circumstances, scientists might be encouraged under the Consent Principle to play the role of issue advocates, and they might be relieved of some of their typical responsibilities as sources of information.

A final objection to the arguments in this chapter might be that this discussion of the Consent Principle has been overly general. For example, we have not explored how the specific maxims proposed earlier by John Hardwig might be supported or questioned based on the concept of informed consent. Furthermore, although I have acknowledged that scientists might have differing responsibilities depending on the contexts in which they provide information, I have not provided a systematic list of the variables that scientists might need to consider when crafting their dissemination of information. (Some of these variables might include the gender, age, and experience level of the scientist; the prestige of the scientist and that person's institution; the dissemination activities of other members of the scientific community; the degree of uncertainty or disagreement in the scientific community; and the potential societal impacts of the decisions that need to be made.) Although a thorough examination of all these issues is beyond the scope of this book, perhaps the best way to initiate a response to this objection is to examine hormesis research as

53. Pielke Jr., *Honest Broker.*

a case study of how the Consent Principle could provide a measure of practical guidance.

## APPLICATION TO THE HORMESIS CASE

The hormesis case illustrates the importance of having an EOE, because researchers studying this phenomenon must consider a number of issues when disseminating information. These questions include how confidently to present their results, how (and whether) to present the views of scientists who disagree with them, how to characterize the value judgments and uncertainties associated with their work, and whether to directly incorporate societal values (e.g., concerns about potential biological harms caused by chemicals or potential economic harms caused by stringent chemical regulations) in the interpretation of their results. This section considers some examples of how the Consent Principle could provide guidelines for hormesis researchers.

For several reasons, however, it is advisable to proceed cautiously and constructively with this endeavor. First, the scientific community continues to debate the precise extent and nature of its ethical responsibilities, especially those associated with social matters.[54] Thus, it is not clear that researchers are culpable for failing to fulfill responsibilities that are currently not well specified. Second, as we will see in the subsequent discussion, a variety of complicated contextual considerations affect the ethical responsibilities of researchers in particular circumstances. Given this complexity and the resulting potential for ethical disagreement about how best to respond to particular situations, it is generally more fruitful to offer constructive suggestions for scientists rather than accusing them of wrongdoing. Finally, in particularly complicated ethical cases, researchers may not be blameworthy for any failings until outside observers help them to consider the dynamics of their situation.

It is important to keep these caveats in mind, because the scientific community often associates ethical concerns with dramatic lapses (e.g., fraud, plagiarism) that merit sanctions. There is less precedent for constructive ethical reasoning about issues that are not entirely clear cut. The purpose of this more subtle reasoning about debated matters is not to threaten researchers but rather to assist them in achieving the ethical values to which they and their colleagues aspire. The goal in this chapter is therefore to demonstrate how the Consent Principle could provide helpful guidance and advice

54. Marris, "Should Conservation Biologists Push Policies?" See also the special section titled "Conservation Biology, Values, and Advocacy," *Conservation Biology* 10 (1996): 904–20.

for contemporary scientists. After all, disseminating information in accordance with this principle is not only *ethically* advisable but also *practically* advantageous, because it is likely to mitigate potentially damaging disputes over controversial areas of research.[55]

In order to be as relevant as possible to current scientists, this section focuses primarily on *contemporary* debates about hormesis. Nevertheless, this is just one segment of a long history of debate. Edward Calabrese and Linda Baldwin have suggested that members of the toxicological community may have acted inappropriately in their dismissal of claim HG throughout the twentieth century. For example, they argue that prominent pharmacologist A. J. Clark's treatment of hormesis in his classic text, *Handbook of Experimental Pharmacology*, was questionable. They claim that "it is apparent that the conclusions of Clark [with respect to hormesis] were not only unsubstantiated but, in fact, were inconsistent with a large and generally available database that preceded his book."[56] If they are correct, then opponents of hormesis such as Clark may have had ethical obligations under the Consent Principle to acknowledge the important experimental results that conflicted with their views.

This chapter focuses on the manner in which contemporary hormesis researchers are disseminating information about the phenomenon. While it might seem here that I am unfairly directing my advice only at scientists who propound positions favorable to industry, we will see in chapter 7 that the Consent Principle also suggests guidelines for endocrine-disruption researchers who make claims favorable to environmentalists. In both cases, my goal is to guide scientists who are staking out new ground and taking controversial positions that are relevant to public policy. One should keep in mind that some hormesis researchers, most notably Edward Calabrese, have made efforts to promote open, critical discussions of the phenomenon.[57] I offer the further suggestion that they should acknowledge in a more consistent and explicit fashion the major, socially significant value judgments that appear in their work. It is

55. For examples of the damaging consequences of promoting controversial theories without adequate care, see Carey, "Criticism of a Gender Theory, and a Scientist under Siege." Another example of the need for careful thinking about how to present conflicting scientific evidence comes from the controversy in late 2009 over the hacked emails of climate scientists who wanted to minimize evidence that could potentially detract from concerns over climate change; see, for example, Revkin, "Hacked E-mail Is New Fodder for Climate Dispute."

56. Calabrese and Baldwin, "Marginalization of Hormesis," 36.

57. For example, Calabrese has invited critics of hormesis to conferences that he has organized, and he has published their work in the *BELLE Newsletter*, which he edits; see Calabrese, "Elliott's Ethics of Expertise Proposal and Application."

encouraging to see that many of Calabrese's recent articles do consider some of these judgments.[58]

In suggesting that major value judgments constitute a category of information that the Consent Principle would call for scientific experts to disclose, I consider any judgment as major if it could have significant ramifications for individual or societal decision making. These sorts of judgments clearly constitute material information that experts ought to disclose in accordance with the reasonable-person standard for disclosure (see the previous section of this chapter).[59] I want to focus on two major and socially significant judgments that some hormesis researchers make while failing to be explicit about their controversial character and the limits to the evidence in favor of them. One judgment is that current evidence strongly supports claim HP (i.e., that the hormetic model predominates over other models, perhaps for both carcinogenic and noncarcinogenic toxicants). A second judgment is that current evidence strongly supports claim HD (i.e., that hormesis justifies regulatory changes, especially employing hormesis as the default model in risk assessment). The first judgment relates to the evaluation and interpretation of studies, and the second has to do with the application of research to public policy (i.e., the third and fourth sorts of judgments discussed in chapter 2).

An important commentary article by Edward Calabrese and Linda Baldwin in *Nature* provides a helpful example of these judgments. Their piece is noteworthy because it has served as one of the highest-profile sources of information about hormesis and because it has been cited extensively. The following five quotations from Calabrese and Baldwin's article illustrate how it makes the two judgments mentioned previously: (a) that hormetic dose-response curves predominate over others (for both carcinogens and noncarcinogens) and (b) that a hormetic model should be the default in risk assessment:

1. "The hormetic model is not an exception to the rule—it is the rule."[60]
2. "Now, we not only know that it [i.e., hormesis] exists but accept its dominance over other models."[61]
3. "Most notably it [i.e., hormesis] challenges the belief and use of low-dose linearity in estimating cancer risks and emphasizes that

58. In particular, Calabrese acknowledges that hormetic effects may often be harmful rather than beneficial. See his article "Hormesis: Why It Is Important," and his essay "Hormesis: Once Marginalized."

59. For other arguments that scientists ought to acknowledge major value judgments in their work, see Douglas, "Role of Values in Expert Reasoning"; Mayo and Spanos, "Risks to Health and Risks to Science"; Shrader-Frechette, *Ethics of Scientific Research*.

60. Calabrese and Baldwin, "Toxicology Rethinks Its Central Belief," 691.

61. Ibid., 692.

there are thresholds for carcinogens. The economic implications of this conclusion are substantial."[62]

4. "As both types of biological response [i.e., the biological responses to noncarcinogens and carcinogens] follow the hormetic paradigm and display similar quantitative features of the dose response, the EPA could use the hormetic model as default to assess risk in both non-carcinogens and carcinogens."[63]
5. "The hormetic perspective also turns upside down the strategies and tactics used for risk communication of toxic substances for the public."[64]

Although Calabrese and Baldwin note that toxicologists were skeptical about hormesis in the past, they do not discuss the range of toxicological opinions about these value judgments at the time of their commentary's publication (see chapter 2). It is conceivable, however, that they already believed this point was sufficiently clear.[65]

Most articles that disseminate information about hormesis are not published in such prominent venues, but many of them make the same judgments as Calabrese and Baldwin, again without clarifying their significance.[66] For example, Robert Sielken and Donald Stevenson claimed, in response to the evidence collected in Calabrese and Baldwin's original literature study, "Low-dose risk characterization will need to reflect the likelihood of beneficial effects at a dose and the likelihood that sufficiently small dose levels may have a reasonable certainty of having no adverse effects.... The authors believe that these changes are needed and long overdue."[67] Although they acknowledged that the need for regulatory changes is *their* position (thus implicitly hinting that some scientists might disagree with them), they did not highlight the controversial judgments involved in coming to their conclusion. In much the same way, Justin Teeguarden and his colleagues claimed that Calabrese's work on hormesis "challenges current approaches

62. Ibid.

63. Ibid.

64. Ibid.

65. For an argument that Calabrese and Baldwin do in fact make it relatively clear in their *Nature* commentary that the toxicology community holds conflicting positions, see Calabrese, "Elliott's Ethics of Expertise"; Hoffmann, "Letter to the Editor."

66. In order to clarify that the practice of making controversial value judgments about hormesis without highlighting them is not isolated to an individual article, I provide several examples of this phenomenon. Nevertheless, my primary goal in this chapter is not to analyze how widespread this practice is but instead to show that the Consent Principle can provide helpful guidance for determining when this sort of practice may be problematic.

67. Sielken Jr. and Stevenson, "Some Implications for Quantitative Risk Assessment," 259.

to carcinogen testing that are limited in their usefulness by their narrow focus on linear dose responses and toxic effects. Indications of hormesis in carcinogenesis further legitimize the notion that current linear low-dose approaches to risk assessment and human drug safety studies are flawed."[68] Ortwin Renn claims that "the evidence collected so far on the hormesis hypothesis justifies a thorough revision of the present paradigms in regulatory philosophy and actions."[69] As an expert in risk communication rather than in toxicology, he may have just been relying on the interpretive judgments made by the scientists with whom he had been in communication, but it would be helpful if he clarified that these judgments were significant and highly debatable.

Calabrese has recently published a clever "fictional obituary" of the threshold dose-response model in the journal *Bioessays*[70] It claims that Calabrese's study of the nearly fifty-seven thousand dose-response relationships in the NCI database (see chapter 2) indicated that the threshold model "just could not get a grip on the problem, failed to predict low-dose responses, and simply stopped functioning," whereas "this challenge proved to be a snap for its hormetic rival."[71] As chapter 2 clarifies, however, interpreting the data from the NCI database requires significant methodological value judgments. For one thing, the extent to which the database conflicts with the threshold model is not entirely clear.[72] Furthermore, the data do not provide precise information about how often the hormetic model occurs relative to the threshold model (see chapter 2), and it is therefore a highly debatable judgment to claim that the threshold model is entirely dead. Of course, it is important to remember that the *Bioessays* piece was written as a light-hearted spoof; one must be sensitive to this context when offering advice to the authors. Nevertheless, because we have seen that scientific language can be rhetorically powerful, it would be unwise to ignore the fact that this article provides a very one-sided perspective on the current evidence for hormesis.

Although I have focused here on just two major and socially significant judgments, one could identify a variety of others associated with hormesis

68. Teeguarden, Dragan, and Pitot, "Implications of Hormesis," 257.

69. Renn, "Hormesis and Risk Communication," 19.

70. Calabrese, "Threshold—Dose—Response Model—RIP."

71. Ibid., 686. For Calabrese's study of the NCI database, see Calabrese et al., "Hormesis Outperforms Threshold Model."

72. For a challenge to Calabrese's study of the NCI database, see Crump, "Limitations in the National Cancer Institute Antitumor Drug Screening Database"; for Calabrese's response, see Calabrese et al., "Hormesis and High Throughput Studies." For the claim that Calabrese's response to Crump is still not entirely adequate, see Mushak, "Ad-hoc and Fast Forward"; for Calabrese's response to Mushak, see Calabrese, "Hormesis: A Conversation with a Critic."

research. For example, Deborah Mayo and Aris Spanos have recently analyzed a number of statistical weaknesses associated with studies that purport to provide evidence for the phenomenon.[73] These involve several of the methodological judgments discussed in chapter 2: (1) deciding how much to trust studies that hunt for supportive data; (2) determining whether stimulatory effects at low doses in previous studies need to be statistically significant in order to count as evidence for hormesis; and (3) considering how to balance seemingly supportive evidence against contradictory findings. In addition to suggesting solutions for what they take to be questionable judgments made in hormesis studies, Mayo and Spanos argue that their criticisms could be mitigated by carefully revealing the judgments made by study authors:

> [E]ven failing to mitigate these threats to validity, . . . clearly revealing this, and taking steps to scrupulously avoid misleading claims would disarm criticisms. However, thus far, the hormetic proponents appear not to have mitigated and rarely fully expose such noteworthy shortcomings. . . . Acknowledging [potential problems with hormesis studies] up front will be the best way to disarm critics and strengthen the evidential credentials of the hormetic research program.[74]

Thus, Mayo and Spanos apparently share my view that proponents of claims HP and HD should be explicit about the major, debatable judgments associated with their studies.

Admittedly, various contextual details still make the dissemination of information about hormesis more complicated than it might initially appear. First, many studies appear in scholarly publications and are directed largely at other scientific researchers. Thus, one might think that it is unnecessary to make all major and socially significant value judgments explicit, because the other scientists who read the articles can probably recognize those judgments. This consideration seems less relevant to Calabrese and Baldwin's essay in *Nature*, because it was clearly designed to popularize the concept of hormesis beyond the realm of the toxicology community. Nevertheless, because the essay was published as a commentary, one might think that the authors should be allowed to take extra liberty to express their personal views.[75]

An argument could also be made that debates about the regulation of toxic chemicals provide the sort of heavily politicized scientific context in which it is to be expected that particular scientists will speak for specific interest groups. Thus, it may be unrealistic to expect individual toxicologists

73. Mayo and Spanos, "Risks to Health and Risks to Science."

74. Ibid., 623.

75. See, for example, Hoffmann, "Letter to the Editor."

to provide careful acknowledgment of the major value judgments that they are making. Rather, one might think that interchanges between scientists with opposing views should be the primary means of clarifying these crucial judgments. To some extent, that does appear to be what is taking place. Proponents of claims HD and HP have taken very strong stances (often without clarifying the judgments associated with those positions), and opponents have then argued that a variety of the judgments made by the proponents are problematic.[76]

Another contextual consideration is that the toxicological community and the EPA have been fairly hesitant to consider changing current risk-assessment practices in response to recent studies of hormesis.[77] Therefore, one might suppose that there is little danger that the value judgments made by the most enthusiastic proponents of claims HP or HD will result in unjustified regulatory changes. In fact, one might argue that the public is very likely to be biased against the notion that pollution can be beneficial,[78] so proponents of hormesis need to be as forceful as possible in order to gain an adequate hearing for their views. Another possible reason to think that it is appropriate for hormesis researchers to make controversial value judgments without highlighting them is that significant economic costs appear to be associated with the regulation of toxic chemicals at low doses. Proponents of claim HD believe that the present regulatory policies impose these serious costs on society while possibly harming public health. Thus, hormesis researchers may have been motivated to shake up the status quo and to interpret the data for hormesis aggressively because of the possible economic and public-health costs of stringent chemical regulations.

These contextual considerations are important to consider, because the Consent Principle provides only a prima facie case for clarifying the major, controversial value judgments of hormesis proponents. Recall the principle's structure:

> *Consent Principle:* Scientists have prima facie duties, in contexts in which their findings are likely to be used for particular individual or group decisions, to disseminate that information in a manner that promotes the ability of those affected by the decisions to provide some form of informed consent to them.

It seems clear that this principle is applicable to the hormesis case insofar as it does involve information that is likely to be used for individual or group

76. For examples of these interchanges, see Axelrod et al., "'Hormesis'—An Inappropriate Extrapolation"; Cook and Calabrese, "Importance of Hormesis to Public Health"; Thayer et al., "Fundamental Flaws"; Weltje, vom Saal, and Oehlmann, "Reproductive Stimulation by Low Doses of Xenoestrogens."

77. See, for example, Davis and Farland, "Biological Effects of Low-level Exposures."

78. Renn, "Hormesis and Risk Communication."

decisions. Many proponents of claims HD and HP argue explicitly that hormesis has significant ramifications for the regulation of toxic chemicals.[79] Nevertheless, it still might not be important for individual scientists to clarify their major, controversial value judgments if contextual considerations override the prima facie duties of hormesis researchers.

Although this case merits further study, there are at least three reasons for believing that hormesis proponents should clarify their major, socially significant judgments, despite the mitigating circumstances that were just mentioned. The first reason is that the claims of proponents are often decoupled from the opposing arguments of their critics. We have already seen that if a paper were part of an adversarial proceeding or a symposium in which a number of eminent scientists with conflicting views on hormesis presented their distinctive viewpoints, those receiving information might have little difficulty recognizing the presence of crucial judgments. However, in many of the contexts in which hormesis researchers publish their work, it appears by itself without opposing views. For example, not only did Calabrese and Baldwin's *Nature* essay stand alone, but the editors of *Nature* do not accept responses to commentaries.[80] Thus, other scientists were unable to formulate quick responses in the same venue in which Calabrese and Baldwin disseminated their opinions. Whenever one decouples the clarification of questionable judgments from the original context in which they are made, decision makers may miss or underestimate their importance. Therefore, the safest course in such a case appears to be at least some acknowledgment of major judgments so that those receiving the information can understand the crucial decisions being made.

A second reason for thinking that hormesis proponents should clarify their value judgments is that interest groups are likely to try to use their claims in misleading ways. This second consideration counts in favor of the suggestion that, even in commentary pieces in scientific journals, it would be wise for scientists to take reasonable steps to prevent their personal opinions from being misinterpreted or twisted in the broader social context in which they might be used. For example, one could draw fruitful comparisons to the plight of evolutionary biologists, who have to be careful how they present challenges to Darwinian orthodoxy in order to avoid having their statements used inappropriately by creationists or intelligent design theorists. Although these scientists cannot completely control how interest groups use their work, they can at least offer well-placed caveats that alert

79. Calabrese and Baldwin, "Toxicology Rethinks Its Central Belief."

80. I obtained this information from a colleague who wrote a reply to Calabrese and Baldwin's article. The response was rejected on the grounds that the original article was a commentary.

nonexperts to their major interpretive judgments or to potential misinterpretations of their claims.[81]

Such safeguards may not be particularly important in most fields of science, but they can be extremely valuable to the public in areas of science that are closely tied to political conflict. Consider, for example, that vested interest groups have a fairly successful record of using small, even unrepresentative bodies of scientific information to influence public-health regulations. We saw in chapters 4 and 6 that a limited number of industry studies on dioxin and BPA proved disproportionately influential in the formulation of public policy despite significant flaws in their methodologies.[82] Dan Fagin and his colleagues at the Center for Public Integrity argue that such strategies are widespread; they suggest that industry groups have a track record of being able to use questionable scientific evidence to slow chemical regulations to a standstill.[83] In contexts like this, the failure of researchers to clarify major interpretive judgments could very well hinder the scientific community's efforts to promote informed consent to public policy decisions.

Another reason for thinking that hormesis proponents should clarify their major, controversial value judgments is that it would require very little effort to provide at least some indication of alternative perspectives. This consideration makes it less likely that other responsibilities or considerations could easily override the responsibility to make these judgments known. Even if some researchers did believe that they have an ethical responsibility to draw greater societal attention to hormesis, it would still be relatively easy for them to acknowledge opposing perspectives at the same time. For example, Calabrese has been clarifying in much of his work that

81. Consider, for example, debates about whether it was unwise for the *New Scientist* journal to publish an issue that featured the heading "Darwin Was Wrong" across the cover (*New Scientist* 2692 [Jan. 24, 2009]), http://www.newscientist.com/issue/2692, accessed on 6/11/09. Although scientists would have little trouble realizing that the material in the journal did not provide significant support for creationism or intelligent design theory (it merely had to do with the appropriateness of Darwin's "tree of life" metaphor as an organizing principle in biology), it was nevertheless employed as a challenge to evolutionary theory; see http://scienceblogs.com/pharyngula/2009/01/new_scientist_says_darwin_was.php, accessed on 6/11/09.

82. Interestingly, industry groups are known for spending up to a million dollars to obtain and share reprints of studies that further their interests. This has come to be a worry, for example, as the marketing departments of pharmaceutical companies have come to see favorably designed scientific studies as an ideal way to promote their products; see Smith, "Trouble with Medical Journals." In the field of public health, an excellent example of how a small body of questionable research can be unjustifiably influential can be found in Myers et al., "Why Public Health Agencies Cannot Depend on Good Laboratory Practices."

83. Fagin, Lavelle, and the Center for Public Integrity, *Toxic Deception*. See also Beder, *Global Spin*; Markowitz and Rosner, *Deceit and Denial*; Shrader-Frechette, *Taking Action, Saving Lives*; Wargo, *Our Children's Toxic Legacy*.

hormetic low-dose effects can turn out to be harmful over the long run.[84] This demonstrates that even in short papers or brief discussions it is possible to acknowledge conflicting perspectives and to point out that there are important judgments to consider. Thus, given the danger that their work will be manipulated by vested interest groups, proponents of claims HD or HP arguably have much to gain (both ethically and epistemically) and little to lose by clarifying the major, socially significant judgments inherent in their work.

## CONCLUSION

Physicist Niels Bohr once quipped that "An expert is someone who has made all the mistakes which can be made in a very narrow field."[85] While this is obviously an exaggeration, it is clear that experts are prone to errors. Therefore, society depends on them to acknowledge (to the extent feasible) the limits, assumptions, and weaknesses associated with their knowledge claims. This chapter has developed an ethical framework that can assist them with this task. Its primary lesson has been that the extensive literature on informed consent in biomedical ethics can provide a set of ethical considerations and guidelines for scientific experts (see figure 6.1). It also has shown how these guidelines could provide advice to hormesis researchers. The chapter has concluded that proponents of claims HD and HP would be wise to clarify the ways in which they are making major judgments that rely on debatable interpretations of the available evidence. By doing so, they will help open up socially relevant research to societal scrutiny.

84. Calabrese, "Hormesis: Why It Is Important."
85. Mackay, *Dictionary of Scientific Quotations*, 35.

# 7

# The MCS and ED Cases

In 1996, while Al Gore was vice president of the United States, he wrote in the foreword to the book *Our Stolen Future*[1] that it was in many respects the sequel to Rachel Carson's famous work, *Silent Spring*. Like Carson's earlier plea for close examination of the health risks associated with synthetic pesticides, *Our Stolen Future* also raises concerns about the potentially damaging biological effects of synthetic chemicals. The focus of the more recent concerns, however, is evidence that a number of substances may mimic estrogen or otherwise interfere with the endocrine systems of humans and other animals. Because the endocrine system is sensitive to extremely low levels of hormones, especially during embryonic and fetal development, endocrine-disrupting chemicals have the potential to cause damage at surprisingly low levels of exposure. This chapter examines endocrine disruption (ED) and another low-dose chemical phenomenon, multiple chemical sensitivity (MCS), as additional case studies of the ways in which societal values can be more successfully brought to bear on contemporary environmental research. The chapter draws heavily from the excellent previous analyses of ED by Sheldon Krimsky and of MCS by Nicholas Ashford and Claudia Miller.[2]

The chapter shows how these additional cases support the major claims that the book draws from the hormesis case in chapters 2 through 6. First, research on MCS and ED supports the claim in chapter 2 that value judgments play an important role in the choice and design of studies, in the development of scientific language, in the interpretation and evaluation of studies, and in the application of research results to policy making. Second, the MCS and ED cases support the lesson in chapter 4 that current COI policies are insufficient to keep academic science from being overly influenced by powerful interest groups. Third, these cases provide further support for the lesson in chapter 5, namely, that concerned citizens and policy makers should diagnose what sorts of deliberative mechanisms are most appropriate

1. Colborn, Dumanoski, and Myers, *Our Stolen Future.*
2. Ashford and Miller, *Chemical Exposures*; Krimsky, *Hormonal Chaos.*

for responding to the value judgments in particular areas of policy-relevant research. Fourth, the MCS and ED cases provide further illustration of the lesson in chapter 6, which is that scientists would benefit from an EOE and that the Consent Principle can provide them with helpful guidance in this regard. Thus, these two additional case studies support the book's major claims by showing that they are well supported by other areas of research in addition to hormesis.

## MULTIPLE CHEMICAL SENSITIVITY

Ashford and Miller estimate that up to 5 percent of the population could suffer from diseases associated with MCS.[3] Individuals affected by this alleged disorder appear to experience an initial sensitization caused either by chronic exposure to toxic chemicals or by an acute exposure to one particular toxicant. These individuals subsequently appear to become extremely sensitive to a wide variety of chemicals and suffer chronic neurological, respiratory, and digestive problems. Interest in the phenomenon has risen during the past twenty years, especially because of its potential connections with the strange symptoms experienced by veterans of the first Gulf War. Nevertheless, physicians and public health researchers continue to disagree about whether it represents a psychological phenomenon akin to posttraumatic stress disorder or a physiological response to chemical exposures.[4]

### Four Kinds of Value Judgments

Chapter 2 argues that the hormesis case illustrates at least four ways in which value judgments permeate scientific practice. These same sorts of value judgments are clearly visible in research on multiple chemical sensitivity. Partly because of the split between psychological and physiological interpretations of the phenomenon, current research on MCS vividly illustrates the first category of value judgments highlighted in chapter 2, namely, values associated with choosing topics, developing hypotheses, and designing studies. Researchers who promote physiological accounts of MCS are taking great care to develop experimental systems that minimize the chance of false negatives. For example, one concern about previous blinded, controlled studies that found no evidence for physiological causes of MCS is that their control environments may still have included conditions to which the patients were sensitive. Therefore, some researchers who are particularly

3. Ashford and Miller, *Chemical Exposures.*
4. Ibid.; Kerns, *Environmentally Induced Illnesses*; Kroll-Smith and Floyd, *Bodies in Protest.*

sympathetic to MCS sufferers have been working with these patients to avoid easily missed design flaws and to develop experiments that have the best chance of uncovering evidence for physiological aspects of the phenomenon.[5] Other researchers have been working to find mechanistic pathways that could produce the symptoms characteristic of MCS.[6]

In contrast, those who prefer psychological interpretations of the phenomenon have pursued very different research approaches. Conflicts between veterans groups and the U.S. Department of Veterans Affairs (VA) have highlighted some of these strategies. Although it is not clear that Gulf War syndrome (GWS) is the same as MCS, it includes many of the same features, including apparent chemical sensitivities that many skeptics attribute to psychological causes. Many veterans believe that the research working group that the VA created in the 1990s was motivated by financial considerations to pursue research in a manner that would minimize evidence for physiological explanations of GWS.[7] One alleged strategy of the research working group was to avoid the provision of grants and needed data to scientists who were advancing physiological interpretations of GWS. Another alleged approach was to provide physical exams of thousands of veterans but to avoid performing tests (e.g., brain scans, genetic tests) that might provide evidence for a physiological problem. Moreover, the U.S. General Accounting Office (GAO) claims that the Department of Defense used questionable models for estimating the plume heights of chemical warfare agents released during the war, thereby underestimating the number of exposed troops.[8] In addition, the GAO claims that the VA emphasized epidemiological studies that were likely to be inconclusive, while minimizing research on possible treatments.[9] The research working group also supposedly funded a great deal of research on stress-related explanations of the phenomenon and on studies designed to downplay veterans' health problems. Furthermore, when it did find evidence for physiological factors at work in GWS, it allegedly resisted publishing the information. More recently, the VA may have become more open to physiological interpretations

5. See, for example, Ashford and Miller, *Chemical Exposures*; Joffres, Sampalli, and Fox, "Physiologic and Symptomatic Responses."

6. Gilbert, "Repeated Exposure to Lindane"; Pall, "Elevated Nitric Oxide/Peroxynitrite Theory."

7. See U.S. General Accounting Office, *Gulf War Illnesses*. See also *Statement of Ross Perot*, testimony before the Subcommittee on National Security, Veterans Affairs and International Relations, Committee on Government Reform, U.S. House of Representatives (Washington, D.C., Jan. 24, 2002), http://home.att.net/~LIGWVets/perot02.htm, accessed on 6/21/07. Many of the allegations in this paragraph are summarized in Perot's testimony.

8. U.S. General Accounting Office, *Gulf War Illnesses*.

9. U.S. General Accounting Office, *Federal Research Strategy*.

of GWS. Interestingly, this appears to be partly because billionaire Ross Perot poured a significant amount of money into preliminary research that could support physiological explanations of the phenomenon.[10]

The MCS case also provides an excellent example of the second category of value judgments identified in chapter 2, namely, those associated with defining phenomena and choosing descriptive terminology. Initially, various syndromes were defined in terms of the distinctive causes that appeared to initiate the intolerance of some chemically sensitive patients. These diseases include sick building syndrome (SBS), Gulf War syndrome, and wood preservative syndrome (WPS).[11] These syndromes are now often grouped under the more general concept of MCS, but this phenomenon has still been difficult to define. For example, Ashford and Miller present six different case definitions that various organizations and individuals have proposed.[12] The definitions vary in terms of the precise number of organ systems that must be affected, whether instances in which other accepted clinical or psychological conditions are present can also count as instances of MCS, and whether a provocative challenge or environmental exposure must be documented. Moreover, the range of terms for the phenomenon (with significant differences in their valences) is striking; they include idiopathic environmental intolerance, mass psychogenic illness, universal allergy, twentieth-century illness, environmental maladaptation syndrome, immunologic illness, and chemical acquired immune deficiency syndrome.[13]

One of the most controversial aspects of these different definitions and terms is their alleged potential to bias policy makers and members of the public toward the conclusion that MCS is either psychologically or physiologically based. For example, at an important 1996 conference in Berlin (sponsored by the International Program on Chemical Safety, or IPCS), the participants proposed that MCS be renamed "idiopathic environmental intolerances" (IEI). According to the conference's final report, the term "multiple chemical sensitivities" is problematic, because "it makes an unsupported judgment on causation [of the phenomenon]."[14] As Ronald Gots, one of the key participants at the conference, argued, "The premature use of the term multiple chemical sensitivities has hampered effective exploration of and response to this phenomenon, because it suggests, to the lay person, a physiological explanation."[15] The conference participants felt that

10. *Statement of Ross Perot*; Urbina, "Gas May Have Harmed Troops."
11. Ashford and Miller, *Chemical Exposures*.
12. Ibid., 314–15.
13. Ibid., 28.
14. Anonymous, "Conclusions and Recommendations."
15. Gots, "Multiple Chemical Sensitivities," S8.

the concept of IEI would be less likely to be misconstrued, and they defined it as follows:

- an acquired disorder with multiple recurrent symptoms
- associated with diverse environmental factors tolerated by the majority of people
- not explained by any known medical or psychiatric/psychologic disorder.[16]

In contrast, Ashford and Miller have expressed opposing concerns about how the concept of IEI could be misinterpreted:

> Soon after the Berlin meeting, certain workshop participants reported to the media and at scientific meetings that the "idiopathic" in IEI meant "self-originated" rather than "being of unknown etiology" (a more familiar meaning of the term as it is used in medicine)—and they erroneously proclaimed that IEI had become WHO's official name for the condition.[17]

Ashford and Miller worry that the IEI concept may have problems of its own that are the opposite of those associated with the MCS concept; in other words, it may facilitate an unjustified interpretation of the phenomenon as *psychogenic*. Because of similar concerns, a number of prominent researchers wrote a letter to the IPCS, denouncing what they perceived as significant conflicts of interest that may have caused the participants at the Berlin meeting to be biased in favor of corporate interests.[18]

One of the reasons for these sharp debates about appropriate scientific terminology in the MCS case is the fact that scientists must make significant value judgments about how to evaluate and interpret available scientific studies (i.e., the third category of value judgments discussed in chapter 2). Researchers currently disagree about the extent to which current evidence supports the conclusion that MCS is caused by psychological as opposed to physiological factors. Those who favor a psychogenic interpretation of the phenomenon claim that too many anomalous features are associated with a physiological interpretation. For example, scientists cannot currently explain why some individuals would exhibit a nonallergenic response to substances at much lower doses than most other people. Furthermore, the alleged fact that those with MCS experience adverse effects on many very different physiological systems at once (e.g., the digestive, endocrine, neurological, and immune systems) does not accord with typical toxicological responses. Finally, some researchers allege that MCS sufferers exhibit adaptation

16. Anonymous, "Conclusions and Recommendations," S188.
17. Ashford and Miller, *Chemical Exposures*, 284.
18. Ibid.

responses in which they initially experience severe reactions but then gradually exhibit lessened *apparent* sensitivity to the toxicants (unless they are separated from the chemicals and then reexposed to them).[19] Because of these anomalous features of the phenomenon, because controlled studies of MCS sufferers have produced conflicting results, because no mechanistic pathways have been conclusively shown to cause the disorder, and because many of the afflicted individuals exhibit psychological disturbances, many researchers regard the phenomenon as a psychologically caused somatization effect or panic response to toxic chemicals.[20]

Despite some researchers' arguments that MCS is primarily psychological in origin, mounting evidence supports further investigations of possible physiological origins. For example, researchers have shown that exposing rats to low doses of chlorinated pesticides can "kindle" components of the limbic system that other scientists have hypothesized to be associated with MCS.[21] In another study, Iris Bell found that women with chemical intolerances had a higher incidence than controls of physical symptoms that are associated with sensitization of the amygdala, which is within the limbic system.[22] More recent work has advanced some of Bell's mechanistic hypotheses,[23] and a group in Canada has provided improved techniques for controlling clinical studies of MCS patients and obtaining data consistent with physiological origins of the phenomenon.[24] The sharp disputes among current researchers regarding the nature of the MCS phenomenon provide another excellent example of the way researchers are forced to make difficult judgments when evaluating evidence for policy-relevant hypotheses.

A fourth category of value judgments associated with the MCS phenomenon involves applying scientific research to decision making. Decision makers must determine what sorts of mistakes they are most concerned to avoid as they choose treatments, make liability decisions, and categorize those who suffer from this mysterious disorder. All these decisions are likely to be influenced by conclusions about whether the disorder is

19. It is important to emphasize that the lessened sensitivity that MCS sufferers exhibit after being exposed to toxic chemicals for a period of time may be only *apparent*. It is possible that the patients are still harmed by the toxicants but that their obvious symptoms subside.

20. Escobar, Hoyos-Nervi, and Gara, "Medically Unexplained Physical Symptoms"; Staudenmayer et al., "Idiopathic Environmental Intolerance"; Tarlo et al., "Responses to Panic Induction Procedures."

21. "Kindling" refers to a sensitization of particular components of the brain, sometimes leading to seizures. See Gilbert, "Repeated Exposure to Lindane." See also Ashford and Miller, *Chemical Exposures*, 256ff.

22. Bell, "Clinically Relevant EEG Studies."

23. Pall, "Elevated Nitric Oxide/Peroxynitrite Theory."

24. Joffres, Sampalli, and Fox, "Physiologic and Symptomatic Responses."

physiological or psychological. For example, a psychological interpretation of the phenomenon would support psychiatric therapy as a crucial mode of treatment, whereas a physiological account would be more likely to encourage avoidance of chemical incitants. Moreover, psychological interpretations might be less likely than physiological ones to support accommodating public places to the requests of MCS patients or holding manufacturers legally liable for their symptoms.[25] We have already seen that many veterans have accused the VA and the Pentagon of promoting psychological interpretations of GWS in an attempt to lessen costs for treating veterans' health problems.[26] Many MCS patients also believe that psychological conceptualizations of their diseases are somewhat dismissive or otherwise derogatory relative to physiological ones.[27]

## Safeguarding Science

Chapters 4 through 6 explore ways of making these judgments associated with scientific research responsive to a representative array of societal values. Chapter 4 focuses on the importance of addressing financial conflicts of interest in university research, because those COIs have the potential to skew important judgments toward the interests of powerful stakeholders. We have seen that none of the three major elements of current university COI policies (i.e., disclosure, elimination of conflicts, management) appears likely to provide both an effective and a practical means of preventing the troublesome effects of COIs. Recall the central argument of the chapter: It seems unlikely that the conflicts can be eliminated; psychological research indicates that disclosure is an inadequate solution; and management attempts are likely to be either too bureaucratic or inadequate. The MCS case further supports this conclusion. If one considers the range of judgments described previously in this section, it seems quite unlikely that worrisome influences could be systematically eliminated via management approaches. Moreover, these value judgments permeate the research process so extensively that those who receive COI disclosures will have difficulty

25. Gots, "Multiple Chemical Sensitivities." Gots does note, however, that at least some policy responses may not be sensitive to the distinction between psychological and physiological origins of the phenomenon. For example, he suggests that one might qualify for Social Security benefits as long as one could provide adequate evidence of disability, regardless of the origins of one's symptoms. Moreover, Ashford and Miller note that, in at least some cases, it may actually be easier to obtain workers' compensation if one is diagnosed with a widely accepted psychiatric problem (e.g., posttraumatic stress disorder) than with a highly disputed physiological problem (such as MCS); see Ashford and Miller, *Chemical Exposures*, 156.

26. *Statement of Ross Perot.*

27. Kroll-Smith and Floyd, *Bodies in Protest.*

figuring out how much to discount information from those who have financial conflicts.

Consider, for example, that researchers appear to make different decisions about the first category of judgments (i.e., choice and design of studies) depending on whether they are inclined to support a psychological or a physiological interpretation of the phenomenon. In particular, powerful groups (e.g., the military, corporate defendants facing litigation) have financial incentives to fund research that promotes psychological accounts of the phenomenon. Nevertheless, COI management committees are quite unlikely to prevent researchers from pursuing studies that tend to support the preferred hypotheses of their study sponsors unless the study designs are flagrantly biased. Therefore, it appears that the overall body of research on MCS runs the risk of being skewed toward psychological interpretations of the phenomenon unless patient advocacy groups can leverage enough funding from the federal government (or from wealthy patrons like Ross Perot) to pursue research projects that address their concerns.

Values associated with the second, third, and fourth categories of value judgments (e.g., choice of terminology, evaluation of studies, application of research to decision making) are also likely to fly under the radar of COI management committees. For example, it seems improbable that management committees would block researchers from employing their preferred terminology for describing the phenomenon, even though the various interest groups debating MCS are very concerned about the connotations of different terms. Moreover, although COI committees could prevent obviously biased interpretations of a researcher's own studies, they would be unlikely to prevent scientists from making questionable judgments in their evaluations of studies performed by others (as we will see later in this section). In addition, to the extent that scientists interpret research in questionable ways, they will contribute to dubious societal decision making. Therefore, COI policies alone will not guarantee an adequate representation of societal perspectives in the production of MCS research or in its interpretation and application to policy. Policy makers should therefore consider whether they need to employ the types of strategies suggested in chapter 4, such as encouraging more funding of MCS research by those who do not have a vested interest in the outcome.

### Diagnosing Deliberation

The MCS case study also supports the lesson in chapter 5, namely, that policy makers would do well to diagnose more carefully the most appropriate forms of deliberation in response to policy-relevant areas of research. The important 1996 Berlin conference mentioned earlier in this chapter illustrates the dangers of organizing a deliberative process without accurately determining the range of stakeholders who ought to be represented. We have already seen that the conference participants suggested that the label "multiple chemical sensitivity" be replaced by the label "idiopathic environmental intolerances." They claimed that the MCS label might provide unjustified support for physiological (as opposed to psychogenic) interpretations of the phenomenon.

The conference was funded by the International Program on Chemical Safety, together with several German agencies. The IPCS is, in turn, funded by the United Nations Environmental Program (UNEP), the International Labor Organization (ILO), and the World Health Organization (WHO). Because policy-making organizations designed the conference, it could have served as a promising opportunity to institute this book's recommendations to engage in a thoughtful diagnosis of appropriate deliberative formats. Unfortunately, their poor design of the deliberative process instead resulted in a great deal of conflict and lack of trust among the stakeholders and scientists involved in MCS debates.

Ashford and Miller argue that the conference was inappropriately skewed toward industry perspectives in at least three ways. First, all four invited representatives from nongovernmental organizations were from industry-oriented NGOs. Second, no representatives of labor, environmental, or MCS patient groups were present. Third, the person invited to present the U.S. perspective on MCS, Ronald Gots, was the director of both a corporate-sponsored research institute and a service that provides medical experts to corporate defendants in legal cases involving MCS.[28] The final report of the Berlin conference,[29] which espouses the concept of IEI, was published in a special supplement of *Regulatory Toxicology and Pharmacology*, which was funded by Gots's corporate-sponsored Environmental Sensitivities Research Institute. Although the journal acknowledged its funding source, it described the institute only as "a charitable, non-profit, scientific, and educational organization dedicated to the open exchange of objective scientific information and data among physicians, scientists, industry, the government, and the general public."[30] Moreover, in addition to the Berlin report, the supplement contains the proceedings of a conference that was partially sponsored by the National Medical Advisory Service, which "provides medical experts to corporate defendants involved in litigation over MCS."[31]

28. Ashford and Miller, *Chemical Exposures*, 284.
29. Anonymous, "Conclusions and Recommendations."
30. Ashford and Miller, *Chemical Exposures*, 285.
31. Ibid., 284.

In part because of the appearance of bias in the design of the conference and its aftermath, it inflamed disputes about MCS rather than generating productive deliberation. As mentioned earlier in this section, a number of scientists later repudiated the "IEI" label and suggested that it was being misused by interest groups who wanted to advance the notion that MCS is a purely psychological phenomenon. As Ashford and Miller report, many of these scientists also illustrated their awareness of the need for more balanced deliberative proceedings by sending a letter to the sponsors of the IPCS after the Berlin meeting:

> [Eighty] prominent and predominantly academic and independent scientists and physicians (including the former directors of the U.S. National Institute of Environmental Health Sciences, the National Institute for Occupational Safety and Health, and the National Cancer Institute)...urged that IPCS and its UN sponsors...[i]mmediately halt work toward the issuance of reports on MCS...[,] assign NGO places to legitimate NGOs and, to the fullest extent possible,...identify and exclude scientists with financial conflicts of interest.[32]

The letter also argued that the IPCS should publicly report conflicts of interest for those who were currently involved in its scientific panels.

Future efforts to diagnose the most appropriate deliberative processes for responding to MCS should also take account of two powerful social dynamics that are affecting the way scientists and physicians respond to the phenomenon. First, MCS is caught in a turf war between two groups of medical doctors: traditional allergists and clinical ecologists. Although the specialty of clinical ecology is closely related to the study of allergy, clinical ecologists have largely separated from the mainstream community of allergists because of their belief that at least some environmental sensitivities (such as MCS) may not be mediated by the antibody IgE. Ashford and Miller note that the study of allergy, which was defined in 1906 as the study of "altered reactivity" of any origin, was not well respected throughout much of the twentieth century.[33] Allergy shots were even called "witchcraft" or "voodoo medicine" by some physicians. The discovery in 1967 that many allergic reactions might be caused by the action of IgE provided a valuable boost to the respectability of the discipline. Thus, Ashford and Miller note that the dismissive attitude of the American Academy of Allergy, Asthma, and Immunology toward clinical ecologists may be due, at least in part, to the challenge that clinical ecology represents to the newfound scientific respectability of the study of allergy.

32. Ibid., 285.
33. Ibid., 20.

A second set of social forces that complicates the design of deliberative proceedings concerning MCS consists of its economic and legal ramifications (e.g., disability benefits, accommodations in housing and employment, compensation). As discussed earlier in this chapter, agencies such as the Department of Defense (which has strong financial interests in the outcome of these debates) have instituted policies that exacerbate the difficulties of Gulf War veterans who seek evidence that their symptoms are physiologically linked to wartime chemical exposures.[34] This second set of factors (i.e., legal and economic ones) has also intertwined with the dispute between allergists and clinical ecologists. Court cases regarding compensation for MCS now typically pit members of these two medical communities against each other as expert witnesses for the opposing sides. Thus, Ashford and Miller worry that "Blind adherence to old paradigms, coupled with vested financial interests, and the reputational consequences of rejecting prior positions are powerful incentives militating against change [toward physiological characterizations of MCS]."[35] Whether or not those who support physiological interpretations of MCS are correct, deliberative proceedings seem unlikely to promote the instrumental benefits of increased trust and acceptance of decisions unless policy makers take care to incorporate an adequate range of perspectives on the phenomenon.

## Ethics for Experts

The MCS case also provides support for the claims of chapter 6, which highlights the importance of developing an ethics of expertise for scientific researchers. It proposes a Consent Principle, according to which scientists have prima facie responsibilities to promote the public's ability to provide informed consent to personal and social decisions that draw on scientific information. The MCS case supports the analysis in chapter 6 in two major ways. First, it provides further evidence that scientists face a variety of situations in which they need ethical guidance concerning their dissemination of information to the public. Second, it illustrates that the Consent Principle has the potential to provide researchers with practical ethical guidance. As in the hormesis case, the goal here is not to judge definitively whether the scientists involved in these cases actually acted inappropriately but rather to show how an ethics of expertise could provide them (and the recipients of scientific information) with helpful guidance.

Let us consider some of the situations related to MCS research in which scientists faced ethical questions about how to disseminate information.

34. Zavestoski et al., "Science, Policy, Activism, and War."
35. Ashford and Miller, *Chemical Exposures*, 287.

Perhaps the most important value judgment facing researchers who investigate MCS is whether to characterize it as a physiological or a psychological phenomenon. Ronald Gots makes this quite explicit:

> The current debates surrounding multiple chemical sensitivities are all rooted in a single question: Is this phenomenon primarily a psychogenic or a toxicodynamic disorder? That is, are symptoms due to an emotional response to perceived chemical toxicity or to a pathological interaction between chemical agents and organ systems?[36]

Thus, those on both sides of the dispute over the origins of MCS face a series of questions when they disseminate information about the phenomenon: (1) Should they acknowledge only their preferred interpretation of the phenomenon, or should they acknowledge other interpretations as well? (2) If they should present alternatives, which ones need to be presented and with how much detail? (3) Should social or ethical considerations (e.g., compassion for MCS sufferers or concern about economic costs) play any role in how these interpretations are presented to the public?

In order to illustrate the applicability of the Consent Principle, let us consider several specific instances of information dissemination. The 1996 Berlin meeting is an excellent case for considering the ethical responsibilities of MCS researchers. As previously mentioned, the participants at the meeting proposed a new term, "idiopathic environmental intolerances," for the MCS phenomenon. Most observers agree that this term is less likely to suggest a physiological etiology for the phenomenon than the "MCS" label; what remains in dispute is whether the IEI term actually provides *too little* emphasis on physiological interpretations.

Without trying to decide which term (if either) is ultimately more acceptable, this chapter has already discussed two ways in which the IEI concept was questionably disseminated. First, some participants at the Berlin meeting, when questioned by members of the media, indicated that the term "idiopathic" in the IEI label means "self-originated" (as opposed to the word's typical medical meaning, "of unknown origin").[37] Such a claim would potentially violate the Consent Principle, insofar as it would inaccurately represent the meeting's official report on the IEI concept,[38] let alone the views of the scientific community as a whole. A second questionable issue is that the report of the Berlin meeting was published in a supplementary issue of the journal *Regulatory Toxicology and Pharmacology* without acknowledging the financial conflicts of interest of the organization that provided

36. Gots, "Multiple Chemical Sensitivities," S8.
37. Ashford and Miller, *Chemical Exposures*, 282ff.
38. See Anonymous, "Conclusions and Recommendations."

the funding for the supplement. Under the Consent Principle, information about financial conflicts of interest would arguably be important to provide, given that the reasonable-person standard of disclosure would probably recommend such information (see chapter 6).[39]

Other cases to consider in the MCS context involve strongly opinionated articles that promote particular judgments regarding the nature of the phenomenon. Two examples include Gots's paper in the same issue of *Regulatory Toxicology and Pharmacology* as the report on the Berlin meeting and a more recent paper by Herman Staudenmayer and his colleagues.[40] Both articles provide very strong endorsements of psychogenic interpretations of MCS. As in the case of the Berlin meeting report, one worry about Gots's paper is that he did not provide any information about his financial conflicts of interest, even though he "is not only the director of an anti-MCS 'research institute' but... also directs the National Medical Advisory Service."[41] His failure to disclose this information is especially worrisome, given that a major theme of his paper is that psychogenic characterizations of the phenomenon weaken claims for compensation and fail to support regulatory controls or accommodations for workers.[42]

Another concern about these papers is that they may have provided insufficient or misleading information about the justification for various interpretations of MCS. For example, Gots claims in the abstract of his paper that "Everything that is known about MCS to date strongly suggests behavioral and psychogenic explanations for symptoms."[43] The final paragraph of the paper returns to the same theme: "There is precious little about the MCS phenomenon which even remotely suggests a physical disease absent at least a major psychogenic component."[44] Staudenmayer et al. make almost the same claim in their paper: "There is no convincing evidence to support the fundamental postulate that IEI has a toxic aetiology; the hypothesized biological processes and mechanisms are implausible."[45] Nevertheless, the notion that "everything" that is known about MCS "strongly" suggests a psychogenic explanation hardly seems to represent the views of many thinkers in the scientific community, either at the time that Gots was writing or at present. Other researchers had published a major criticism of psychogenic

39. See Wilkinson, "Research, Informed Consent, and the Limits of Disclosure."

40. Gots, "Multiple Chemical Sensitivities"; Staudenmayer et al., "Idiopathic Environmental Intolerance."

41. Ashford and Miller, *Chemical Exposures*, 284. Recall that the National Medical Advisory Service provides medical experts to corporate defendants.

42. Gots, "Multiple Chemical Sensitivities," S13.

43. Ibid., S8.

44. Ibid., S14.

45. Staudenmayer et al., "Idiopathic Environmental Intolerance," 235.

characterizations just two years before Gots's publication.[46] Claudia Miller and Howard Mitzel had also recently published evidence that favored a physiological etiology for the phenomenon.[47] More recently, numerous authors have argued that psychogenic characterizations are by no means the only plausible ones, given current evidence.[48]

Gots and Staudenmayer et al. could respond by noting that they do mention a good deal of work by thinkers who promote physiological characterizations of MCS;[49] they merely argue that it is unconvincing. They could also claim that their articles were written not for the general public but for other scientific researchers, who are already aware of the scientific community's mixed perspectives on psychogenic interpretations of MCS. The goal of this chapter is not to make definitive claims about whether Gots and Staudenmayer et al. disseminated information about MCS in an unacceptable manner. Nevertheless, there are at least two reasons for thinking that the Consent Principle would encourage a less dismissive description of alternative judgments about MCS. First, the claim that virtually all the evidence strongly supports a psychogenic origin for the phenomenon could plausibly be interpreted as false, given that numerous other researchers believe that the available evidence supports physiological characterizations and that the evidence for psychogenic characterizations is still incomplete. Second, given the current social context for chemical regulation, in which large vested-interest groups can heavily emphasize small bodies of information (see chapter 6), the claims of Gots and Staudenmayer et al. may be widely disseminated among those who do not have an adequate sense of opposing perspectives within the scientific community.

Other important scenarios in which information about MCS is disseminated involve clinical discussions between physicians and their patients. Although this book focuses on the ethical responsibilities of scientific researchers and policy makers, it is important to note that other contexts become relevant when controversial scientific research involves a disease phenomenon that directly impacts patients. Some of these scenarios can be adequately addressed by appealing to physicians' traditional responsibilities to obtain informed consent before commencing major medical interventions.

46. Davidoff and Fogarty, "Psychogenic Origins of Multiple Chemical Sensitivities Syndrome."

47. Miller and Mitzel, "Chemical Sensitivity Attributed to Pesticide Exposures versus Remodeling."

48. See, for example, Caress and Steinemann, "Review of a Two-phase Population Study"; Joffres, Sampalli, and Fox, "Physiologic and Symptomatic Responses"; Pall, "Elevated Nitric Oxide/Peroxynitrite Theory."

49. For example, both Gots and Staudenmayer et al. cite papers by Iris Bell, a leading advocate of physiological interpretations of MCS.

In other cases, physicians informally provide advice about phenomena like MCS to patients, and it is in these settings that the Consent Principle could provide valuable guidance. For example, it would support Ashford and Miller's suggestion that physicians should provide their patients with a wide variety of perspectives on MCS so that they can choose for themselves how they want to respond to the phenomenon.[50] The ability of an MCS patient to make informed decisions would be challenged by a physician who made an overly confident claim that the patient's symptoms were psychogenic (or physiological) in origin without acknowledging that the nature of MCS is highly disputed. Open acknowledgment of these value judgments is particularly important, given that some studies suggest that psychotherapies can be quite harmful (at least for some MCS patients), whereas other MCS patients appear to respond well to psychiatric interventions.[51] Thus, in both clinical and research settings, it appears that an ethics of expertise would be valuable in the MCS case and that the Consent Principle would provide helpful guidance.

## ENDOCRINE DISRUPTION

As in the hormesis and MCS cases, the endocrine disruption phenomenon initially surfaced in the form of data that researchers did not expect. Some of these data involved traditional laboratory investigations, but other data came from observations in the field. For example, bird watchers in the 1950s noticed that bald eagles in Florida were "loafing" rather than engaging in their normal mating rituals.[52] Near Lake Michigan in the 1960s, researchers gathered data that seemed to reflect dropping mink reproduction rates, and soon many mink had no surviving children.[53] In the 1970s, female western gulls occupied nests together in southern California.[54] In the 1980s, researchers collected data that reflected surprisingly low hatching and survival rates for alligator eggs in Lake Apopka, Florida.[55] And, during the latter half of the twentieth century, researchers gathered results that seemed to reflect dropping sperm counts in human males.[56]

50. Ashford and Miller, *Chemical Exposures*.

51. Psychiatric therapies appear to be quite problematic in the following study: Gibson, Elms, and Ruding, "Perceived Treatment Efficacy." In contrast, they seem to show more promise in the following: Lacour et al., "Interdisciplinary Therapeutic Approach."

52. Broley, "Plight of the American Bald Eagle."

53. Aulerich, Ringer, and Iwamoto, "Reproductive Failure and Mortality in Mink."

54. Hunt and Hunt, "Female-female Pairing in Western Gulls."

55. Woodward et al., "Low Clutch Viability of American Alligators."

56. Carlsen et al., "Evidence for Decreasing Quality of Semen."

Sheldon Krimsky argues that, because these phenomena occurred across a wide range of disciplinary boundaries, it was difficult for researchers to recognize them all as examples of the same underlying causal processes (i.e., the disruptive effects of estrogenic substances).[57] Theo Colborn, a zoologist who worked in environmental NGOs, played the crucial role of synthesizing information from a number of fields and bringing together interdisciplinary groups of researchers to reflect on the findings. According to Krimsky, the ED hypothesis crystallized from three different bodies of evidence. First, clinicians found that the children of women who were given the synthetic estrogen DES during pregnancy displayed a variety of health problems, including reproductive cancers and damaged sperm. Second, biologists were observing a wide variety of problems (many linked to the endocrine system) in wildlife exposed to environmental pollutants. Third, epidemiologists were finding evidence that global human sperm counts might be declining.

Colborn suggested that a wide variety of these phenomena might be the consequence of pollutants that mimicked or otherwise interfered with the endocrine system, thus producing harmful effects on wildlife and possibly also on humans. An especially frightening feature of this hypothesis is that organisms are very sensitive to hormones, especially during the early stages of pre- and postnatal development, which suggests that endocrine-disrupting chemicals could cause harmful effects at particularly low levels of exposure. Researchers have speculated that these effects could include reproductive cancers, behavioral changes, low sperm counts in male organisms, alteration of immune function, and decline in species populations.[58]

## Four Kinds of Value Judgments

As with MCS, it is striking in the case of ED how environmentalists and industry groups have developed exceedingly different approaches to the first category of value judgments identified in chapter 2 (i.e., choosing research topics, asking questions, and designing studies). For example, values associated with public health and environmental well-being played a major role in the development of the ED hypothesis as a research project. From the 1950s to the 1980s, scientists had noticed numerous anomalous and seemingly disconnected environmental phenomena, including problems with wildlife such as alligators, mink, and bald eagles.[59] Partly because these phenomena

57. Krimsky, *Hormonal Chaos.*

58. For further information about endocrine disruption, see Colborn, Dumanoski, and Myers, *Our Stolen Future*; Krimsky, *Hormonal Chaos*; NRC, *Hormonally Active Agents in the Environment.*

59. See Colborn, Dumanoski, and Myers, *Our Stolen Future.*

crossed various disciplinary boundaries, it was difficult to draw connections between them. Sheldon Krimsky suggests that it was Theo Colborn's passionate desire to investigate environmental problems that encouraged her to connect the dots between multiple, seemingly disconnected phenomena in order to develop a unifying explanatory hypothesis.[60]

In sharp contrast to Colborn's values, many industry groups appear to be choosing and designing studies in a manner that tries to minimize concerns related to endocrine disruption. Frederick vom Saal suggests, for example, that much of the motivation to engage in hormesis research has stemmed from the chemical industry as it tries to minimize worries about endocrine disruption. By investigating the hypothesis that many chemicals may have beneficial rather than adverse effects at low doses, he suggests that they are trying to deflect attention from the harmful low-dose effects associated with endocrine disruption.[61] Vom Saal also reports that the industry studies that do address ED appear to be designed to minimize the likelihood of identifying harmful effects. He reports on a major discrepancy between various studies of bisphenol A (BPA), an endocrine disruptor that is used in the manufacture of many plastics: "For government-funded published studies, 94 of 104 (90 percent) report significant effects at doses of BPA < 50 mg/kg/day. No industry-funded studies (0 of 11, or 0 percent) report significant effects at these same doses."[62] He argues that the discrepancy between these studies can be attributed to four design features that tended to produce negative results in the industry studies: "strain of experimental animal [i.e., using an especially insensitive strain], misinterpretation of finding no significant effects for the positive controls, animal feed, and specific end point examined."[63] Considering this correlation between study results on endocrine disruptors and funding sources, it is worrisome that the chemical industry is building "a formidable war chest to combat the theory of endocrine-disrupting chemicals," including an astonishing $500 million from the Chemical Manufacturers Association devoted to screening chemicals for endocrine effects.[64]

Like the hormesis and MCS cases, ED research also illustrates the second set of value judgments associated with scientific research (i.e., the choice of categories and terminology). For example, defining "endocrine disruption" continues to involve difficult choices. When the EPA developed its Endocrine Disruptor Research Program in 1996, it defined an endocrine disruptor as

60. Krimsky, *Hormonal Chaos.*
61. Vom Saal, "Hormesis Controversy."
62. Vom Saal and Hughes, "Extensive New Literature," 928.
63. Ibid., 928.
64. Krimsky, *Hormonal Chaos*, 98.

"any exogenous agent that *interferes* with the production, release, transport, metabolism, binding action, or elimination of natural hormones in the body."[65] At an important meeting in 1996 that was organized by the international Organization for Economic Cooperation and Development (OECD), the European Union, and the World Health Organization, endocrine disruptors were defined somewhat differently as "any exogenous substance that *causes adverse health effects* in an intact organism, or its progeny, consequent to changes in endocrine function."[66]

The differences between the EPA and OECD definitions of ED appear to be significant not just for scientific research but also for society at large. Whereas the EPA merely requires interference with the endocrine system, the OECD explicitly requires evidence that a substance actually causes harm to the organism. Therefore, as Krimsky emphasizes, one might think that the OECD definition sets too high a standard of proof for identifying endocrine disruptors, especially for the purposes of formulating public policy.[67] Because of this worry, the U.S. Endocrine Disruptor Screening and Testing Advisory Committee (EDSTAC) failed to achieve consensus when it tried to define the term "endocrine disruptor."[68] Those involved in the proceedings recognized that, on one hand, choosing a definition (like the EPA's) that refers to any chemical interference with the endocrine system would make it easier to classify agents as endocrine disruptors. It would potentially place the burden of proof on industrial manufacturers and users of those chemicals to show that their chemicals should not be stringently regulated. On the other hand, choosing a definition (like the OECD's) that requires evidence of adverse health effects could potentially place the burden of proof on consumer and public-health organizations to show that chemicals should be regulated as endocrine disruptors. Thus, choices about how to define an endocrine disruptor could perhaps affect whether the burden of proof for identifying harmful chemicals is placed on industry groups or on the public.

As in the hormesis and MCS cases, the terminology employed in describing ED is also controversial, in part because it may have societal consequences. Even the term "endocrine disruptor" is debated. When a National Academy of Sciences panel analyzed the issue, it chose to use the term "'hormonally active agent" (HAA) in place of "endocrine disruptor" because it believed that "the term [endocrine disruptor] is fraught with emotional overtones and was tantamount to a prejudgment of potential outcomes."[69] Moreover, no matter

65. Ibid., 82; italics added.
66. Ibid., 88; italics added.
67. Ibid.
68. Ibid., 214.
69. NRC, *Hormonally Active Agents*, 21.

whether one refers to "endocrine disruptors" or "hormonally active agents," Theo Colborn's effort to unify previously diverse findings under a single term is itself significant. As Krimsky has emphasized, the attempt to unify disparate phenomena can have a significant influence on public attitudes:

> The significance of the integrative concept [i.e., endocrine disruption or HAA] is that it magnifies the importance of many otherwise disparate, less notable events. In some respects, the term *environmental endocrine disrupter* is for the media analogous to the term *cancer*. Many variant diseases are all categorized under the rubric of cancer because they have in common abnormally formed, unregulated, and invasive cells. Their causes, mechanisms, and outcomes may be vastly different. But having a single concept that unites these variant diseases heightens the public's attention to each individual disease.... Because so many outcomes are linked to the term [endocrine disruptor or HAA], the mere frequency with which the term is used in the media reifies the concept in the public mind.[70]

Krimsky reports that public concern, which was arguably influenced by Colborn's efforts to develop a unifying hypothesis, promoted congressional attention to ED. This congressional concern in turn yielded increased research funding to study it. Thus, the ED phenomenon, which formerly fell largely between the cracks of mainstream scientific disciplines, became a major topic for scientific research.

Turning to the third category of value judgments discussed in chapter 2 (i.e., interpretation and evaluation of studies), the most significant questions in the ED case concern the likelihood that endocrine-disrupting chemicals are currently having particular harmful effects on humans.[71] For a good example of the complex range of judgments involved in assessing human health risks from endocrine disruptors, we can consider the question of whether (and, if so, why) human sperm counts are declining. As Krimsky reports, the Danish researcher Niels Skakkebaek initially promoted the notion that human sperm counts were in decline on the basis of a meta-analysis of sixty-one papers published between 1938 and 1990, including data from twenty-one countries and fifteen thousand men.[72] Some evidence (including lowered sperm count and sperm quality in pesticide workers, children of mothers exposed to DES, and rats exposed to endocrine disruptors) suggested that endocrine-disrupting chemicals might play a role in this apparent decline. Nevertheless, this evidence was not entirely compelling. Skakkebaek and his coworkers resisted full-scale acceptance of the judgment that ED was the explanation for human sperm declines, and they

70. Krimsky, *Hormonal Chaos*, 104.
71. NRC, *Hormonally Active Agents*; Safe, "Endocrine Disruptors and Human Health."
72. Krimsky, *Hormonal Chaos*, 32.

dissociated themselves from groups like Greenpeace, which actively promoted such a conclusion.

In fact, even the claim that human sperm counts are declining rests on a number of interpretive choices. Some studies published in the journal *Fertility and Sterility* around the same time as Skakkebaek's work suggested that the sperm levels of men in several U.S. cities had remained relatively constant over a period of twenty years.[73] One of the authors of these papers argued that apparent sperm declines could be explained on the basis of geographic variability around the world. Others argued that the apparent decline could be the result of confounding factors (e.g., different sperm-counting methods) or an artifact of the statistical modeling procedures used for analyzing data in previous studies. One review study concluded that the data examined by Skakkebaek did show a significant trend of declining sperm counts (despite some conflicting data in specific locations) in at least some parts of the world (namely, the United States and northern Europe).[74] Nevertheless, these debates (as well as comparable disagreements about whether endocrine-disrupting chemicals might be associated with increased breast cancer risks) illustrate the range of methodological judgments involved in interpreting scientific data on pollution and evaluating results from multiple studies.

These judgments about the extent to which current evidence supports the existence of health effects on humans (in addition to the more obvious effects on wildlife) also inform the fourth category of choices discussed in chapter 2 (namely, those associated with applying scientific research to public policy). In particular, decision makers have to decide how much evidence to demand for endocrine-disrupting effects on humans before taking particular actions in response to the phenomenon. For example, Krimsky reports that New York senator Alphonse D'Amato was the first public official to promote the routine screening of pesticides for estrogenic effects, and he was motivated by concerns among his constituents about unusually high breast cancer rates.[75] Although the evidence of a link between endocrine-disrupting chemicals and breast cancer was not decisive, he was willing to promote further research by proposing a screening proposal that was adopted in an amendment to the 1996 Food Quality Protection Act (FQPA).

This screening proposal provides a good example of value judgments associated with the application of scientific research to policy. For instance, in a background paper developed as part of its preparatory process for

73. Ibid., 35–36.
74. Swan, Elkin, and Fenster, "Have Sperm Densities Declined?"
75. Krimsky, *Hormonal Chaos*, 70.

responding to the FQPA, the EPA claimed: "While we are working to answer these important scientific questions... EPA believes the potential implications of endocrine disruptors for our children and for our future are serious enough to warrant the agency taking prudent, preventive steps, without waiting for the research to be complete."[76] This judgment (i.e., that at least some human health threats are sufficiently serious that they warrant action in the absence of conclusive scientific information about their causes) closely resembles the "precautionary principle," a concept that policy makers and citizen groups have debated heavily in recent years.[77]

## Safeguarding Science

As in the cases of hormesis and MCS, COI policies appear unlikely to prevent worrisome influences on ED research. With respect to the first category of value judgments (i.e., design of studies), we have seen evidence that industry-funded studies tend to come to conclusions that differ from those of independently funded studies. Nevertheless, if vom Saal is correct that these discrepancies are sometimes the result of subtle design features such as the strain of rat or the type of feed chosen for a study, it seems unlikely that COI committees would catch worrisome value judgments of this sort. In fact, it took an extensive review by the National Toxicology Program to settle debates about the trustworthiness of vom Saal's studies of BPA; a generic COI committee could hardly be expected to appreciate the range of judgments associated with endocrine-disruption studies.[78] Moreover, as in the hormesis and MCS cases, it seems quite likely that management committees will completely ignore the categories and terminology that university researchers choose to promote (i.e., judgments of the second type identified in chapter 2).

When it comes to the interpretation and evaluation of studies (i.e., the third category of value judgments), Krimsky's analysis of the ED case well illustrates how financial COIs can raise concerns about the way researchers interpret and evaluate studies. Stephen Safe, a prominent toxicologist at

76. Environmental Protection Agency, Office of Pollution Prevention and Toxic Substances, *EPA Activities on Endocrine Disrupters: Background Paper*, prepared for the meeting "Endocrine Disruption by Chemicals: Next Steps in Chemical Screening and Testing," May 15–16, 1996, Washington, D.C.; quoted in Krimsky, *Hormonal Chaos*, 207–208.

77. See, for example, Manson, "Formulating the Precautionary Principle"; Morris, ed., *Rethinking Risk and the Precautionary Principle*; Raffensperger and Tickner, *Protecting Public Health and the Environment*; Sandin, "Dimensions of the Precautionary Principle"; Sunstein, *Laws of Fear*.

78. National Toxicology Program, *National Toxicology Program's Report*, accessed on 11/29/08.

Texas A&M University, has questioned various elements of the ED hypothesis. Invited to write an editorial for the *New England Journal of Medicine*, he penned a response to a study that appeared to show no link between estrogenic compounds and breast cancer.[79] Krimsky complains that "The journal's editors had an opportunity to yield the editorial page to someone who could point out the limitations of the study or emphasize the difficulty of finding such links. Instead they chose Safe, who cast the study as the definitive case against the industrial link to breast cancer."[80] It is worrisome that Safe had recently been receiving research funds from the Chemical Manufacturers Association, and he had also received money from the Chemical Industry Institute of Toxicology at various points during his career. The journal's editor in chief provided several justifications for allowing Safe to write the editorial despite having these financial COIs: The editor did not know about Safe's funding, Safe had stopped receiving the funding a few months before publishing the piece, and he was also receiving funding (in fact, a majority of his funds) from neutral sources.[81] Nevertheless, as chapter 4 points out, psychological research indicates that the influences of COIs can remain even after they have been eliminated.[82] Because review essays and editorials incorporate a particularly wide range of value judgments, it is difficult to decide how much to discount Safe's perspective. The ED case therefore illustrates once again how industry funding has the unfortunate effect of reducing the availability of relatively neutral sources of scientific information, even from public universities.

Another worry in the ED case is that interest groups may exert pressure on university researchers who do not themselves have financial conflicts. After Frederick vom Saal published his classic study, which first linked BPA with endocrine disruption, he was assailed both personally and publicly by chemical-industry representatives even though his results were ultimately vindicated by a National Toxicology Program review.[83] Other prominent scientists who have uncovered apparent endocrine-disrupting effects have dealt with almost the same pattern of industry skepticism, including apparent efforts to prevent or delay publication of the research.[84] Because of this

79. Safe, "Editorial: Xenoestrogens and Breast Cancer."

80. Krimsky, *Hormonal Chaos*, 43.

81. Ibid.

82. Miller, "Commentary."

83. Nagel et al., "Relative Binding Affinity-Serum Modified Access"; Krimsky, *Hormonal Chaos*, 166–67; National Toxicology Program, *National Toxicology Program's Report*, accessed on 11/29/08.

84. See, for example, Hayes, "There Is No Denying This"; Lee, "Popular Pesticide Faulted." For an extensive discussion of the harassment of scientists who obtain results that conflict with industry interests, see McGarity and Wagner, *Bending Science*.

pressure, less courageous or well-positioned researchers might simply avoid publishing their findings or propose weaker conclusions on the basis of their studies, thereby allowing industry groups to influence the judgments of scientists who do not themselves have financial COIs.

## Diagnosing Deliberation

As in the MCS case, policy makers have already organized some deliberative forums on ED. Fortunately, the deliberations on endocrine disruption illustrate the advantages of engaging in a thoughtful diagnosis process, as opposed to the disadvantages associated with failing to engage in adequate diagnosis (as seen in the MCS case). We have already observed that the EPA developed an Endocrine Disruptor Screening and Testing Advisory Committee in response to the Food Quality Protection Act of 1996. The EDSTAC had to make controversial decisions about which chemicals to test for endocrine-disrupting effects and what sorts of tests to perform. Fortunately, the EPA took at least four steps to incorporate an adequate array of stakeholder perspectives in its deliberative processes.[85] First, the agency engaged in an initial process of diagnosis by meeting with crucial stakeholders to discuss how to work cooperatively in developing a screening strategy. Second, once the EDSTAC was put together, the committee's meetings were open to the public and located in multiple parts of the country. Third, the committee's membership included a wide array of affiliations that represented an array of interested and affected parties, including "EPA, other federal agencies, state agencies, various sectors of industry, water providers, worker protection, national environmental groups, environmental justice groups, public health groups, and research scientists."[86] Fourth, the EDSTAC's deliberations included public-comment sessions that incorporated input from numerous constituents. Thus, although the decision-making process did not involve any of the more dramatic approaches for incorporating public participation (such as a citizens' advisory council or a citizens' jury), it was grounded in a diagnostic process that was adequate to facilitate successful deliberation.

The results of this deliberative process appear to illustrate not only the instrumental benefits of thoughtful diagnosis (namely, relatively widespread acceptance of the EDSTAC's proposals) but also the substantive benefit of a well-nuanced screening plan that included four important features. First, the committee ultimately decided to provide a general description of endocrine

85. See Endocrine Disruptor Screening and Testing Advisory Committee (EDSTAC), *Final Report*.

86. Ibid., I-2.

disruption but to avoid providing a precise definition of the phenomenon. As mentioned earlier, this compromise was a response to disagreement about whether a chemical must cause *adverse* effects in order to be considered an endocrine disruptor or whether it need only *alter* endocrine function.[87] Second, they designed testing and screening for *both* human *and* wildlife endocrine disruptors. Third, they decided that the testing and screening should cover estrogenic, androgenic, and thyroid-related endocrine effects in the short term, while recommending that other hormonal effects be examined over the long term.[88] Fourth, they suggested testing for multiple-hormone interactions, effects on multiple species, and long-term or delayed effects. Overall, the EDSTAC developed a screening proposal that thoughtfully balanced the tremendous need for more information about potential endocrine disruptors with the limits in time and money available for performing tests.

## Ethics for Experts

The ED case, like the hormesis and MCS cases, also supports the potential for the Consent Principle developed in chapter 6 to help those who provide and receive scientific information. Whereas the central value judgments in the MCS case involve the question of whether to employ psychogenic or physiological interpretations, the divisive judgments regarding ED concern the extent to which it affects humans, as well as nonhuman organisms. This was a particularly contentious issue during the 1980s and 1990s, when few human studies were available other than those on DES and sperm counts. Over the past fifteen years, an increasing body of evidence has come to support endocrine-disrupting effects on human beings.[89] Some of these effects include altered menstrual cycles, increased breast cancer risk, early breast development, reduced duration of lactation, neurobehavioral problems (e.g., increased aggression, learning difficulties, ADHD, autism), and lowered sperm quality.[90]

Nevertheless, many research gaps remain, in part because it is generally unethical to perform experiments on humans if they are likely to be harmed in the process.[91] Some scientists and policy makers, especially those with

87. Ibid., III-4.

88. Krimsky, *Hormonal Chaos*, 215.

89. For an excellent summary of much of this research, especially on the effects of endocrine disruptors on human females, see Crain et al., "Female Reproductive Disorders."

90. Ibid.; see also S. Swan et al., "Semen Quality in Relation to Biomarkers of Pesticide Exposure"; Y. Guo et al., "Semen Quality after Prenatal Exposure"; J. Braun et al., "Prenatal Bisphenol A Exposure and Early Childhood Behavior"; vom Saal et al., "Chapel Hill Bisphenol A Expert Panel Consensus Statement."

91. Shrader-Frechette, "Evidentiary Standards and Animal Data."

ties to industry, regularly appeal to these sorts of weaknesses in order to challenge public-health regulations until human data on specific effects are available.[92] Many others note that good animal tests provide probable evidence for human health effects and are actually more reliable than most human epidemiological studies (which frequently have significant methodological limitations).[93] For example, Adam Finkel, the executive director of the University of Pennsylvania Program on Regulation, insists that positive animal tests are "highly correlated" with human toxicity.[94]

With this context in mind, it is enlightening to consider debates over the manner in which Theo Colborn and her coauthors disseminated information about the endocrine-disruption hypothesis in *Our Stolen Future*,[95] a popular book published in 1996. A crucial question about the book is whether, given the evidence available to the authors at that time, it went too far in its aggressive advocacy for the notion that ED was affecting humans. The editors of the journal *Environmental Health Perspectives* (which has published numerous articles on ED) made this worry explicit. On one hand, they agreed with the authors of *Our Stolen Future* that a great deal of evidence indicated that "environmental substances that mimic or block actions of hormones are producing many of the widespread adverse effects on reproductive capacity and development in *wildlife*."[96] On the other hand, they cautioned that "Readers…should be mindful…and recognize that *Our Stolen Future* is neither a balanced nor an objective presentation of the scientific evidence on…whether exposure to endocrine-disrupting environmental chemicals is causing significant increases in *human* disease."[97]

To be fair to Colborn and her coauthors, it is important to acknowledge that they included a number of caveats throughout their discussion of human health effects. Typical of this tone is their response to studies on human breast cancer: "Because of our poor understanding of what causes

92. For discussions of this skepticism about animal studies in the ED case, see Colborn, Dumanoski, and Myers, *Our Stolen Future*, 22, 57–58. For skepticism about animal studies in general, see Ames and Gold, "Causes and Prevention of Cancer"; Whelan, "Ratty Test Rationale." Despite her skepticism about animal studies, Elizabeth Whelan acknowledges that positive tests on several different animal species, including at low- and medium-range doses, may be sufficient to justify regulations.

93. For a discussion of the relevance of animal tests to human health effects, see Shrader-Frechette, "Evidentiary Standards and Animal Data." It is also important to note that some of the classic criticisms of animal tests, such as those by Bruce Ames and Lois Gold, are directed primarily at high-dose cancer studies and may be less applicable to low-dose studies of endocrine disruptors.

94. Finkel, "Rodent Tests Continue."

95. Colborn, Dumanoski, and Myers, *Our Stolen Future*.

96. Lucier and Hook, "Anniversaries and Issues," 350; italics added.

97. Ibid.; italics added.

breast cancer and significant uncertainties about exposure, it may take some time to satisfactorily test the hypothesis and discover whether synthetic chemicals are contributing to rising breast cancer rates."[98] Again, in a summary chapter of human health risks, they noted, "At the moment, there are many provocative questions and few definitive answers, but the potential disruption to individuals and society is so serious that these questions bear exploration."[99]

Nevertheless, a significant worry about their presentation is that, despite these caveats, they had a tendency to use somewhat alarmist language to speculate about the possibility that endocrine-disrupting chemicals were contributing to a wide variety of human social ills. Consider, for example, their strong rhetoric in a chapter on "looming" health threats:

> What we fear most immediately is not extinction, but the insidious erosion of the human species. We worry about an invisible loss of human potential. We worry about the power of hormone-disrupting chemicals to undermine and alter the characteristics that make us uniquely human—our behavior, intelligence, and capacity for social organization.[100]

While Colborn and her coauthors had discussed some suggestive studies on endocrine-disrupting effects on human behavior, they had very limited evidence to support such dramatic concerns. Several pages later they returned to a more careful tone, acknowledging that "at the moment it is impossible to know whether hormone-disrupting chemicals are contributing to any of the disturbing social and behavioral problems besetting our society and, if so, how much."[101] Given the available evidence on animals, however, they concluded that "we should consider chemical contamination as a factor contributing to the increasing prevalence of dysfunctional behavior in human society as well."[102]

Considering the number of caveats throughout their book, it is not clear that Colborn and her coauthors misled their readers in a manner that would violate the Consent Principle. Nevertheless, the controversy over their book suggests a lesson for authors of popular books like *Our Stolen Future*. Namely, in order to promote the ability of members of the public to provide consent to decisions that affect their well-being, such authors should be particularly careful to acknowledge when they are making controversial judgments. Because most of those who read popular books are not themselves scientists, it is unlikely that such readers will have many other

98. Colborn, Dumanoski, and Myers, *Our Stolen Future*, 185.
99. Ibid., 231.
100. Ibid., 234.
101. Ibid., 238.
102. Ibid.

opportunities to recognize major, socially significant value judgments on the topic under consideration. Thus, the authors arguably have special responsibilities to clarify these judgments for their readers so that they can pursue alternative perspectives. One might argue, of course, that the authors of *Our Stolen Future* genuinely believed that endocrine disruption had the potential to cause dramatic harm to human societies. However, as in the case of MCS researchers like Gots and Staudenmayer et al., who seem convinced that psychogenic descriptions of MCS are correct, it seems doubtful that genuine commitment to one's judgments is ethically sufficient. If one is making a major, socially relevant value judgment, the Consent Principle suggests that (all else being equal) one should make those controversial judgments clear.

The book *Our Stolen Future* is an enlightening case not only because of its content but also because of the responses to it. In fact, these responses illustrate how the Consent Principle may be relevant to the science media, as well as to scientists and policy makers themselves. For example, an investigative report by Mark Dowie criticized the *New York Times*'s coverage of endocrine disruption.[103] According to Dowie, *Times* science reporter Gina Kolata emphasized critics of ED, such as Bruce Ames, in a news story on endocrine disruption while downplaying supporters of the hypothesis.[104] Krimsky also suggests that Kolata's story was somewhat misleading.[105] Another questionable journalistic treatment of ED comes from Ronald Bailey, a television reporter who wrote an opinion piece for the *Washington Post*. Bailey quoted John Giesy, a toxicologist from Michigan State University, as expressing a very negative attitude toward the ED hypothesis. Nevertheless, a piece published about six weeks later in *Chemical and Engineering News* appeared to contradict Bailey's account, because it quoted Giesy as being somewhat positive about the ED hypothesis, at least in wildlife populations.[106] Of course, it is not clear that either Kolata or Bailey presented information in a problematic fashion. They may have been reporting their best understanding of the scientific community's views. Nevertheless, to the extent that journalists, like scientists, have responsibilities to promote autonomous decision making by the public, the Consent Principle would appear to provide guidance for them as well. For example, it would presumably call for them to be as careful as possible about acknowledging when they or their sources have major conflicting interests or are making significant judgments.

103. Dowie, "What's Wrong with the *New York Times* Science Reporting?"
104. Kolata, "Chemicals That Mimic Hormones Spark Alarm and Debate."
105. Krimsky, *Hormonal Chaos*, 135.
106. Ibid., 136.

Another set of scenarios in the ED case that illustrates the importance of an ethics of expertise involves industry studies that dispute the evidence for ED. Industry groups have published numerous pieces in an effort to discredit claims about harmful effects from endocrine-disrupting chemicals, but there appear to be good reasons to think that many of these studies are problematic.[107] Besides the studies on bisphenol A described in previous parts of this section, another set of apparently flawed industry studies was designed to discredit the work of University of California–Berkeley endocrinologist Tyrone Hayes, who studied harmful biological effects of the herbicide atrazine.[108] One way in which the content of these studies appears to differ from the recommendations of the Consent Principle is that the studies do not acknowledge the design elements that incline them toward false negative results.

Depending on the precise motivations of the industry scientists who published these studies, they could also conflict with the Consent Principle in an even deeper way. Namely, if the scientists *deliberately* designed their studies so as to yield results that *successfully* convinced decision makers to act in accordance with industry interests, they would appear to be *manipulating* information in a way that prevents decision makers from meeting the voluntariness component of informed consent (see chapter 6). It would be extremely difficult to determine whether these scientists are deliberately manipulating the results of their studies. Nevertheless, it is worrisome in the atrazine and bisphenol A cases that the industry studies obtain negative results almost without exception (in contrast to the work of scientists unaffiliated with industry) and that they appear to involve fairly blatant experimental-design flaws.[109] The Consent Principle thus raises significant concerns about these cases.

## CONCLUSION

We began this chapter with Al Gore's foreword to *Our Stolen Future*, in which he asserts that the book is, in many ways, a successor to *Silent Spring*. Near the end of that foreword Gore writes, "We can never construct a society that is completely free of risk. At a minimum, however, the American people have a right to know the substances to which they and their children are being exposed and to know everything that science can tell us about the hazards."[110] This book has argued that, while scientific information is indeed

107. See vom Saal and Hughes, "Extensive New Literature."
108. See Hayes, "There Is No Denying This."
109. Ibid.; vom Saal and Hughes, "Extensive New Literature."
110. Gore, "Foreword," ix.

crucial for making good environmental decisions, it would be unwise for the American people to stand back and uncritically allow science to inform them about hazards. We have seen that significant judgments permeate the practice of policy-relevant science, and vested-interest groups exert major influences on many of these judgments. Therefore, it is important to safeguard scientific research from some of the worst abuses associated with private funding, to diagnose appropriate deliberative formats for reflecting on research, and to hold experts to ethical standards for disseminating information to decision makers.

This chapter has examined the MCS and ED cases in order to support these major claims of the book's earlier chapters. First, the four major classes of value judgments identified in the hormesis case also play a crucial role in these other areas of research. Second, financial COIs are widespread, and it is difficult to block their worrisome influences with current university COI policies. Third, examination of the MCS and ED cases indicates that diagnosing appropriate forms of deliberation in these contexts is quite valuable (both from an instrumental and a substantive perspective). Fourth, an ethics of expertise such as the Consent Principle provides much-needed guidance for those who disseminate information about these phenomena to policy makers and to the public. This analysis suggests that the book's major claims are applicable to a range of policy-related research projects in addition to the hormesis case.

# 8

# Conclusion

Two recent articles illustrate contemporary scientists' widely divergent perspectives on the hormesis phenomenon. On one hand, Edward Calabrese claims that "[T]he preponderance of evidence supports the consideration of hormesis as the default dose-response model for all types of endpoints."[1] On the other hand, Kristina Thayer and her colleagues state the following:

> The claims and projections of health benefits from exposures to environmental toxicants and carcinogens are based on untested assumptions and disregard numerous well-established scientific principles that underpin a public health–protective approach to regulating exposure to toxic substances. If hormesis were used in the decision-making process to allow higher exposures to toxic and carcinogenic agents, this would substantially increase health risks for many, if not most, segments of the general population.[2]

This book has emphasized that these disagreements are aggravated by the significant amounts of money at stake in scientific conclusions on hormesis. For example, the industrial community tends to be much more sympathetic than the environmental and public-health communities to claims HG, HP, and HD.

We saw in chapter 4 that powerful stakeholders with deep pockets can pursue a variety of strategies to obtain research results that serve their interests in policy-relevant cases like hormesis. Partly because of this, scholars in the science-policy community argue that collecting more information is not always sufficient to resolve disputes. In fact, Roger Pielke Jr. and Daniel Sarewitz make the surprising claim that, rather than scientific uncertainty breeding political conflicts over how to act, the causal arrow often runs in the opposite direction—disagreements over social values breed scientific uncertainty. As Sarewitz puts it:

> [T]he growth of considerable bodies of scientific knowledge, created especially to resolve political dispute and enable effective decision-making, has often been accompanied instead by growing political controversy and gridlock.

1. Calabrese, "Hormesis: From Marginalization to Mainstream," especially 134.
2. Thayer et al., "Fundamental Flaws."

> Science typically lies at the center of the debate, where those who advocate some line of action are likely to claim a scientific justification for their position, while those opposing the action will either invoke scientific uncertainty or competing scientific results to support their position.[3]

Pielke claims that, when scientists attempt to be purely objective in response to these heavily value-laden areas of research, they often become "stealth issue advocates."[4] In other words, despite their best attempts to stick to the science, their work can incorporate implicit value judgments that surreptitiously favor one side of a controversy.

This book has explored several strategies for responding to the influences of powerful interest groups on policy-relevant research. Chapters 2 and 3 performed two preliminary tasks: They clarified the major categories of value judgments that contribute to differing evaluations of claims HG, HD, and HP, and they argued that societal values should not be completely excluded from influencing any of these categories of judgments. Chapters 4 through 6 developed the book's three primary lessons, corresponding to the three "bodies" that Sheila Jasanoff has emphasized as central to obtaining trustworthy public-policy guidance from scientific experts. These lessons concerned how to safeguard the *body of scientific knowledge* from interest groups, how to diagnose the best *advisory bodies* for guiding policy makers and directing the course of future research, and how to provide the *bodies of experts* themselves with an ethics of expertise. Chapter 7 argued that the lessons drawn in chapters 2 through 6 are applicable not only to the hormesis case but also to other areas of policy-relevant research, such as endocrine disruption and multiple chemical sensitivity. This brief final chapter reviews the book's major claims and considers important directions for future work.

## REVIEW

Chapter 2 examined hormesis research as an important case study of the ways in which methodological and interpretive judgments enter scientific practice. The chapter organized these choices into four major categories (see figure 2.1). First, judgments pervade the choice of research projects and the design of studies. One of the important questions in this regard is what kind of studies to prioritize, given the limited funding available to examine the low-dose effects of toxicants. Second, crucial decisions are involved in developing scientific language. The hormesis, MCS, and ED case studies all

3. Sarewitz, "How Science Makes Environmental Controversies Worse."
4. Pielke Jr., *Honest Broker.*

provide vivid examples of how the choice of scientific terms and categories can subtly influence policy discussions. Third, judgments play a crucial role in the interpretation and evaluation of studies. This third category of methodological choices is especially important to understand in the hormesis case, because it is largely responsible for the disagreements between proponents and opponents of claims HG, HD, and HP. Fourth, there are important decisions to make about how to apply research results in the context of formulating public policy. For example, efforts to apply hormesis to regulatory policy must come to grips with difficult questions about how to balance potentially beneficial and harmful effects of toxic chemicals.

Chapter 3 argued that contextual values should not be systematically excluded from any of the four categories of judgments considered in chapter 2. The argument rested on three major principles. First, the "ethics" principle is that scientists have ethical responsibilities to consider the major societal consequences of their work and to take reasonable steps to mitigate harmful effects that it might have. Second, the "uncertainty" principle is that those researching policy-relevant topics often face situations in which scientific information is uncertain and incomplete, and they have to decide what standard of proof to demand before drawing conclusions. Third, the "no-passing-the-buck" principle is that it is frequently socially harmful or impracticable for scientists to respond to uncertainty by completely withholding their judgment or providing uninterpreted data to decision makers. With this third principle in mind, we saw that scientists cannot always leave difficult value judgments about interpreting uncertain evidence up to policy makers. Therefore, scientists sometimes have ethical reasons to factor societal considerations into their responses to uncertainty, even when they address judgments about choosing scientific language or interpreting evidence. The upshot of this chapter is that administrators and policy makers need to find ways to limit the influences of powerful interest groups without naively trying to seal scientific research off from all societal influences and considerations.

Chapters 4 through 6 developed the book's three lessons for promoting a more representative range of societal values in policy-relevant research. Chapter 4 argued that current financial COI policies are severely limited in their ability to prevent powerful interest groups from hijacking university research. It considered the three major elements of these policies (i.e., elimination of conflicts, disclosure, and management) and argued that none of them is likely to be both effective and practical. Given the current economic emphasis on creating links between universities and industry, outright elimination of conflicts will generally not be feasible. Moreover, despite the popularity of disclosure policies, psychologists warn that those who receive information about conflicts are often unable to employ that information effectively. By highlighting the wide array of value judgments that permeate scientific practice, this book strengthens these psychological arguments by highlighting how difficult it would be for the recipients of information to estimate how financial conflicts might be influencing such a diverse array of judgments. Finally, the prevalence of these judgments makes it unlikely that management committees could prevent questionable influences on science without instituting an unreasonable amount of bureaucratic oversight. Chapter 4 suggested that, instead of depending only on COI policies, university administrators and policy makers would do well to consider at least five additional options. These include providing more funding for independent research, preventing particularly egregious institutional conflicts, creating trial registries, developing adversarial deliberative proceedings, and promoting consensual deliberative forums.

Chapter 5 explored the last of these options, that of creating consensual deliberative forums. It argued that there are normative, substantive, and instrumental reasons for pursuing broadly based deliberative venues to guide the value judgments associated with policy-relevant science. Nevertheless, because these forums can involve a wide range of mechanisms and strategies for representing affected parties, and because deliberative proceedings have weaknesses as well as strengths, the chapter called for greater "diagnosis" of the mechanisms appropriate to particular areas of research. It developed a three-step diagnostic model inspired by the account proposed in the NRC volume *Understanding Risk*.

Applying this diagnostic procedure to the hormesis case, chapter 5 called for a mixed deliberative approach. In the near term, it recommended that policy makers examine the hormesis phenomenon in either an existing scientific advisory committee or a special advisory council created to represent the range of important stakeholder perspectives on hormesis. This council could address some of the major judgments identified in chapter 2, such as prioritizing future areas of research, proposing definitions for key terms under debate, and evaluating the evidence for claims HG, HD, and HP. If the advisory council were to conclude, now or in the future, that the evidence warranted considering regulatory changes in response to hormesis, chapter 5 recommended another step of deliberation. This would involve a consensus conference or other citizens' panel that would elicit a range of informed citizen perspectives on the proposed regulatory changes. These formal exercises could provide a valuable starting point for informal political action by concerned citizens' groups.

Chapter 6 turned to the bodies of scientific experts themselves. It argued that, if scientists are to avoid railroading their own values into individual and societal decision-making processes, they need to follow an ethics of expertise when disseminating information. The chapter suggested that an

EOE based on the principle of informed consent would help decision makers to formulate choices according to their own values and priorities, and it would also help them to evaluate the trustworthiness of various experts. On the basis of this principle, it advised proponents of hormesis to be as explicit as possible in acknowledging the major and controversial value judgments present in their work. Two of these crucial judgments are that claims HP and HD are well supported by current evidence (i.e., that hormesis is the predominant dose-response relationship and that it should be the default dose-response model in risk assessment). Clarifying these judgments would help decision makers to recognize the key sources of uncertainty and controversy in the information supplied to them, and it would prevent interest groups from misusing the claims of hormesis proponents.

Chapter 7 showed how the major lessons of the preceding chapters apply to cases of policy-relevant research other than hormesis. It argued that those who investigate endocrine disruption and MCS also encounter at least four major categories of value judgments: (1) choices about what topics to investigate and how to design studies; (2) decisions about what scientific terminology and definitions to employ; (3) choices about how to interpret and evaluate studies; and (4) questions about how to incorporate scientific research in policy decisions. The chapter also showed, in accordance with chapter 4, that current university COI policies are unlikely to prevent interest groups from exerting powerful influences on these judgments. Chapter 7 also supported the central contention of chapter 5 (i.e., that diagnosing deliberative forums is important) by showing the problematic effects of poorly designed deliberation in the MCS case and the positive consequences of well-designed deliberation in response to endocrine disruption. Finally, the chapter showed that experts who study MCS and endocrine disruption could also gain valuable guidance by reflecting on the ethics of expertise developed in chapter 6.

## ONGOING QUESTIONS

The analyses in the preceding chapters suggest at least three promising avenues for future work: (1) further philosophical studies of the roles that various sorts of values should play in scientific research; (2) new scientific investigations of the biological effects of toxicants at low doses; and (3) ongoing social-scientific research on how to incorporate a representative range of societal values in science. First, although value judgments are clearly important in many areas of scientific research, chapter 3 indicated that much more work is required to advance our understanding of the roles that specific sorts of values ought to play in particular contexts. For example, leading philosophers of science disagree both about the extent to which scientific theory choice is underdetermined by epistemic values and about the conditions under which nonepistemic values should be employed in resolving this underdetermination.[5] One issue at the core of these debates is whether the conceptual distinction between epistemic and nonepistemic (or constitutive and contextual) values holds up to critical scrutiny.[6] Another central question is whether it is possible to draw a convincing distinction between *practical* decisions about how to act, as opposed to *epistemic* judgments about what to believe.[7] Addressing such issues will obviously require careful conceptual analyses of these sorts of values and epistemic attitudes. It will also require further studies of the behavior and traditions of scientists (in a wide variety of basic and applied domains of research) to determine the precise conditions under which these distinctions hold up in actual practice.[8] Chapters 4 through 6 showed that this sort of philosophical understanding of the roles that value judgments play in science can assist practical efforts to address conflicts of interest, to develop appropriate deliberative exercises, and to communicate scientific information to the public.

A second crucial area for future research involves the biological effects of toxic chemicals at low concentrations. In particular, research on endocrine disruptors and chemical mixtures should be especially high priorities. As chapter 7 emphasized, the available evidence regarding endocrine disruption suggests that low concentrations of many chemicals may be more harmful than previously thought, especially when exposures occur during critical periods of human development.[9] More information about these low-dose effects is urgently needed. For example, an extensive review of existing work on female reproductive disorders and endocrine disruption recently identified three large-scale needs: (1) long-term research on the connections

5. See, for example, Giere, "New Program for Philosophy of Science?"; Haack, "Science as Social?"; Intemann, "Feminism, Underdetermination, and Values in Science"; Kourany, "Reply to Giere"; Longino, *Fate of Knowledge*.

6. For arguments for and against the distinction between epistemic and nonepistemic values, see Dorato, "Epistemic and Nonepistemic Values in Science"; Lacey, "Is There a Significant Distinction between Cognitive and Social Values?"; Longino, "Cognitive and Non-cognitive Values in Science"; Rooney, "On Values in Science"; Steel, "Epistemic Values."

7. See, for example, Cohen, *Essay on Belief and Acceptance*; Giere, "New Program for Philosophy of Science?"; Kourany, "Reply to Giere"; McKaughan, *Toward a Richer Vocabulary*.

8. Philosophers of science need to pay attention to the actual behavior of scientists because, as Ron Giere points out, much of the philosophy of science has become "naturalized." In other words, philosophers draw conclusions about proper scientific practice based not simply on logical or conceptual analyses but also on the actual practice of science; see Giere, "New Program for Philosophy of Science?"

9. See, for example, Nagel et al., "Relative Binding Affinity-Serum Modified Access"; Wetherill et al., "Xenoestrogen Bisphenol A."

between early-life chemical exposures and adult diseases; (2) coordination of relevant data, both nationally and internationally; and (3) development of an interdisciplinary consortium to coordinate research, public policy, and education.[10]

In addition to these needed studies of endocrine disruption, recent scientific work suggests that it is also crucial to investigate the biological effects of low-dose chemical mixtures.[11] A 2008 report from the National Academy of Sciences, *Phthalates and Cumulative Risk Assessment*, urges agencies such as the EPA to explore more fully the combined effects of multiple chemical exposures.[12] In particular, it emphasizes that these effects should be studied not only for sets of chemicals with similar structures or mechanisms but also for combinations of substances that induce similar biological outcomes. For example, scientists could explore the combined effects of lead, methylmercury, and polychlorinated biphenyls (PCBs), all of which affect human cognitive development. Another suggestion in the report is to investigate combinations of endocrine-disrupting chemicals that could be contributing to male reproductive abnormalities.[13]

Further research to establish the generalizability or predominance of hormesis (i.e., claims HG or HP) appear to be less of a priority than these other topics, largely because its relevance to regulatory policy is dubious. As chapter 2 emphasized, most human populations (and especially vulnerable groups, such as minorities and poor people) are exposed to extensive mixtures of toxic chemicals.[14] Therefore, sensitive humans (such as children) are probably already exposed to concentrations of chemical mixtures that exceed the hormetic range.[15] Nevertheless, some subsets of hormesis research may have greater social relevance.[16] For example, Calabrese and Mattson suggest that numerous pharmaceutical agents act via hormetic mechanisms.[17] Therefore, appropriate administration of many drugs (and

10. Crain et al., "Female Reproductive Disorders."

11. Biello, "Mixing It Up."

12. NRC, *Phtalates and Cumulative Risk Assessment.*

13. Ibid., 11.

14. See, for example, Shabecoff and Shabecoff, *Poisoned Profits*, ch. 4; Shrader-Frechette, "Ideological Toxicology"; Shrader-Frechette, *Taking Action, Saving Lives.*

15. See Shrader-Frechette, *Taking Action, Saving Lives*, especially 21–29, where she provides statistics from the World Health Organization, American Public Health Association, and U.S. National Cancer Institute, documenting health risks from the pollutants to which children and minorities are already exposed. See also Shabecoff and Shabecoff, *Poisoned Profits*, especially ch. 4.

16. For an overview of ways in which the hormesis phenomenon could contribute to or be associated with research on better health care, drug development, lifestyle, and diet, see the essays in Mattson and Calabrese, eds., *Hormesis.*

17. Calabrese and Mattson, "Hormetic Pharmacy."

successful development of new pharmaceuticals) might require attention to the hormesis phenomenon. Failure to do so could result in a variety of problems, including the stimulation of tumors or disease-causing organisms.[18]

Partly because of industry interest in hormesis and partly because of the phenomenon's potential relevance in fields such as pharmaceutical development, further research on this topic seems likely. Those who pursue such work should remain cognizant of the major interpretive judgments identified in chapter 2, especially the possibility that Calabrese's literature-study methodologies could result in false positive errors and the concern that seemingly beneficial effects on individual endpoints may not translate into benefits for the whole organism over the long term.[19] One of the ways to respond to such concerns would be to fund new, well-controlled experiments specifically designed to test particular chemicals for hormetic effects at low doses.[20] As chapter 4 emphasized, however, industry has a very worrisome track record of pursuing questionable research methodologies in the pharmaceutical and public-health domains. Moreover, calling for hormesis research in the regulatory domain can be a ploy for causing further delays in our already backlogged regulatory apparatus. Therefore, it is important that further studies of hormesis be carefully evaluated, perhaps via the sorts of deliberative mechanisms proposed in chapter 5, before using them to justify policy changes.

More generally, scientists, industry leaders, citizens, and policy makers should be looking for creative research projects that could lessen our society's use of potentially toxic substances. While chemical risk assessment is a valuable tool, there are dangers involved in focusing too much regulatory energy on efforts to determine the doses at which toxic chemicals are safe. Warring interest groups frequently produce conflicting studies that create endless delays in the regulatory process. Rather than providing ever more funding to try to reduce uncertainty about toxic effects, it is sometimes more effective to fund research projects that identify safer alternatives to potentially toxic substances. Dan Sarewitz lauds the Toxics Use Reduction Institute (TURI) at the University of Massachusetts, Lowell, as a model for these efforts, and he notes that industry has happily adopted some of the alternatives that TURI developed.[21] Similarly, some agroecological

18. Calabrese and Baldwin, "Hormesis: U-shaped Dose Responses"; Hoffmann, "Perspective on the Scientific, Philosophical, and Policy Dimensions of Hormesis."

19. Mayo and Spanos, "Risks to Health and Risks to Science"; Mushak, "Hormesis and Its Place."

20. Douglas, "Science, Hormesis, and Regulation"; Jonas, "Critique of 'The Scientific Foundations of Hormesis.'"

21. Sarewitz, "Tale of Two Sciences." See also Tickner, ed., *Precaution, Environmental Science.*

researchers are attempting to make agriculture more environmentally friendly not by endlessly testing the toxicity of existing pesticides but rather by developing new agricultural practices that require much less pesticide application.[22]

The third body of research supported by the present book consists of social-scientific work on avenues for integrating a broader range of societal values into scientific judgments. We saw in chapter 4 that psychological research can help to identify weaknesses of current university COI policies. Further social-scientific studies would be extremely valuable to administrators as they try to develop better strategies. In the introduction to a recent edited volume that introduces policy makers to empirical research on COIs, the authors note that "there are few clear or inexpensive solutions to conflicts of interest."[23] As chapter 4 emphasized, the strategy of disclosure appears to be limited in its effectiveness. The existing empirical research suggests that many of the other appealing responses (including penalties, procedural regulation, moral suasion, and peer review) also have significant limitations.[24] As the authors of the edited volume note, a significant need exists to synthesize existing research findings from multiple applied domains in order to glean general insights for responding to COIs.[25]

Further social-science research could also help policy makers who aim to diagnose the most effective deliberative processes for responding to particular policy-relevant research topics (see chapter 5). A recent NRC report, *Public Participation in Environmental Assessment and Decision Making*, states that "Research on the public participation process has lagged far behind the need."[26] It calls for further attention to questions such as the following:

- How can technical analyses be made more understandable to participants who do not have extensive technical backgrounds?
- How can diverse bodies of knowledge, including the local knowledge of nonscientists, be more effectively integrated into deliberative exercises?
- What are the best strategies for achieving closure in deliberative settings and for determining when closure is appropriate and feasible?

22. See, for example, Lacey, *Is Science Value Free?*

23. Moore et al., "Introduction," 3.

24. Ibid., 5–8.

25. Ibid., 3.

26. NRC, *Public Participation in Environmental Assessment and Decision Making*, 240. Additional calls for research on broadly based deliberative mechanisms can be found in Beierle, "Quality of Stakeholder-based Decisions"; NRC, *Understanding Risk*; Rowe and Frewer, "Public Participation Methods"; Irvin and Stansbury, "Citizen Participation in Decision Making."

The report especially emphasizes that there is inadequate evidence concerning the sorts of deliberative mechanisms that are most effective in particular contexts. To address this problem, the NRC calls for a wide range of social-scientific methodologies, including formal experiments, modeling, and detailed comparisons of public participation efforts from a wide variety of cases.[27]

Finally, as chapter 6 noted, more empirical scholarship is needed regarding the ethical responsibilities of scientific experts who provide information to policy makers and to the public. Consider the concerns raised in a recent publication from the American Public Health Association:

> There is limited research on the dissemination and use of public health information. For example, what are the best communication formats and channels for public health practitioners to communicate with certain audiences, such as the news media, elected officials, or private health organizations? There is a large "knowledge-generating" research establishment.... In contrast, there is a very small "knowledge-use" research establishment, and much of its effort has concentrated on proactive campaigns, especially those directed toward mass media or individual change in limited research situations.[28]

The editors of the report call for further research on how members of the public obtain public-health information, on whether particular dissemination formats work best for specific audiences, and on how members of the public interpret the information that they receive.[29] Further empirical research of this sort, regarding the ways in which citizens collect and interpret scientific information, would be of great value to those pursuing normative work on the ethics of expertise.

## CONCLUSION

In the *Federalist Papers* James Madison wrote, "To secure the public good... and at the same time to preserve the spirit and the form of popular government, is then the great object to which our inquiries are directed."[30]

27. NRC, *Public Participation in Environmental Assessment and Decision Making,* 240–42. Diana Mutz's essay "Is Deliberative Democracy a Falsifiable Theory?" provides another call for research on the specific characteristics of deliberative forums that yield particular desired outcomes.

28. Nelson et al., "Future Directions," 207.

29. Ibid. Of course, we already have some information about how members of the public respond to particular sorts of information. See, for example, Nisbet and Mooney, "Framing Science"; Scheufele and Lewenstein, "Public and Nanotechnology." As the APHA report makes clear, however, there is still a long way to go in providing practitioners in many areas of science with adequate information about how to disseminate their findings.

30. Madison, "Federalist No. 10," 80.

This book aims at the same goals. On one hand, the public good depends on competent and reliable scientific and technical information about environmental issues, including the public-health effects of pollution. On the other hand, preserving the spirit of popular government depends on keeping decision makers accountable to ordinary citizens, not just to technical experts. Thus, the question that we have explored throughout this book is how to integrate the societal values of citizens with the scientific research that informs public policy. We have encountered three major suggestions: (1) safeguarding university research from powerful interest groups; (2) diagnosing deliberative forums in response to policy-relevant research; and (3) developing an ethics of expertise that helps scientists to communicate with the public. Admittedly, it will take effort to implement these strategies. Nevertheless, given the central contributions that both science and democracy make to our society, it is well worth making the effort to harmonize these endeavors.

# References

Abelson, R., and A. Levi. 1985. Decision Making and Decision Theory. In *The Handbook of Social Psychology*, 3rd ed., vol. 1, ed. G. Linzey and E. Aronson, 231–310. New York: Random House.

Alonso-Magdalena, P., S. Morimoto, C. Ripoll, E. Fuentes, and A. Nadal. 2006. The Estrogenic Effect of Bisphenol-A Disrupts the Pancreatic ß-Cell Function *in vivo* and Induces Insulin Resistance. *Environmental Health Perspectives* 114: 106–12.

Als-Nielsen, B., W. Chen, C. Gluud, and L. Kjaergard. 2003. Association of Funding and Conclusions in Randomized Drug Trials. *Journal of the American Medical Association* 290: 921–28.

American Public Health Association (APHA). 2003. *Supporting Legislation for Independent Post-marketing Phase IV Comparative Evaluation of Pharmaceuticals.* Washington, D.C.: APHA. http://www.apha.org/advocacy/policy/policysearch/default.htm?id=1265 (accessed September 12, 2007).

Ames, B., and L. Gold. 1994. The Causes and Prevention of Cancer. *Environmental Health Perspectives* 105, suppl. 4: 865–74.

Ames, B., R. Magaw, and L. Gold. 1987. Ranking Possible Carcinogenic Hazards. *Science* 236: 271–80.

Anderson, E. 1995. Feminist Epistemology: An Interpretation and a Defense. *Hypatia* 10: 50–84.

———. 2004. Uses of Value Judgments in Science: A General Argument, with Lessons from a Case Study of Feminist Research on Divorce. *Hypatia* 19: 1–24.

Angell, M. 2004a. Time for a Drug Registry. *Washington Post* (August 13).

———. 2004b. *The Truth about the Drug Companies: How They Deceive Us and What to Do about It.* New York: Random House.

Anonymous. 1996. Conclusions and Recommendations of a Workshop on Multiple Chemical Sensitivities (MCS). *Regulatory Toxicology and Pharmacology* 24: S188–89.

Arnall, A., and D. Parr. 2005. Moving the Nanoscience and Technology (NST) Debate Forwards: Short-term Impacts, Long-term Uncertainty and the Social Constitution. *Technology in Society* 27: 23–38.

Ashford, N., and C. Miller. 1998. *Chemical Exposures: Low Levels and High Stakes*, 2nd ed. New York: Van Nostrand Reinhold.

Aulerich, R., R. Ringer, and S. Iwamoto. 1973. Reproductive Failure and Mortality in Mink Fed on Great Lakes Fish. *Journal of Reproduction and Fertility Supplement* 19: 365–76.

Axelrod, D., K. Burns, D. Davis, and N. Von Larebeke. 2004. "Hormesis"—An Inappropriate Extrapolation from the Specific to the Universal. *International Journal of Occupational and Environmental Health* 10: 335–39.

Bailar, J. 2006. How to Distort the Scientific Record without Actually Lying: Truth and the Arts of Science. *European Journal of Oncology* 11: 217–24.

Barben, D., E. Fisher, C. Selin, and D. Guston. 2008. Anticipatory Governance of Nanotechnology: Foresight, Engagement, and Integration. In *The Handbook of Science and Technology Studies*, ed. E. Hackett, O. Amsterdamska, M. Lynch, and J. Wajcman, 979–1000. Cambridge, Mass.: MIT Press.

Barnes, D. 2000. Reference Dose (RfD): The Possible Impact of Hormesis. *Journal of Applied Toxicology* 20: 127–30.

Barnes, D. and L. Bero. 1998. Why Review Articles on the Health Effects of Passive Smoking Reach Different Conclusions. *Journal of the American Medical Association* 279: 1566–70.

Beauchamp, T., and J. Childress. 2001. *Principles of Biomedical Ethics*, 5th ed. New York: Oxford University Press.

Bechtel, W., and R. Richardson. 1993. *Discovering Complexity: Decomposition and Localization as Strategies in Scientific Research*. Princeton: Princeton University Press.

Beder, S. 2000. *Global Spin*, rev. ed. White River Junction, Vt.: Chelsea Green.

Begley, S. 2003. Scientists Revisit Idea That Little Poisons Could Be Beneficial. *Wall Street Journal*, December 19.

Beierle, T. 1999. Using Social Goals to Evaluate Public Participation in Environmental Decisions. *Policy Studies Review* 16: 76–103.

———. 2002. The Quality of Stakeholder-based Decisions. *Risk Analysis* 22: 739–49.

Bekelman, J., Y. Lee, and C. Gross. 2003. Scope and Impact of Financial Conflicts of Interest in Biomedical Research. *Journal of the American Medical Association* 289: 454–65.

Bell, I. 1996. Clinically Relevant EEG Studies and Psychophysiological Findings: Possible Neural Mechanisms for Multiple Chemical Sensitivity. *Toxicology* 111: 101–17.

Berry, W. 1986. *The Unsettling of America: Culture and Agriculture*. San Francisco: Sierra Club Books.

Biddle, J. 2006. "Socializing Science: On the Epistemic Significance of the Institutional Context of Science." PhD diss., University of Notre Dame.

Biello, D. 2006. Mixing It Up. *Scientific American*, May 10, http://www.sciam.com/article.cfm?id=mixing-it-up (accessed April 16, 2009).

Boyce, N. 2004. Is There a Tonic in the Toxin? *U.S. News and World Report*, October 10.

Braun, J., K. Yolton, K. N. Dietrich, R. Hornung, Y. Xiaoyun, A. M. Calafat, and B. P. Lanphear, et al. 2009. Prenatal Bisphenol A Exposure and Early Childhood Behavior. *Environmental Health Perspectives* 117: 1945–52.

Bridgman, P. 1927. *The Logic of Modern Physics*. New York: Macmillan.

Broley, C. 1958. The Plight of the American Bald Eagle. *Audubon Magazine* 60: 162–63, 171.

Brown, H. 1977. *Perception, Theory, and Commitment: The New Philosophy of Science*. Chicago: University of Chicago Press.

Brown, J. R. 2002. Funding, Objectivity, and the Socialization of Medical Research. *Science and Engineering Ethics* 8: 295–308.

Brown, P., and E. Mikkelsen. 1990. *No Safe Place: Toxic Waste, Leukemia, and Community Action*. Berkeley: University of California Press.

Browning, L. 2007. Makers of Artificial Sweeteners Go to Court. *New York Times*, April 6.

Bryan, C., T. Call, and K. Elliott. 2007. The Ethics of Infection Control: Philosophical Frameworks. *Infection Control and Hospital Epidemiology* 28: 1077–84.

Busenberg, G. 1999. Collaborative and Adversarial Analysis in Environmental Policy. *Policy Sciences* 32: 1–11.

Cain, D., G. Loewenstein, and D. Moore. 2005. The Shortcomings of Disclosure as a Solution to Conflicts of Interest. In *Conflicts of Interest: Challenges and Solutions in Business, Law, Medicine, and Public Policy*, ed. D. Moore, D. Cain, G. Loewenstein, and M. Bazerman, 104–25. New York: Cambridge University Press.

Calabrese, E. 1999. Evidence That Hormesis Represents an "Overcompensation" Response to a Disruption in Homeostasis. *Ecotoxicology and Environmental Safety* 42: 135–37.

———. 2001. Overcompensation Stimulation: A Mechanism for Hormetic Effects. *Critical Reviews in Toxicology* 31: 425–70.

———. 2004. Hormesis: From Marginalization to Mainstream: A Case for Hormesis as the Default Dose-response Model in Risk Assessment. *Toxicology and Applied Pharmacology* 197: 125–36.

———. 2005. Paradigm Lost, Paradigm Found: The Re-emergence of Hormesis as a Fundamental Dose Response Model in the Toxicological Sciences. *Environmental Pollution* 138: 378–411.

———. 2007. Elliott's Ethics of Expertise Proposal and Application: A Dangerous Precedent. *Science and Engineering Ethics* 13: 139–45.

———. 2007. Threshold—Dose—Response Model—RIP: 1911 to 2006. *BioEssays* 29: 686–88.
———. 2008. Hormesis: Why It Is Important to Toxicology and Toxicologists. *Environmental Toxicology and Chemistry* 27: 1451–74.
———. 2009. Hormesis: A Conversation with a Critic. *Environmental Health Perspectives* 117: 1339–43.
———. 2010. Hormesis: Once Marginalized, Evidence Now Supports Hormesis as the Most Fundamental Dose Response. In *Hormesis: A Revolution in Biology, Toxicology, and Medicine*, ed. M. Mattson and E. Calabrese, 15–56. New York: Springer.
———. 2010. Hormesis: Calabrese Responds. *Environmental Health Perspectives* 118: a153–4.
Calabrese, E., K. A. Bachmann, A. J. Bailer, P. M. Bolger, J. Borak, L. Cai, N. Cedergreen, et al. 2007. Biological Stress Response Terminology: Integrating the Concepts of Adaptive Response and Preconditioning Stress within a Hormetic Dose-response Framework. *Toxicology and Applied Pharmacology* 222: 122–28.
Calabrese, E., and L. Baldwin. 1997. The Dose Determines the Stimulation (and Poison): Development of a Chemical Hormesis Database. *International Journal of Toxicology* 16: 545–59.
———. 1998a. *Chemical Hormesis: Scientific Foundations*. College Station: Texas Institute for the Advancement of Chemical Technology.
———. 1998b. A General Classification of U-shaped Dose-response Relationships in Toxicology and Their Mechanistic Foundations. *Human and Experimental Toxicology* 17: 353–64.
———. 2000a. Chemical Hormesis: Its Historical Foundations as a Biological Hypothesis. *Human and Experimental Toxicology* 19: 2–31.
———. 2000b. The Marginalization of Hormesis. *Human and Experimental Toxicology* 19: 32–40.
———. 2000c. Tales of Two Similar Hypotheses: The Rise and Fall of Chemical and Radiation Hormesis. *Human and Experimental Toxicology* 19: 85–97.
———. 2001a. The Frequency of U-shaped Dose Responses in the Toxicological Literature. *Toxicological Sciences* 62: 330–38.
———. 2001b. Hormesis: U-shaped Dose Responses and Their Centrality in Toxicology. *Trends in Pharmacological Sciences* 22: 285–91.
———. 2002a. Applications of Hormesis in Toxicology, Risk Assessment, and Chemotherapeutics. *Trends in Pharmacological Sciences* 23: 331–37.
———. 2002b. Defining Hormesis. *Human and Experimental Toxicology* 21: 91–97.
———. 2003a. Hormesis at the National Toxicology Program (NTP): Evidence of Hormetic Dose Responses in NTP Dose-range Studies. *Nonlinearity in Biology, Toxicology, and Medicine* 1: 455–67.

———. 2003b. Hormesis: The Dose-response Revolution. *Annual Review of Pharmacology and Toxicology* 43: 175–97.

———. 2003c. The Hormetic Dose-response Model Is More Common than the Threshold Model in Toxicology. *Toxicological Sciences* 71: 246–50.

———. 2003d. Toxicology Rethinks Its Central Belief. *Nature* 421: 691–92.

Calabrese, E., L. Baldwin, and C. Holland. 1999. Hormesis: A Highly Generalizable and Reproducible Phenomenon with Important Implications for Risk Assessment. *Risk Analysis* 19: 261–81.

Calabrese, E., and R. Blain. 1999. The Single Exposure Carcinogen Database: Assessing the Circumstances under Which a Single Exposure to a Carcinogen Can Cause Cancer. *Toxicological Sciences* 50: 169–85.

Calabrese, E., and M. Mattson. 2010. The Hormetic Pharmacy: The Future of Natural Products and Man-made Drugs in Disease Prevention and Treatment. In *Hormesis: A Revolution in Biology, Toxicology, and Medicine*, ed. M. Mattson and E. Calabrese, 177–98. New York: Springer.

Calabrese, E., M. McCarthy, and E. Kenyon. 1987. The Occurrence of Chemically Induced Hormesis. *Health Physics* 52: 531–41.

Calabrese, E., J. Staudenmayer, E. Stanek, and G. Hoffmann. 2006. Hormesis Outperforms Threshold Model in National Cancer Institute Antitumor Drug Screening Database. *Toxicological Sciences* 94: 368–78.

———. 2007. Hormesis and High Throughput Studies: Crump's Analysis Lacks Credibility. *Toxicological Sciences* 98: 602–603.

Callahan, M., and J. Tercier. 2007. The Relationship of Previous Training and Experience of Journal Peer Reviewers to Subsequent Review Quality. *PLOS Medicine* 4: 32–40.

Camerer, C., and R. Hogarth. 1999. The Effects of Financial Incentives in Experiments: A Review and Capital-labor-production Framework. *Journal of Risk and Uncertainty* 19: 7–42.

Capek, S. 2000. Reframing Endometriosis: From "Career Women's Disease" to Environment/Body Connections. In *Illness and the Environment: A Reader in Contested Medicine*, ed. S. Kroll-Smith, P. Brown, and V. Gunter, 345–63. New York: New York University Press.

Caress, S., and A. Steinemann. 2003. A Review of a Two-phase Population Study of Multiple Chemical Sensitivities. *Environmental Health Perspectives* 111: 1490–97.

Carey, B. 2007. Criticism of a Gender Theory, and a Scientist under Siege. *New York Times*, August 21.

Carlsen, E., A. Giwercman, N. Keiding, and N. Skakkebaek. 1992. Evidence for Decreasing Quality of Semen during the Past 50 Years. *British Medical Journal* 305: 609–13.

Chapman, P. 2002. Defining Hormesis: Comments on Calabrese and Baldwin (2002). *Human and Experimental Toxicology* 21: 99–101.

Chugh, D., M. Bazerman, and M. Banaji. 2005. Bounded Ethicality as a Psychological Barrier to Recognizing Conflicts of Interest. In *Conflicts of Interest: Challenges and Solutions in Business, Law, Medicine, and Public Policy*, ed. D. Moore, D. Cain, G. Loewenstein, and M. Bazerman, 74–95. New York: Cambridge University Press.

Churchman, C. 1948. Statistics, Pragmatics, and Induction. *Philosophy of Science* 15: 249–68.

———. 1956. Science and Decision-making. *Philosophy of Science* 23: 247–49.

Cohen, L. J. 1992. *An Essay on Belief and Acceptance*. New York: Oxford University Press.

Colborn, T., D. Dumanoski, and J. Myers. 1996. *Our Stolen Future*. New York: Dutton.

Cole, S., J. Cole, and G. Simon. 1981. Chance and Consensus in Peer Review. *Science* 214: 881–86.

Conant, J. B. 1951. *Science and Common Sense*. New Haven: Yale University Press.

Connolly, R., and W. Lutz. 2004. Nonmonotonic Dose-response Relationships: Mechanistic Basis, Kinetic Modeling, and Implications for Risk Assessment. *Toxicological Sciences* 77: 151–57.

Cook, R., and E. Calabrese. 2006. The Importance of Hormesis to Public Health. *Environmental Health Perspectives* 114: 1631–35.

Couch, S., and S. Kroll-Smith. 2000. Environmental Movements and Expert Knowledge: Evidence for a New Populism. In *Illness and the Environment: A Reader in Contested Medicine*, ed. S. Kroll-Smith, P. Brown, and V. Gunter, 384–404. New York: New York University Press.

Crain, D., S. J. Janssen, T. M. Edwards, J. Heindel, S-M. Ho, P. Hunt, T. Iguchi, et al. 2008. Female Reproductive Disorders: The Roles of Endocrine-disrupting Compounds and Developmental Timing. *Fertility and Sterility* 90: 911–40.

Cranor, C. 1990. Some Moral Issues in Risk Assessment. *Ethics* 101: 123–43.

———. 1993. *Regulating Toxic Substances: A Philosophy of Science and the Law*. New York: Oxford University Press.

———. 1995. The Social Benefits of Expedited Risk Assessment. *Risk Analysis* 15: 353–58.

———. 2008. *Toxic Torts: Science, Law, and the Possibility of Justice*. New York: Cambridge University Press.

Crump, K. 2001. Evaluating the Evidence for Hormesis: A Statistical Perspective. *Critical Reviews in Toxicology* 31: 669–79.

———. 2007. Limitations in the National Cancer Institute Antitumor Drug Screening Database for Evaluating Hormesis. *Toxicological Sciences* 98: 599–601.

Daston, L., and P. Galison. 2007. *Objectivity*. New York: Zone.

Davidoff, A., and L. Fogarty. 1994. Psychogenic Origins of Multiple Chemical Sensitivities Syndrome: A Critical Review of the Research Literature. *Archives of Environmental Health* 49: 316–25.

Davidson, R. 1986. Source of Funding and Outcomes of Clinical Trials. *Journal of General Internal Medicine* 3: 155–58.

Davis, D. 2003. *When Smoke Ran like Water: Tales of Environmental Deception and the Battle against Pollution*. New York: Basic Books.

———. 2007. *The Secret History of the War on Cancer*. New York: Basic Books.

Davis, J. M., and W. Farland. 1998. Biological Effects of Low-level Exposures: A Perspective from U.S. EPA Scientists. *Environmental Health Perspectives* 106: 380–81.

Davis, J. M., and D. Svendsgaard. 1990. U-shaped Dose-response Curves: Their Occurrence and Implications for Risk Assessment. *Journal of Toxicology and Environmental Health* 30: 71–83.

———. 1994. Nonmonotonic Dose-response Relationships in Toxicological Studies. In *Biological Effects of Low Level Exposures: Dose-Response Relationships*, ed. E. Calabrese, 67–85. Boca Raton, Fla.: Lewis.

DeAngelis, C., J. Drazen, F. Frizelle, C. Haug, J. Hoey, R. Horton, S. Kotzin, et al. 2004. Clinical Trial Registration: A Statement from the International Council of Medical Journal Editors. *Journal of the American Medical Association* 292: 1363–64.

Derenzo, E. 2005. Conflict-of-interest Policy at the National Institutes of Health: The Pendulum Swings Wildly. *Kennedy Institute of Ethics Journal* 45: 199–208.

Dietz, T. 1995. Preface: Democracy and Science. In *Fairness and Competence in Citizen Participation*, ed. O. Renn, T. Webler, and P. Wiedemann, xvii–xix. Boston: Kluwer.

Donnelly, M. 2002. *Consent: Bridging the Gap between Doctor and Patient*. Cork: Cork University Press.

Dorato, M. 2004. Epistemic and Nonepistemic Values in Science. In *Science, Values, and Objectivity*, ed. P. Machamer and G. Wolters, 52–77. Pittsburgh: University of Pittsburgh Press.

Douglas, H. 2000. Inductive Risk and Values in Science. *Philosophy of Science* 67: 559–79.

———. 2003. The Moral Responsibilities of Scientists: Tensions between Autonomy and Responsibility. *American Philosophical Quarterly* 40: 59–68.

———. 2004. The Irreducible Complexity of Objectivity. *Synthese* 138: 453–73.

———. 2007. Inserting the Public into Science. In *Democratization of Expertise? Exploring Novel Forms of Scientific Advice in Political Decision-Making*, ed. S. Maasen and P. Weingart, 153–69. New York: Springer.

———. 2008a. The Role of Values in Expert Reasoning. *Public Affairs Quarterly* 22: 1–18.

———. 2008b. Science, Hormesis, and Regulation. *Human and Experimental Toxicology* 27: 603–607.

———. 2009. *Science, Policy, and the Value-free Ideal.* Pittsburgh: University of Pittsburgh Press.

Dowie, M. 1998. What's Wrong with the *New York Times* Science Reporting? *Nation,* July 6, 13–14, 16–19.

Drazen, J., and G. Curfman. 2002. Financial Associations of Authors. *New England Journal of Medicine* 346: 1901–1902.

Dryzek, J. 2002. *Deliberative Democracy and Beyond.* New York: Oxford University Press.

Dupré, J. 2007. Fact and Value. In *Value-free Science? Ideals and Illusions,* ed. H. Kincaid, J. Dupré, and A. Wylie, 27–41. New York: Oxford University Press.

EDSTAC (Endocrine Disrupter Screening and Testing Advisory Committee). 1998. *Final Report.* Washington, D.C.: Environmental Protection Agency.

Efron, E. 1984. *The Apocalyptics.* New York: Simon and Schuster.

Einstein, A. 1998. Science and Religion. In *Ideas and Opinions.* New York: Bonanza.

Elliott, C. 2004. Pharma Goes to the Laundry: Public Relations and the Business of Medical Education. *Hastings Center Report* 34: 18–23.

Elliott, K. 2000. A Case for Caution: An Evaluation of Calabrese and Baldwin's Studies of Chemical Hormesis. *Risk: Health, Safety, and Environment* 11: 177–96.

———. 2004. Error as Means to Discovery. *Philosophy of Science* 71: 1–24.

———. 2006. A Novel Account of Scientific Anomaly: Help for the Dispute over Low-dose Biochemical Effects. *Philosophy of Science* 73 (Proceedings): 790–802.

———. 2008. Hormesis, Ethics, and Public Policy: An Overview. *Human and Experimental Toxicology* 27: 659–62.

———. 2009. The Ethical Significance of Language in the Environmental Sciences: Case Studies from Pollution Research. *Ethics, Place, and Environment* 12: 157–73.

Elliott, K., and D. McKaughan. 2009. How Values in Discovery and Pursuit Alter Theory Appraisal. *Philosophy of Science* 76 (December): 598–611.

EPA (Environmental Protection Agency). 2000. *Comments on the Use of Data from the Testing of Human Subjects: A Report by the Science Advisory Board and the FIFRA Scientific Advisory Panel.* Washington, D.C.: Author.

Epstein, S. 2000. Democracy, Expertise, and AIDS Treatment Activism. In *Science, Technology, and Democracy*, ed. D. Kleinman, 15–32. Albany: SUNY Press.

Escobar, J., C. Hoyos-Nervi, and M. Gara. 2002. Medically Unexplained Physical Symptoms in Medical Practice: A Psychiatric Perspective. *Environmental Health Perspectives* 110 (suppl. 4): 631–36.

Faden, R., and T. Beauchamp. 1986. *A History and Theory of Informed Consent*. New York: Oxford University Press.

Fagin, D., M. Lavelle, and the Center for Public Integrity. 1999. *Toxic Deception*, 2nd ed. Monroe, Maine: Common Courage.

Finkel, A. 1994. Rodent Tests Continue to Save Human Lives—Use of Rodents in Testing Possible Carcinogens. *Insight on the News* (December 12), http://findarticles.com/p/articles/mi_m1571/is_n50_v10/ai_15981072/?tag=content;col1 (accessed April 4, 2009).

Fiorino, D. 1990. Citizen Participation and Environmental Risk: A Survey of Institutional Mechanisms. *Science, Technology, and Human Values* 15: 226–43.

———. 1995. Regulatory Negotiation as a Form of Public Participation. In *Fairness and Competence in Citizen Participation*, ed. O. Renn, T. Webler, and P. Wiedemann, 223–37. Boston: Kluwer.

Fischer, F. 1993. Citizen Participation and the Democratization of Policy Expertise: From Theoretical Inquiry to Practical Cases. *Policy Sciences* 26: 165–87.

Fishkin, J., and P. Laslett. 2003. *Debating Deliberative Democracy*. Oxford: Blackwell.

Foran, J. 1998. Regulatory Implications of Hormesis. *Human and Experimental Toxicology* 17: 441–43.

Franklin, P. 2006. EPA's Drinking Water Standards and the Shaping of Sound Science. In *Shaping Science and Technology Policy: The Next Generation of Research*, ed. D. Guston and D. Sarewitz, 102–23. Madison: University of Wisconsin Press.

Friedberg, M., B. Saffran, T. Stinson, W. Nelson, and C. Bennett. 1999. Evaluation of Conflict of Interest in Economic Analyses of New Drugs Used in Oncology. *Journal of the American Medical Association* 282: 1453–57.

Fujiwara, Y., T. Tomoko, Y. Toshie, and N. Fusao. 2002. Changes in Egg Size of the Diamondback Moth *Plutella Xylostella* (Lepidoptera: Yponomeutidae) Treated with Fenvalerate at Sublethal Doses and Viability of the Eggs. *Applied Entomology and Zoology* 37: 103–109.

Fumento, M. 1993. *Science under Siege: Balancing Technology and the Environment*. New York: Morrow.

Futrell, R. 2003. Technical Adversarialism and Participatory Collaboration in the U.S. Chemical Weapons Disposal Program. *Science, Technology, and Human Values* 28: 451–82.

Galinsky, A., and T. Mussweiler. 2001. First Offers as Anchors: The Role of Perspective-taking and Negotiator Focus. *Journal of Personality and Social Psychology* 81: 657–69.

GAO (General Accounting Office). 1998. *Gulf War Illnesses: Federal Research Strategy Needs Reexamination.* Washington, D.C.: Author, http://www.gao.gov/archive/1998/ns98104t.pdf (accessed June 22, 2007).

———. 2001. *Air Pollution: EPA Should Improve Oversight of Emissions Reporting,* GAO-01–46. Washington, D.C.: Author.

———. 2003. *University Research: Most Federal Agencies Need to Better Protect against Financial Conflicts of Interest.* Washington, D.C.: Author.

———. 2004. *Gulf War Illnesses: DOD's Conclusions about U.S. Troops' Exposure Cannot Be Adequately Supported.* Washington, D.C.: Author, http://www.gao.gov/new.items/d04159.pdf (accessed June 22, 2007).

Gardiner, S. 2004. Ethics and Global Climate Change. *Ethics* 114: 555–600.

Gerber, L., G. Williams, and S. Gray. 1999. The Nutrient-toxin Dosage Continuum in Human Evolution and Modern Health. *Quarterly Review of Biology* 74: 273–89.

Gert, B., C. Culver, and K. Clouser. 1997. *Bioethics: A Return to Fundamentals.* New York: Oxford University Press.

Gewirth, A. 1986. Professional Ethics: The Separatist Thesis. *Ethics* 96: 282–300.

Gibson, P., A. Elms, and L. Ruding. 2003. Perceived Treatment Efficacy for Conventional and Alternative Therapies Reported by Persons with Multiple Chemical Sensitivity. *Environmental Health Perspectives* 111: 1498–1504.

Giere, R. 2003. A New Program for Philosophy of Science. *Philosophy of Science* 70: 15–21.

Gieryn, T. 1999. *Cultural Boundaries of Science: Credibility on the Line.* Chicago: University of Chicago Press.

Gilbert, M. 1995. Repeated Exposure to Lindane Leads to Behavioral Sensitization and Facilitates Electrical Kindling. *Neurotoxicology and Teratology* 17: 143–50.

Goldman, A. 1980. *The Moral Foundations of Professional Ethics.* Totowa, N.J.: Rowman and Littlefield.

Gore, A. 1996. Foreword. In *Our Stolen Future,* by T. Colborn, D. Dumanoski, and J. Myers, vii–ix. New York: Dutton.

Gots, R. 1996. Multiple Chemical Sensitivities: Distinguishing between Psychogenic and Toxicodynamic. *Regulatory Toxicology and Pharmacology* 24: S8–15.

Greenberg, D. 2007. *Science for Sale: The Perils, Rewards, and Delusions of Campus Capitalism.* Chicago: University of Chicago Press.

Guo, Y., P. C. Hsu, C. C. Hsu, and G. H. Lambert. 2000. Semen Quality after Prenatal Exposure to Polychlorinated Biphenyls and Dibenzofurans. *Lancet* 356: 1240–41.

Guston, D. 1999. Evaluating the First U.S. Consensus Conference: The Impact of the Citizen's Panel on Telecommunications and the Future of Democracy. *Science, Technology, and Human Values* 24: 451–82.

———. 2004. Forget Politicizing Science. Let's Democratize Science! *Issues in Science and Technology* 21: 25–28.

———. 2005. Institutional Design for Socially Robust Knowledge: The National Toxicology Program's Report on Carcinogens. In *Democratization of Expertise? Exploring Novel Forms of Scientific Advice in Political Decision Making,* ed. S. Maasen and P. Weingart, 63–79. Dordrecht: Springer.

———. 2008. Innovation Policy: Not Just a Jumbo Shrimp. *Nature* 454: 940–41.

Haack, S. 1996. Science as Social? Yes and No. In *Feminism, Science, and the Philosophy of Science,* ed. L. Hankinson Nelson and J. Nelson, 79–94. Boston: Kluwer.

Hansson, S. O. 2008. Ethical Principles for Hormesis Policies. *Human and Experimental Toxicology* 27: 609–12.

Hardell, L., M. Walker, B. Walhjalt, L. Friedman, and E. Richter. 2007. Secret Ties to Industry and Conflicting Interests in Cancer Research. *American Journal of Industrial Medicine* 50: 227–233.

Hardwig, J. 1994. Toward an Ethics of Expertise. In *Professional Ethics and Social Responsibility,* ed. D. Wueste. Lanham, Md.: Rowman and Littlefield.

Harre, R., J. Brockmeier, and P. Muhlhauser. 1999. *Greenspeak: A Study of Environmental Discourse.* Thousand Oaks, Calif.: Sage.

Harris, G., and A. Berenson. 2005. 10 Voters on Panel Backing Pain Pills Had Industry Ties. *New York Times,* February 25, A1.

Hayes, T. 2004. There Is No Denying This: Defusing the Confusion about Atrazine. *BioScience* 54: 1138–39.

Healy, D., and D. Cattell. 2003. Interface between Authorship, Industry, and Science in the Domain of Therapeutics. *British Journal of Psychiatry* 183: 22–27.

Hempel, C. 1965. Science and Human Values. In *Aspects of Scientific Explanation and Other Essays in the Philosophy of Science,* 81–96. New York: Free Press.

Henschler, D. 2006. The Origin of Hormesis: Historical Background and Driving Forces. *Human and Experimental Toxicology* 25: 347–51.

Herbers, J. 2007. Watch Your Language! Racially Loaded Metaphors in Scientific Research. *BioScience* 57: 104–105.

Ho, S.-M., W.-Y. Tang, J. Belmonte de Frausto, and G. S. Prins. 2006. Developmental Exposure to Estradiol and Bisphenol A Increases Susceptibility to Prostate Carcinogenesis and Epigenetically Regulates Phosphodiesterase Type 4 Variant 4. *Cancer Research* 66: 5624–32.

Hoffmann, G. 2007. Letter to the Editor on Ethics of Expertise, Informed Consent, and Hormesis. *Science and Engineering Ethics* 13: 135–37.

———. 2009. A Perspective on the Scientific, Philosophical, and Policy Dimensions of Hormesis. *Dose-Response* 7: 1–51.

Hoffmann, G., and W. E. Stempsey. 2008. The Hormesis Concept and Risk Assessment: Are There Unique Ethical and Policy Considerations? *Human and Experimental Toxicology* 27: 613–20.

Howard, D. 2003. Two Left Turns Make a Right: On the Curious Political Career of North-American Philosophy of Science at Mid-century. In *Logical Empiricism in North America,* ed. A. Richardson and G. Hardcastle, 25–93. Minneapolis: University of Minnesota Press.

———. 2006. Lost Wanderers in the Forest of Knowledge: Some Thoughts on the Discovery-justification Distinction. In *Revisiting Discovery and Justification: Historical and Philosophical Perspectives on the Context Distinction,* ed. J. Schickore and F. Steinle, 3–22. New York: Springer.

Hunt, G., and M. Hunt. 1977. Female-female Pairing in Western Gulls (*Larus occidentalis*) in Southern California. *Science* 196: 1466–67.

Intemann, K. 2005. Feminism, Underdetermination, and Values in Science. *Philosophy of Science* 72: 1001–12.

Intersociety Working Group. 2006. *Congressional Action on Research and Development in the FY 2006 Budget,* http://www.aaas.org/spp/rd/ca06main.htm (accessed November 24, 2008).

Irvin, R., and J. Stansbury. 2004. Citizen Participation in Decision Making: Is It Worth the Effort? *Public Administration Review* 64: 55–65.

Irwin, A. 1995. *Citizen Science: A Study of People, Expertise, and Sustainable Development.* New York: Routledge.

Jamieson, D. 1996. Scientific Uncertainty: How Do We Know When to Communicate Research Findings to the Public? *Science of the Total Environment* 184: 103–107.

———, ed. 1999. *Singer and His Critics.* Oxford: Blackwell.

Jasanoff, S. 1990. *The Fifth Branch: Science Advisors as Policymakers.* Cambridge, Mass.: Harvard University Press.

———. 1993. Procedural Choices in Regulatory Science. *Risk: Issues in Health and Safety* 4: 143–60.

———. 2003. Technologies of Humility: Citizen Participation in Governing Science. *Minerva* 41: 223–44.

———. 2005. Judgment under Siege: The Three-body Problem of Expert Legitimacy. In *Democratization of Expertise? Exploring Novel Forms of*

*Scientific Advice in Political Decision Making*, ed. S. Maasen and P. Weingart, 209–24. Dordrecht: Springer.

Jasanoff, S., G. Markle, J. Peterson, and T. Pinch, eds. 2001. *Handbook of Science and Technology Studies*, rev. ed. Thousand Oaks, Calif.: Sage.

Jefferson, T., E. Wager, and F. Davidoff. 2002. Measuring the Quality of Editorial Peer Review. *Journal of the American Medical Association* 287: 2786–90.

Jeffrey, R. 1956. Valuation and Acceptance of Scientific Hypotheses. *Philosophy of Science* 23: 237–46.

Joffres, M., T. Sampalli, and R. Fox. 2005. Physiologic and Symptomatic Responses to Low-level Substances in Individuals with and without Chemical Sensitivities: A Randomized Controlled Blinded Pilot Booth Study. *Environmental Health Perspectives* 113: 1178–83.

Johnson, A. 2004. The End of Pure Science: Science Policy from Bayh-Dole to the NNI. In *Discovering the Nanoscale*, ed. D. Baird, A. Nordmann, and J. Schummer, 217–30. Amsterdam: IOS Press.

Jonas, W. 2001. A Critique of "The Scientific Foundations of Hormesis." *Critical Reviews in Toxicology* 31: 625–29.

Joss, S., and J. Durant. 1995. *Public Participation in Science: The Role of Consensus Conferences in Europe*. London: Science Museum.

Kahan, D., P. Slovic, D. Braman, and J. Gastil. 2006. Fear of Democracy: A Cultural Evaluation of Sunstein on Risk. *Harvard Law Review* 119: 1071–1109.

Kaiser, J. 2003. Sipping from a Poisoned Chalice. *Science* 302: 376–79.

Kantrowitz, A. 1967. Proposal for an Institution for Scientific Judgment. *Science* 156: 763–64.

———. 1976. The Science Court Experiment: An Interim Report. *Science* 193: 653–56.

Kassirer, J. 2005. *On the Take: How Medicine's Complicity with Big Business Endangers Your Health*. New York: Oxford University Press.

Kerns, T. 2001. *Environmentally Induced Illnesses*. Jefferson, N.C.: McFarland.

Kincaid, H., J. Dupré, and A. Wylie. 2007a. Introduction. In *Value-free Science? Ideals and Illusions*, ed. H. Kincaid, J. Dupré, and A. Wylie, 3–26. New York: Oxford University Press.

———, eds. 2007b. *Value-free Science? Ideals and Illusions*. New York: Oxford University Press.

Kitcher, P. 1985. *Vaulting Ambition*. Cambridge, Mass.: MIT Press.

———. 2001. *Science, Truth, and Democracy*. New York: Oxford University Press.

———. 2007. Scientific Research—Who Should Govern? *NanoEthics* 1: 177–84.

Kitchin, K., and J. W. Drane. 2005. A Critique of the Use of Hormesis in Risk Assessment. *BELLE Newsletter* 12: 8–12.

Klaassen, C. 2007. *Casarett and Doull's Toxicology: The Basic Science of Poisons*, 7th ed. New York: McGraw-Hill.

Kleinman, D. 2000. *Science, Technology, and Democracy*. Albany: State University of New York Press.

———. 2005. *Science and Technology in Society: From Biotechnology to the Internet*. Malden, Mass.: Blackwell.

Koertge, N. 1998. *A House Built on Sand: Exposing Postmodernist Myths about Science*. New York: Oxford University Press.

Koizumi, K. 2008. Federal R&D in the FY 2009 Budget: An Introduction. In *AAAS Report XXXIII: Research and Development FY 2009*, by Intersociety Working Group, http://www.aaas.org/spp/rd/rd09main.htm (accessed November 24, 2008).

Kolata, G. 1996. Chemicals That Mimic Hormones Spark Alarm and Debate. *New York Times*, March 19, C1, C10.

Kourany, J. 2003. A Philosophy of Science for the Twenty-first Century. *Philosophy of Science* 70: 1–14.

Krimsky, S. 2000a. Environmental Endocrine Hypothesis and Public Policy. In *Illness and the Environment: A Reader in Contested Medicine*, ed. S. Kroll-Smith, P. Brown, and V. Gunter, 95–107. New York: New York University Press.

———. 2000b. *Hormonal Chaos: The Scientific and Social Origins of the Environmental Endocrine Hypothesis*. Baltimore: Johns Hopkins University Press.

———. 2003. *Science in the Private Interest*. Lanham, Md.: Rowman and Littlefield.

Krimsky, S., and L. S. Rothenberg. 2001. Conflict of Interest Policies in Science and Medical Journals: Editorial Practices and Author Disclosure. *Science and Engineering Ethics* 7: 205–18.

Krimsky, S., P. Stott, and G. Kyle. 1996. Financial Interests of Authors in Scientific Journals: A Pilot Study of 14 Publications. *Science and Engineering Ethics* 2: 395–410.

Kroll-Smith, J. S., and H. Floyd. 1997. *Bodies in Protest: Environmental Illness and the Struggle over Medical Knowledge*. New York: New York University Press.

Kuhn, T. 1977. Rationality, Value Judgment, and Theory Choice. In *The Essential Tension*, 320–39. Chicago: University of Chicago Press.

Lacey, H. 1999. *Is Science Value Free?* London: Routledge.

———. 2004. Is There a Significant Distinction between Cognitive and Social Values? In *Science, Values, and Objectivity*, ed. P. Machamer and G. Wolters, 24–51. Pittsburgh: University of Pittsburgh Press.

Lacour, M., T. Zunder, K. Schmidtke, P. Vaith, and C. Scheidt. 2005. Multiple Chemical Sensitivity Syndrome (MCS)—Suggestions for an Extension of the U.S. MCS-Case Definition. *International Journal of Hygiene and Environmental Health* 208: 141–51.

Lappé, M. 1991. *Chemical Deception.* San Francisco: Sierra Club Books.

Larson, B. 2005. The War of the Roses: Demilitarizing Invasion Biology. *Frontiers in Ecology and the Environment* 3: 495–500.

———. 2006. The Social Resonance of Competitive and Progressive Evolutionary Metaphors. *BioScience* 56: 997–1004.

Laudan, L. 1984. *Science and Values.* Berkeley: University of California Press.

Lave, L. 2000. Hormesis: Policy Implications. *Journal of Applied Toxicology* 20: 141–45.

———. 2001. Hormesis: Implications for Public Policy regarding Toxicants. *Annual Review of Public Health* 22: 63–67.

Lave, L., and E. Seskin. 1970. Air Pollution and Human Health. *Science* 169: 723–33.

Lee, J. 2003. Popular Pesticide Faulted for Frogs' Sexual Abnormalities. *New York Times,* June 19.

Leonhardt, D. 2007. A Battle over the Costs of Global Warming. *New York Times,* February 21, A20.

Longino, H. 1990. *Science as Social Knowledge.* Princeton: Princeton University Press.

———. 1994. Gender and Racial Biases in Scientific Research. In *Ethics of Scientific Research,* ed. K. Shrader-Frechette, 139–52. Lanham, Md.: Rowman and Littlefield.

———. 1995. Gender, Politics, and the Theoretical Virtues. *Synthese* 104: 383–97.

———. 1997. Cognitive and Non-cognitive Values in Science: Rethinking the Dichotomy. In *Feminism, Science, and the Philosophy of Science,* ed. L. Hankinson Nelson and J. Nelson, 39–58. Boston: Kluwer.

———. 2002a. *The Fate of Knowledge.* Princeton: Princeton University Press.

———. 2002b. Science and the Common Good: Thoughts on Philip Kitcher's *Science, Truth, and Democracy. Philosophy of Science* 69: 560–68.

Lucier, G., and G. Hook. 1996. Anniversaries and Issues. *Environmental Health Perspectives* 104: 350.

Macedo, S., ed. 1999. *Deliberative Politics: Essays on Democracy and Disagreement.* New York: Oxford University Press.

Machamer, P., L. Darden, and C. Craver. 2000. Thinking about Mechanisms. *Philosophy of Science* 67: 1–25.

Machamer, P., and G. Wolters. 2004a. Introduction: Science, Values, and Objectivity. In *Science, Values, and Objectivity*, ed. P. Machamer and G. Wolters, 1–13. Pittsburgh: University of Pittsburgh Press.

———, eds. 2004b. *Science, Values, and Objectivity*. Pittsburgh: University of Pittsburgh Press.

Mackay, A. 1991. *A Dictionary of Scientific Quotations*. Bristol: Institute of Physics Publishing.

Madison, J. 1961. The Federalist No. 10. In *The Federalist Papers*, ed. C. Rossiter, 77–84. New York: Signet.

Maker, W. 1994. Scientific Autonomy, Scientific Responsibility. In *Professional Ethics and Social Responsibility*, ed. D. Wueste, 219–42. Lanham, Md.: Rowman and Littlefield.

Manson, N. 2002. Formulating the Precautionary Principle. *Environmental Ethics* 24: 263–74.

Markowitz, G., and D. Rosner. 2002. *Deceit and Denial: The Deadly Politics of Industrial Pollution*. Berkeley: University of California Press.

Marris, E. 2006. Should Conservation Biologists Push Policies? *Nature* 442: 13.

Martin, E. 1996. The Egg and the Sperm: How Science Has Constructed a Romance Based on Stereotypical Male-female Roles. In *Feminism and Science*, ed. E. Fox Keller and H. Longino, 103–17. New York: Oxford University Press.

Martin, M., and R. Schinzinger. 2004. *Ethics in Engineering*, 4th ed. New York: McGraw-Hill.

Matthews, A., and B. Martinez. 2004. Emails Suggest Merck Knew Vioxx's Dangers at Early Stage. *Wall Street Journal* (November 1).

Mattson, M. 2008. Hormesis Defined. *Ageing Research Review* 7: 1–7.

———. 2010a. The Fundamental Role of Hormesis in Evolution. In *Hormesis: A Revolution in Biology, Toxicology, and Medicine*, ed. M. Mattson and C. Calabrese, 57–68. New York: Springer.

———. 2010b. Preface. In *Hormesis: A Revolution in Biology, Toxicology, and Medicine*, ed. M. Mattson and E. Calabrese, v–vii. New York: Springer.

Mattson, M., and E. Calabrese, eds. 2010a. *Hormesis: A Revolution in Biology, Toxicology, and Medicine*. New York: Springer.

———. 2010b. "Hormesis: What It Is and Why It Matters. In *Hormesis: A Revolution in Biology, Toxicology, and Medicine*, ed. M. Mattson and E. Calabrese, 1–13. New York: Springer.

Mattson, M., T. Son, and S. Camandola. 2007. Viewpoint: Mechanisms of Action and Therapeutic Potential of Neurohormetic Phytochemicals. *Dose Response* 5: 174–86.

May, T. 2002. *Bioethics in a Liberal Society*. Baltimore: Johns Hopkins University Press.

Mayo, D. 1991. Sociological vs. Metascientific Views of Risk Assessment. In *Acceptable Evidence: Science and Values in Risk Management*, ed. D. Mayo and R. Hollander, 249–80. New York: Oxford University Press.

Mayo, D., and R. Hollander. 1991. *Acceptable Evidence: Science and Values in Risk Management*. New York: Oxford University Press.

Mayo, D., and A. Spanos. 2008. Risks to Health and Risks to Science: The Need for a Responsible "Bioevidential" Scrutiny. *Human and Experimental Toxicology* 27: 621–25.

Mazur, D. 2003. *The New Medical Conversation*. Lanham, Md.: Rowman and Littlefield.

McGarity, T., and W. Wagner. 2008. *Bending Science: How Special Interests Corrupt Public Health Research*. Cambridge, Mass.: Harvard University Press.

McGinn, A. 2002. Reducing Our Toxic Burden. In *State of the World 2002*, ed. Linda Starke, 75–100. New York: Norton.

McKaughan, D. 2007. "Toward a Richer Vocabulary for Epistemic Attitudes: Mapping the Cognitive Landscape." PhD diss., University of Notre Dame.

McMullin, E. 1983. Values in Science. In *PSA 1982*, vol. 2, ed. P. Asquith and T. Nickles, 3–28. East Lansing: Philosophy of Science Association.

———. 2000. Values in Science. In *A Companion to the Philosophy of Science*, ed. W. Newton-Smith, 550–60. Oxford: Blackwell.

Meffe, G., C. R. Carroll, and Contributors. 1997. *Principles of Conservation Biology*, 2nd ed. Sunderland, Mass.: Sinauer.

Menzie, C. 2001. Hormesis in Ecological Risk Assessment: A Useful Concept, a Confusing Term, and/or a Distraction? *Human and Experimental Toxicology* 20: 521–23.

Merton, R. 1942. *The Sociology of Science*. Chicago: University of Chicago Press.

Michaels, D. 2008. *Doubt Is Their Product: How Industry's Assault on Science Threatens Your Health*. New York: Oxford University Press.

Miller, C., and H. Mitzel. 1995. Chemical Sensitivity Attributed to Pesticide Exposures versus Remodeling. *Archives of Environmental Health* 50: 119–29.

Miller, D. 2005. Commentary: Psychologically Naïve Assumptions about the Perils of Conflicts of Interest. In *Conflicts of Interest: Challenges and Solutions in Business, Law, Medicine, and Public Policy*, ed. D. Moore, D. Cain, G. Loewenstein, and M. Bazerman, 126–29. New York: Cambridge University Press.

Milloy, S. 2001. *Junk Science Judo: Self-defense against Health Scams and Scares*. Washington, D.C.: Cato Institute.

Mitchell, S. 2004. The Prescribed and Proscribed Values in Science Policy. In *Science, Values, and Objectivity*, ed. P. Machamer and G. Wolters, 245–55. Pittsburgh: University of Pittsburgh Press.

Moore, D., G. Loewenstein, D. Cain, and M. Bazerman. 2005. Introduction. In *Conflicts of Interest: Challenges and Solutions in Business, Law, Medicine, and Public Policy*, ed. D. Moore, D. Cain, G. Loewenstein, and M. Bazerman, 1–12. New York: Cambridge University Press.

Morris, J., ed. 2000. *Rethinking Risk and the Precautionary Principle*. Boston: Butterworth-Heinemann.

Munn Sanchez, E. 2004. The Expert's Role in Nanoscience and Technology. In *Discovering the Nanoscale*, ed. D. Baird, A. Nordmann, and J. Schummer, 257–68. Amsterdam: IOS Press.

Mushak, P. 2007. Hormesis and Its Place in Nonmonotonic Dose-response Relationships: Some Scientific Reality Checks. *Environmental Health Perspectives* 115: 500–506.

———. 2009. Ad-hoc and Fast Forward: The Science of Hormesis Growth and Development. *Environmental Health Perspectives* 117: 1333–38.

———. 2010. Hormesis: A Brief Reply to an Advocate. *Environmental Health Perspectives* 118: a153.

Mutz, D. 2008. Is Deliberative Democracy a Falsifiable Theory? *Annual Review of Political Science* 11: 521–38.

Myers, J., F. vom Saal, B. Akingbemi, K. Arizono, S. Belcher, T. Colborn, I. Chahoud, et al. 2009. Why Public Health Agencies Cannot Depend on Good Laboratory Practices as a Criterion for Selecting Data: The Case of Bisphenol A. *Environmental Health Perspectives* 117: 309–15.

Nagel, S., F. vom Saal, K. Thayer, M. Dhar, M. Boechler, and W. Welshons. 1997. Relative Binding Affinity-Serum Modified Access (RBA-SMA) Assay Predicts the Relative *In Vivo* Activity of the Xenoestrogens Bisphenol A and Octylphenol. *Environmental Health Perspectives* 105: 70–76.

Neafsey, P. J., H. Boxenbaum, D. A. Ciraulo, and D. J. Fournier. 1988. A Gompertz Age-specific Mortality Rate Model of Aging, Hormesis, and Toxicity: Fixed Dose Studies. *Drug Metabolism Reviews* 19: 369–401.

Nelson, D., R. Brownson, P. Remington, and C. Parvanta. 2002. Future Directions. In *Communicating Public Health Information Effectively*, ed. D. Nelson, R. Brownson, P. Remington, and C. Parvanta. Washington, D.C.: American Public Health Association.

Nisbet, M., and C. Mooney. 2007. Framing Science. *Science* 316: 56.

Norton, B. 2003. *Searching for Sustainability*. New York: Cambridge University Press.

———. 2005. *Sustainability: A Philosophy of Adaptive Ecosystem Management*. Chicago: University of Chicago Press.

NRC (National Research Council). 1994. *Science and Judgment in Risk Assessment*. Washington, D.C.: National Academy Press.

———. 1996. *Understanding Risk: Informing Decisions in a Democratic Society*. Washington, D.C.: National Academy Press.

———. 1999. *Hormonally Active Agents in the Environment*. Washington, D.C.: National Academy Press.

———. 2005. *Decision Making for the Environment*. Washington, D.C.: National Academies Press.

———. 2006. *Health Effects from Exposure to Low Levels of Ionizing Radiation*. BEIR VII Phase 2. Washington, D.C.: National Academy Press.

———. 2008a. *Phtalates and Cumulative Risk Assessment*. Washington, D.C.: National Academies Press.

———. 2008b. *Public Participation in Environmental Assessment and Decision Making*. Washington, D.C.: National Academies Press.

NTP (National Toxicology Program). 2001. *National Toxicology Program's Report of the Endocrine Disruptors Low Dose Peer Review*. Research Triangle Park, N.C.: National Toxicology Program.

Oleskey, C., A. Fleischman, L. Goldman, K. Hirschhorn, P. Landrigan, M. Lappé, M. F. Marhsall, et al. 2004. Pesticide Testing in Humans: Ethics and Public Policy. *Environmental Health Perspectives* 112: 914–19.

Owen, B., and R. Braeutigam. 1978. *The Regulation Game*. New York: HarperCollins.

Pall, M. 2003. Elevated Nitric Oxide/peroxynitrite Theory of Multiple Chemical Sensitivity: Central Role of *N*-Methyl-D-Aspartate Receptors in the Sensitivity Mechanism. *Environmental Health Perspectives* 111: 1461–64.

Parsons, P. 2001. The Hormetic Zone: An Ecological and Evolutionary Perspective Based upon Habitat Characteristics and Fitness Selection. *Quarterly Review of Biology* 76: 459–67.

Paustenbach, D. 1989. A Survey of Health Risk Assessment. In *The Risk Assessment of Environmental and Human Health Hazards*, ed. D. Paustenbach, 27–124. New York: Wiley.

Pielke, R., Jr. 2007. *The Honest Broker: Making Sense of Science in Policy and Politics*. New York: Cambridge University Press.

Pimple, K. 2002. Six Domains of Research Ethics: A Heuristic Framework for the Responsible Conduct of Research. *Science and Engineering Ethics* 8: 191–205.

Poumadere, M. 2002. Hormesis: Public Health Policy, Organizational Safety, and Risk Communication. *BELLE Newsletter* 11: 33–35.

Pratkanis, A., A. Greenwald, M. Leippe, and M. Baumgardner. 1988. In Search of Reliable Persuasion Effects: The Sleeper Effect Is Dead: Long Live the Sleeper Effect. *Journal of Personality and Social Psychology* 54: 203–18.

Press, E., and J. Washburn. 2000. The Kept University. *Atlantic Monthly*, http://www.theatlantic.com/issues/2000/03/press.htm (accessed February 16, 2007).

Raffensperger, C., and J. Tickner. 1999. *Protecting Public Health and the Environment*. Washington, D.C.: Island.

Raloff, J. 2007. Counterintuitive Toxicology. *Science News* 171: 40–42.

Rampton, S., and J. Stauber. 2001. *Trust Us, We're Experts!* New York: Putnam.

Reiss, J., and P. Kitcher. 2008. *Neglected Diseases and Well-ordered Science.* Technical Report 06/08 from the LSE Centre for the Philosophy of Natural and Social Science, Contingency and Dissent in Science, http://www.lse.ac.uk/collections/CPNSS/projects/ContingencyDissentInScience/DP/DPReissKitcher0608 Online.pdf (accessed April 26, 2009).

Renn, O. 1998. Implications of the Hormesis Hypothesis for Risk Perception and Communication. *BELLE Newsletter* 7: 2–9.

———. 1999. Model for an Analytic-deliberative Process in Risk Management. *Environmental Science and Technology* 33: 3049–55.

———. 2002. Hormesis and Risk Communication. *BELLE Newsletter* 11: 2–24.

———. 2008. An Ethical Appraisal of Hormesis: Toward a Rational Discourse on the Acceptability of Risks and Benefits. *Human and Experimental Toxicology* 27: 627–32.

Renn, O., T. Webler, and P. Wiedemann, eds. 1995. *Fairness and Competence in Citizen Participation.* New York: Springer.

Renner, R. 2003. Hormesis: Nietzsche's Toxicology. *Scientific American* (September 28–30).

Resnik, D. 1996. Social Epistemology and the Ethics of Research. *Studies in History and Philosophy of Science* 27: 565–86.

———. 1998. *The Ethics of Science.* Routledge, London.

———. 2001. Ethical Dilemmas in Communicating Medical Information to the Public. *Health Policy* 55: 129–49.

———. 2006. *The Price of Truth: How Money Affects the Norms of Science.* New York: Oxford University Press.

Revkin, A. 2009. Hacked E-mail Is New Fodder for Climate Dispute. *New York Times*, November 20.

Roberts, S. 2001. Another View of the Scientific Foundations of Hormesis. *Critical Reviews in Toxicology* 31: 631–35.

Rodricks, J. 2003. Hormesis and Toxicological Risk Assessment. *Toxicological Sciences* 71: 134–36.

Rogers-Hayden, T., and N. Pidgeon. 2006. Reflecting upon the UK's Citizens' Jury on Nanotechnologies: Nano Jury UK. *Nanotechnology Law and Business* 2: 167–78.

———. 2008. Developments in Nanotechnology Public Engagement in the UK: "Upstream" towards Sustainability? *Journal of Cleaner Production* 16: 1010–13.

Rooney, P. 1992. On Values in Science: Is the Epistemic/non-epistemic Distinction Useful? In *PSA: Proceedings of the Biennial Meeting of the Philosophy of Science Association*, vol. 1, ed. D. Hull, K. Okruhlik, and M. Forbes, 13–22. Chicago: University of Chicago Press.

Ross, L., and R. Nisbett. 1991. *The Person and the Situation: Perspectives of Social Psychology*. New York: McGraw-Hill.

Roth, A., J. Dunsby, and L. Bero. 2003. Framing Processes in Public Commentary on U.S. Federal Tobacco Control Regulation. *Social Studies of Science* 33: 7–44.

Rothwell, P., and C. Martyn. 2000. Reproducibility of Peer Review in Clinical Neuroscience: Is Agreement between Reviewers Better than Would Be Expected by Chance Alone? *Brain* 123: 1964–69.

Rowe, G., and L. Frewer. 2000. Public Participation Methods: A Framework for Evaluation. *Science, Technology, and Human Values* 25: 3–29.

Rudner, R. 1953. The Scientist qua Scientist Makes Value Judgments. *Philosophy of Science* 20: 1–6.

Ruphy, S. 2006. "Empiricism All the Way Down": A Defense of the Value-neutrality of Science in Response to Helen Longino's Contextual Empiricism. *Perspectives on Science* 14: 189–214.

Safe, S. 1997. Editorial: Xenoestrogens and Breast Cancer. *New England Journal of Medicine* 337: 1303–1304.

———. 2000. Endocrine Disruptors and Human Health—Is There a Problem? An Update. *Environmental Health Perspectives* 108: 487–93.

Sandin, P. 1999. Dimensions of the Precautionary Principle. *Human and Ecological Risk Assessment* 5: 889–907.

———. 2008. The Ethics of Hormesis—No Fuss? *Human and Experimental Toxicology* 27: 643–46.

Sarewitz, D. 2004. How Science Makes Environmental Controversies Worse. *Environmental Science and Policy* 7: 385–403.

———. 2009. A Tale of Two Sciences. *Nature* 462: 566.

Saul, S. 2007. Doctor Says Drug Maker Tried to Quash His Criticism of Avandia. *New York Times*, June 2.

Scanlon, T. 1998. *What We Owe to Each Other*. Cambridge, Mass.: Harvard University Press.

Scheufele, D., and B. Lewenstein. 2005. The Public and Nanotechnology: How Citizens Make Sense of Emerging Technologies. *Journal of Nanoparticle Research* 7: 659–67.

Schiappa, E. 1996. Towards a Pragmatic Approach to Definition: "Wetlands" and the Politics of Meaning. In *Environmental Pragmatism*, ed. A. Light and E. Katz, 209–230. New York: Routledge.

———. 2003. *Defining Reality: Definitions and the Politics of Meaning*. Carbondale: Southern Illinois University Press.

Sclove, R., and M. Scammell. 1999. Practicing the Principle. In *Protecting Public Health and the Environment*, ed. C. Raffensperger and J. Tickner, 252–65. Washington, D.C.: Island.

Scriven, M. 1974. The Exact Role of Value Judgments in Science. In *PSA 1972*, ed. K. Schaffner and R. Cohen, 219–47. Dordrecht: Reidel.

Shabecoff, P., and A. Shabecoff. 2008. *Poisoned Profits: The Toxic Assault on Our Children*. New York: Random House.

Shamoo, A., and D. Resnik. 2002. *Responsible Conduct of Research*. New York: Oxford University Press.

Shock, N. 1962. *Biological Aspects of Aging*. New York: Columbia University Press.

Shrader-Frechette, K. 1985. *Science Policy, Ethics, and Economic Methodology*. Dordrecht: Reidel.

———. 1991. *Risk and Rationality: Philosophical Foundations for Populist Reforms*. Berkeley: University of California Press.

———. 1993. Consent and Nuclear Waste Disposal. *Public Affairs Quarterly* 7: 363–77.

———. 1994. *The Ethics of Scientific Research*. Lanham, Md.: Rowman and Littlefield.

———. 1995. Evaluating the Expertise of Experts. *Risk: Health, Safety, and Environment* 6: 115–26.

———. 1997. Hydrogeology and Framing Questions Having Policy Consequences. *Philosophy of Science* 64 (suppl.): S149–60.

———. 2000. Radiobiological Hormesis, Methodological Value Judgments, and Metascience. *Perspectives on Science* 8: 367–79.

———. 2002. *Environmental Justice: Creating Equality, Reclaiming Democracy*. New York: Oxford University Press.

———. 2004. Review of *Risk and Reason* by Cass Sunstein. *Ethics* 114: 376.

———. 2007a. Nanotoxicology and Ethical Conditions for Informed Consent. *Nanoethics* 1: 47–56.

———. 2007b. *Taking Action, Saving Lives: Our Duties to Protect Environmental and Public Health*. New York: Oxford University Press.

———. 2008a. Evidentiary Standards and Animal Data. *Environmental Justice* 1: 1–6.

———. 2008b. Ideological Toxicology: Invalid Logic, Science, Ethics about Low-dose Pollution. *Human and Experimental Toxicology* 27: 647–57.

Shrader-Frechette, K., and E. McCoy. 1994. How the Tail Wags the Dog: How Value Judgments Determine Ecological Science. *Environmental Values* 3: 107–20.

Sielken, R., Jr., and D. Stevenson. 1998. Some Implications for Quantitative Risk Assessment If Hormesis Exists. *Human and Experimental Toxicology* 17: 259–62.

Silbergeld, E. 1991. Risk Assessment and Risk Management: An Uneasy Divorce. In *Acceptable Evidence: Science and Evidence in Risk Assessment*, ed. D. Mayo and R. Hollander, 99–114. New York: Oxford University Press.

Singer, P. 1972. Famine, Affluence, and Morality. *Philosophy and Public Affairs* 1: 229–42.

Smith, R. 2006. The Trouble with Medical Journals. *Journal of the Royal Society of Medicine* 99: 115–19.

Solomon, M. 2001. *Social Empiricism*. Cambridge, MA: MIT Press.

Southam, C., and J. Ehrlich. 1943. Effects of Extracts of Western Red-cedar Heartwood on Certain Wood-decaying Fungi in Culture. *Phytopathology* 33: 517–24.

Staudenmayer, H., K. Binkley, A. Leznoff, and S. Phillips. 2003a. Idiopathic Environmental Intolerance: Part 1: A Causation Analysis Applying Bradford Hill's Criteria to the Toxicogenic Theory. *Toxicological Reviews* 22: 235–46.

———. 2003b. Idiopathic Environmental Intolerance: Part 2: A Causation Analysis Applying Bradford Hill's Criteria to the Psychogenic Theory. *Toxicological Reviews* 22: 247–61.

Stebbing, A. 1982. Hormesis—The Stimulation of Growth by Low Levels of Inhibitors. *Science of the Total Environment* 22: 213.

———. 1998. A Theory for Growth Hormesis. *Mutation Research* 403: 249–58.

Steel, D. 2010. Epistemic Values and the Argument from Inductive Risk. *Philosophy of Science* 77: 14–34.

Stelfox, H., G. Chua, K. O'Rourke, and A. Detsky. 1998. Conflict of Interest in the Debate over Calcium-channel Antagonists. *New England Journal of Medicine* 338: 101–106.

Stipp, D. 2003. A Little Poison Can Be Good for You. *Fortune* 147: 53–55.

Stokes, D. 1997. *Pasteur's Quadrant*. Washington, D.C.: Brookings Institution Press.

Sunstein, C. 2002. *Risk and Reason*. New York: Cambridge University Press.

———. 2005. *Laws of Fear: Beyond the Precautionary Principle*. New York: Cambridge University Press.

Swan, S., E. Elkin, and L. Fenster. 1997. Have Sperm Densities Declined? A Reanalysis of Global Trend Data. *Environmental Health Perspectives* 105: 128–32.

Swan, S., R. L. Kruse, F. Liu, D. B. Barr, E. Z Drobnis, J. B. Redmon, C. Wang, et al. 2003. Semen Quality in Relation to Biomarkers of Pesticide Exposure. *Environmental Health Perspectives* 111: 1478–84.

Tarlo, S., N. Poonai, K. Binkley, M. Antony, and R. Swinson. 2002. Responses to Panic Induction Procedures in Subjects with Multiple Chemical Sensitivity/Idiopathic Environmental Intolerance: Understanding the Relationship with Panic Disorder. *Environmental Health Perspectives* 110 (suppl. 4): 669–71.

Task Force on Financial Conflicts of Interest in Clinical Research. 2001. *Protecting Subjects, Preserving Trust, Promoting Progress: Policy and Guidelines for the Oversight of Individual Financial Interests in Human Subjects Research.* Association of American Medical Colleges.

Task Force on Research Accountability. 2001. *Report on Institutional and Individual Conflict of Interest.* Association of American Universities.

Teeguarden, J., Y. Dragan, and H. Pitot. 1998. Implications of Hormesis on the Bioassay and Hazard Assessment of Chemical Carcinogens. *Human and Experimental Toxicology* 17: 254–58.

———. 2000. Hazard Assessment of Chemical Carcinogens: The Impact of Hormesis. *Journal of Applied Toxicology* 20: 113–20.

Thayer, K., R. Melnick, K. Burns, D. Davis, and J. Huff. 2005. Fundamental Flaws of Hormesis for Public Health Decisions. *Environmental Health Perspectives* 113: 1271–76.

Thompson, D. 1993. Understanding Financial Conflicts of Interest. *New England Journal of Medicine* 329: 573–76.

Thompson, P. 1995. *The Spirit of the Soil: Agriculture and Environmental Ethics.* New York: Routledge.

———. 1999. The Ethics of Truth Telling and the Problem of Risk. *Science and Engineering Ethics* 5: 489–510.

Tickner, J. ed. 2003. *Precaution, Environmental Science, and Preventive Public Policy.* Washington, DC: Island Press.

Toumey, C. 1996. *Conjuring Science: Scientific Symbols and Cultural Meanings in American Life.* New Brunswick, N.J.: Rutgers University Press.

———. 2006. Science and Democracy. *Nature Nanotechnology* 1: 6–7.

Tuller, D. 2007. Chronic Fatigue No Longer Seen as "Yuppie Flu." *New York Times,* July 17.

Turner, S. 2001. What Is the Problem with Experts? *Social Studies of Science* 31: 123–49.

———. 2003. *Liberal Democracy 3.0.* Thousand Oaks, Calif.: Sage.

Upton, A. 2002. Comments on the Article "Defining Hormesis," by EJ Calabrese and LA Baldwin. *Human and Experimental Toxicology* 21: 111.

Urbina, I. 2007. Gas May Have Harmed Troops, Scientists Say. *New York Times,* May 17.

U.S. Census Bureau. 2008. *Pollution Abatement Costs and Expenditures: 2005,* MA200(05). Washington, D.C.: U.S. Government Printing Office, http://www.census.gov/prod/2008pubs/ma200-05.pdf (accessed October 22, 2008).

van der Woude, H., G. Alink, and I. Rietjens. 2005. The Definition of Hormesis and Its Implications for In Vitro to In Vivo Extrapolation and Risk Assessment. *Critical Reviews in Toxicology* 35: 603–607.

van Fraassen, B. 1980. *The Scientific Image.* Oxford: Clarendon.

Vedantam, S. 2006. Comparison of Schizophrenia Drugs Often Favors Firm Funding Study. *Washington Post,* April 12, A1.

Vichi, P., and T. Tritton. 1989. Stimulation of Growth in Human and Murine Cells by Adriamycin. *Cancer Research* 49: 2679–82.

vom Saal, F. 2007. Hormesis Controversy. *Environmental Science and Technology* 41: 3.

vom Saal, F., S. M. Belcher, L. J. Guillette, R. Hauser, J. P. Myers, G. S. Prins, W. V. Welshons, et al. 2007. Chapel Hill Bisphenol A Expert Panel Consensus Statement: Integration of Mechanisms, Effects in Animals, and Potential to Impact Human Health at Current Levels of Exposure. *Reproductive Toxicology* 24: 131–38.

vom Saal, F., and C. Hughes. 2005. An Extensive New Literature concerning Low-dose Effects of Bisphenol A Shows the Need for a New Risk Assessment. *Environmental Health Perspectives* 113: 926–33.

Wager, E., and T. Jefferson. 2001. Shortcomings of Peer Review in Biomedical Journals. *Learned Publishing* 14: 257–63.

Wargo, J. 1996. *Our Children's Toxic Legacy*. New Haven: Yale University Press.

Wear, S. 1993. *Informed Consent: Patient Autonomy and Physician Beneficence within Clinical Medicine*. Boston: Kluwer.

Weeks, E. 2000. The Practice of Deliberative Democracy: Results from Four Large-scale Trials. *Public Administration Review* 60: 360–72.

Weiss, R. 2005. Many Scientists Admit to Misconduct. *Washington Post*, June 9, A3.

Weltje, L., F. vom Saal, and J. Oehlmann. 2005. Reproductive Stimulation by Low Doses of Xenoestrogens Contrasts with the View of Hormesis as an Adaptive Response. *Human and Experimental Toxicology* 24: 431–37.

Wetherill, Y., C. E. Petre, K. R. Monk, A. Puga, and K. E. Knudsen. 2002. The Xenoestrogen Bisphenol A Induces Inappropriate Androgen Receptor Activation and Mitogenesis in Prostatic Adenocarcinoma Cells. *Molecular Cancer Therapeutics* 1: 515–24.

Whelan, E. 1993. *Toxic Terror*. Buffalo, N.Y.: Prometheus.

———. 2005. Ratty Test Rationale. *Washington Times*, January 11, http://www.washingtontimes.com/news/2005/jan/11/20050111–083925–7283r/ (accessed April 4, 2009).

Wigley, D., and K. Shrader-Frechette. 1996. Environmental Justice: A Louisiana Case Study. *Journal of Agricultural and Environmental Ethics* 9: 61–82.

Wilholt, T. 2006. Design Rules: Industrial Research and Epistemic Merit. *Philosophy of Science* 73: 66–89.

———. 2009. Bias and Values in Scientific Research. *Studies in History and Philosophy of Science* 40: 92–101.

Wilkinson, T. 2001. Research, Informed Consent, and the Limits of Disclosure. *Bioethics* 15: 341–63.

Wilson, J., and R. Willis. 2004. *See-through Science: Why Public Engagement Needs to Move Upstream*. London: Demos.

Woodward, A., H. Percival, M. Jennings, and C. Moore. 1993. Low Clutch Viability of American Alligators on Lake Apopka. *Florida Science* 56: 52–63.

Wueste, D. 1994. Role Moralities and the Problem of Conflicting Obligations. In *Professional Ethics and Social Responsibility*, ed. D. Wueste, 103–20. Lanham, Md.: Rowman and Littlefield.

Wynne, B. 1989. Sheep Farming after Chernobyl: A Case Study in Communicating Scientific Information. *Environment* 31: 10–39.

Zapponi, G., and I. Marcello. 2006. Low-dose Risk, Hormesis, Analogical and Logical Thinking. *Annals of the New York Academy of Sciences* 1076: 839–57.

Zavestoski, S., P. Brown, M. Linder, S. McCormick, and B. Mayer. 2002. Science, Policy, Activism, and War: Defining the Health of Gulf War Veterans. *Science, Technology, and Human Values* 27: 171–205.

Zegart, D. 2000. *Civil Warriors*. New York: Delacorte.

# Index